CW00670473

JOSE RAMOS HORTA (2007–2012) and Nobel Pea
The "Liverpool Four" who action in disabling a British Aerospace aircraft paid for by Indonesia and being readied to be delivered, were part of Timor-Leste's network of friends around the world who with courage and imagination contributed significantly in raising awareness in the UK about British arms sales to Indonesia.

I remain till this very day in admiration and gratitude for the "Liverpool Four".

CAROLINE LUCAS Green MP, Brighton Pavilion
The heroic actions of this small, but determined, group of women is told brilliantly in Andrea Needham's fascinating account.

What's apparent from this book is the utter dedication that these women had to the cause. In a deeply moving account, that spans the time from their action at the British Aerospace hangar to their final court date, you can sense just how much human life matters to each and every one of these women.

Anyone interested in social change, or campaigning for peace, should read this book and take inspiration from the brave actions of these amazing women.

MICATO FERNANDES ALVES Founder of the East Timorese women's NGO, Fokupers, and fighter for an independent Timor-Leste
When writing some paragraphs on this book, I feel overwhelmed with tears and happiness, with profound

privilege and honor to all my activist colleagues for your generosities, courage and solidarities that you have shown us during our fight for independence.

As a freedom fighter who aspired for a free and independent nation, when everyone else had turned their back on our fight, we received courage, support and solidarities as shown in your actions at the British Aerospace. Even with constant repression, we were inspired with your action in order to continue the fight until the end.

Today, everything is worthwhile. We cannot repay all your sublime action, no ways to measure your sacrifice and determination from this action of solidarities. With this endorsement, I express my profound gratitude and acknowledgement.

HANNAH LEWIS Grassroots environmental campaigner, part of the "No Dash For Gas" week-long occupation of West Burton gas power station in 2012
I'm delighted this story is now finally available for the rest of us to learn from. This is a beautifully-written first-hand account of a legendary action that has deeply inspired me many times. These women are experts in meticulous planning, taking effective direct action, developing a tight-knit team, and winning a court battle, which are timeless and essential skills that are every bit as relevant to grassroots organisers today as they were 20 years ago. It is incredibly rare for such detailed information about an action of this scale to be shared in public, which is a testament to the continually open attitude of the women who carried out the action. So

let's make the most of it! For anyone who is curious about the inner workings of someone who carries out direct action, here's your answer. And for those of us who are ready to take action ourselves, this book is a must-read.

PAUL ROGERS Professor of Peace Studies, University of Bradford

The Hawk Ploughshares Trial was one of the most remarkable instances of a jury accepting the defence of preventing a greater crime, and Andrea Needham's story of the four women campaigners is a hugely informative account. It is an amazing narrative, not least in the manner in which they planned the action and went through with it while evading what should have been stringent security measures.

This is not just a thoroughly readable book but is, more importantly, an inspiration.

BENJAMIN ZEPHANIAH Poet

The occupation of East Timor was one of the biggest injustices of our time. I was frustrated by the lack of coverage this occupation got in the British press, and at the same time I was angry with our government for being an apologist for the Indonesians, and for selling them arms. Then I heard about a group of women that undertook a piece of cool and effective direct action. They disrupted the sale of a major piece of military hardware, and in doing so they inspired me (and many others) to continue.

This book is an honest, personal account of how, when and why. It goes without saying that it is an important piece of history, but what's more important is that it shows other women and men what's possible when we stand together for a just cause. These women really did increase the peace.

PAT GAFFNEY Secretary General, Pax Christi UK
To convey the depth, pain and joys of nonviolent actions of civil disobedience is no easy thing. Yet this is what Andrea Needham does in her reflections, twenty years on, of the Seeds of Hope Ploughshares action in 1996.

The strains of secrecy and its invasion into everyday life; the hours of scrupulous planning and observation; the tensions of community building – both with those immediately involved in the action and the wider networks; the ability to grapple with legal challenges and arguments and the hilarious madness of all-night stake-outs are all part of this story. Preparation for actions such as this is essential and painstaking – definitely unglamorous.

And where it would be easy to wallow in self-pity, Andrea presents clear and unsentimental insights into prison life too. Good to be reminded that while these women were variously labelled as fanatics and full of self-delusion during the court case, their witness reached out to the ordinary people of East Timor, to the ordinary people of Liverpool and to thousands more, offering real hope that change is possible and that the war machine can be stopped.

MIKE SCHWARZ Partner, Bindmans solicitors
This is a compelling story, well told, about the triumph of the pen and ploughshare over sword and State. And it's not

just a story. It's a landmark case about the triumph of selfless, collective and high-risk direct action. It has had far-reaching consequences beyond the lives and livelihood of those who would have been bombed by weapons of mass destruction.

CHRIS COLE Founder, Drone Wars UK

The Hammer Blow is a detailed and thrilling account from the inside of one of the most important and inspirational pieces of recent British nonviolent history. *The Hammer Blow* is a must read for scholars, activists and all those committed to nonviolent political change.

ROB NEWMAN Comedian

An excellently written, fast-paced, emotional roller-coaster, this is the story of how four courageous women prevented Hawk jets from gunning down innocent East Timorese. This vivid and inspiring tale is especially relevant in the post-Snowden era as governments around the world step up attempts to criminalise protest.

RACHEL JULIAN Senior Lecturer in Peace Studies, Leeds Metropolitan University

A brilliantly-written book that has such a depth of detail that the power of the Seeds of Hope Hawk action becomes alive in its pages. It is rare to have such a guide to what happened before the action, written with a frankness of the fears and joys and time it took from the day of realising what needed to be done, to hearing "not guilty". Andrea captures both the enormity of the action and the everyday details of how direct action changes lives. It will inspire, guide and inform those who wonder what action they can take.

VIRGINIA MOFFATT Chief Operating Officer, Ekklesia
The 1996 Seeds of Hope Ploughshares was an inspiring and effective act of civil disobedience on behalf of the people of East Timor. Andrea Needham's excellent book provides us with a unique insight of that action from start to finish. Gripping, funny and moving by turns, this is an essential read for anyone wanting to understand how four ordinary women used household hammers to change the world.

BELLA GALHOS Timorese human rights activist
I was in Canada when I heard the news about four women in England who had disarmed a Hawk jet being sold to Indonesia. I was the only Timorese woman living in Canada and had struggled to liberate my country from Indonesian occupation, their action had indeed inspired and made me realize that there were many people around the world, men and women who were also fighting for justice and peace.

These four women not only inspired us, the Timorese, but people around the world to not fold our hands and ignore human rights abuse in this planet. Seeds of Hope was a wonderful act of solidarity with the people of East Timor threatened by British weapons.

The support of people around the world throughout our long struggle for independence was crucial, and this action raised the profile of Britain's role in arming Indonesia, and raised the spirits of the Timorese people.

The Hammer Blow gives a fascinating inside account of the whole story, and should be read by anyone concerned about solidarity and justice. This is the kind of book that we all should read to be reminded that we are one, no matter where we come from, and it is our responsibility to make sure our world is safe and humanity should be highly upheld.

THE HAMMER BLOW

How ten women disarmed a warplane

Andrea Needham

PEACE NEWS PRESS

Published by Peace News Press
5 Caledonian Road, London N1 9DY

Copyright © 2016 Andrea Needham
Andrea Needham asserts her moral right to be
identified as the author of this book
ISBN: 978-0-946409-20-4

Inquiries regarding requests to reprint part of *The Hammer Blow* should
be addressed to *Peace News*, 5 Caledonian Road, London N1 9DY, UK
editorial@peacenews.info

Andrea Needham would like to thank University of New South
Wales Press for allowing her to use extracts from *Telling East Timor:
Personal Testimonies 1942-1992* by Michele Turner. She would also like
to acknowledge the quotations from *Challenge to the New God: The
Resistance to Nuclear Weapons*, by Don Mason and Catherine Robinson,
published by Gooday Publishers, which is no longer operational.

Printed by Catford Print Centre
Cover design by Erica Smith, Wordsmith
Layout by Emily Johns, Gensing Workers Co-op

Peace News Press is a project of *Peace News*
a radical nonviolence project based in London
http://peacenews.info

For Esme

with all my love

CONTENTS

═══════════

AUTHOR'S NOTE

The Seeds of Hope East Timor Ploughshares action was carried out by ten women. Not all of us were in the hangar that January night in 1996; not all of us went to prison. But all of us were equally part of this action, and each one of us was important to the whole.

This is not "the" story of Seeds of Hope: it is simply my story. Each of us could write her own story; each of those stories would be different, but each would have its own truth. Inevitably, as it's my story, it focuses more on the action, the time in prison and the trial than on what was happening inside the support group. This in no way reflects on the importance of the support group, but is simply a function of the fact that I'm writing from my own experience.

I hope that one day someone from the support group will write their story, which would be a tremendous resource for campaigners.

I wrote much of this book some years ago, mostly from my own diaries, prison letters and Seeds of Hope meeting minutes. The trial chapters are based on the verbatim transcript supplied by the court. All mistakes are mine.

In this book, I've tended to give things the names that we used at the time. I've called the country "East Timor", rather than "Timor-Leste", which is the name it took when it gained its independence in 2002. I've also referred to the arms manufacturer who made (and still make) Hawk jets as "British Aerospace" (BAe) even though the company changed its name in 1999, three years after the events in this book, when it became "BAE Systems" (after merging with Marconi Electronic Systems).

TEN YEARS

"Vera says that if we're convicted, Judge Wickham will give us ten years", Angie reported on her return to prison. She'd been representing herself at a bail hearing; Jo, Lotta and I had not been at court as we were represented by our barrister, Vera.

I stared at Angie, speechless. My world was suddenly starting to tip upside down.

"Ten years? Ten years?", I said eventually. "That can't be right. Ten years?"

Ever the optimist, Angie said that at least now we knew where we stood: it was all or nothing. Either we were acquitted, or we were going to spend a very long time in prison.

That night, I couldn't sleep. Ten years, ten years, ten years. It was going through my head like a drumbeat. I lay on my bed in my tiny cell, looking out through the narrow windows at the prison wall and the razor wire and the security lights, listening to the clinking of keys as the night officer patrolled the corridor. Ten years. Eventually, in the early hours of the morning, I turned my aching head over on my wet pillow and went to sleep.

CHAPTER 1

"PEACE PROTEST NURSE JAILED"

Nobody in my early life – myself included – would have suspected that I had a future as a troublemaker ahead of me. Growing up in rural Suffolk in the 1970s, the youngest of four siblings, there didn't seem to be much wrong with the world. I don't recall my family discussing politics, and although my father listened to the news every day, I never paid it much attention.

My interests lay outside: playing with my best friend Louise on her family farm, galloping her ponies round the fields, bike riding through the country lanes.

The outside world finally impinged on me in the early 1980s, when I was in the sixth form at school. The Falklands war started, and I remember thinking that it might be the beginning of something much bigger. I tried not to listen to the news, too scared in case something terrible – the third world war, perhaps – was going to happen. I didn't question the prevailing narrative: the Argentinians had invaded our islands, and it was right and proper that they be evicted, by force if necessary.

The other political event that I became aware of around that time was the Greenham Common women's peace camp. Unfortunately I got most of my information about it from my grandfather's *Daily Mail*, and was horrified: it seemed like a collection of crazed lesbians (lesbians! we didn't have them in Suffolk) hanging sanitary towels on the fences of the base. Again, I didn't think about the issues, about nuclear weapons or American bases or NATO or gender politics: all I knew was that there were a bunch of scary women doing rather unpleasant things in Berkshire. No more needed to be said.

From school, I went on to Newcastle upon Tyne Polytechnic to study physiotherapy. I really wanted to be a doctor, but didn't think I was good enough at science, so chose physiotherapy as a compromise. As it turned out, that decision, made at fifteen, arguably determined the whole course of my life. Had I been happy in my chosen career, I might still be in it now, in a senior position, earning good money and being in every way the respectable citizen I could have been.

However, I hated physiotherapy. I was a shy, unconfident young woman; I found rapport with patients difficult, and felt uncomfortable with many of the other students, who all seemed sporty and confident and popular, like a public school hockey team. It was the days of full grants for students and changing courses would have been easy enough, but having made my bed, I thought I'd better lie in it, although I'm not entirely sure why.

I struggled through to the end, passed my exams and found a job at Kirkwall hospital in Orkney, off the north coast of Scotland, almost as far from Suffolk as it was possible to be without leaving the country. Orkney was a fantastic place to be; the beauty of the islands, the amazing archaeology, the seabirds, the sense of living on the edge of the world. But having a job I hated overshadowed the wonders of the landscape, and after six months, I resigned.

I needed time to re-evaluate my life, to decide my next move. I had not the faintest idea what I wanted to do, so I made the decision to go to the USA to spend some time with my sister Siobhan, who was then studying at the University of Indiana in Bloomington.

Indiana was wonderful; a chance for my sister and me to get to know each other properly as adults, to spend days doing nothing more than thinking what to cook for dinner, volunteer at the local hospital, distributing flowers to patients, cycle round country roads and swim in lakes, and just hang out as summer turned to autumn. Bloomington was where I took part in my first-ever protest, against the US funding of the Contras of Nicaragua, responsible for grotesque violations of human rights. Siobhan and I walked through the middle of town with a small crowd of others, holding signs and feeling somewhat self-conscious. Little did I know that resisting the state would become a key part of my life in the future, and demonstrations would become as natural as breathing.

My plan was to stay for four months, and to do a bit of travelling. Being short of money (my only income was the few dollars I earned each week for selling blood), I needed to find cheap places to visit. A library book suggested a homeless shelter in Washington DC which accepted live-in volunteers.

Perfect: I could do a bit of work, and see the capital for free. I'd stay for three weeks then go home in time for Christmas. As it turned out, the next few weeks would change my life forever.

I saw very little of DC during those first weeks; at the Community for Creative Nonviolence leisure time was looked on as something of an indulgence. The whole operation – a 1,350-bed shelter and a soup kitchen – was run by about fifty live-in volunteers, a mixture of older activists, ex-residents, and idealistic young people like myself. Nobody was paid, and everybody worked far more than full time to keep this enormous ship from running into the rocks.

CCNV was set up in 1970 as a community focused on social change and resisting the Vietnam war. A couple of years later they opened a soup kitchen as a way of tackling issues of injustice closer to home, followed by houses of hospitality and a medical clinic. In the 1980s, CCNV occupied an abandoned government building in downtown DC, and later – through a long campaign which included prolonged fasting as well as more conventional protests – forced the right-wing administration of President Ronald Reagan to renovate it, to become the huge shelter it was in 1987.

To say it was like nothing I had ever experienced would be an understatement. I had grown up in the country in a middle-class family and attended a grammar school where most children were like me. I had never seen poverty, probably never considered it as something which existed outside of charity appeals for famine relief. Yet here I was, in the capital of one of the richest countries in the world, just a few blocks from the White House, and I was surrounded by people who had absolutely nothing. No home, no money, no food, no health care, nothing.

Reagan's war on drugs was in full swing, but seemed to be having little effect in our part of town, where crack cocaine could be bought outside the shelter for a couple of dollars. The huge drug problem in the city led to an epidemic of violent crime, and DC was known as the murder capital of the country. At night, we would often hear gunfire on the streets around the shelter, and occasionally people would stumble through the door still bleeding from gunshot wounds. It would have been hard to find a sharper contrast with the life I had known until that point.

As well as trying to respond to the huge need in front of them, the people at CCNV were organising civil disobedience in support of better conditions for homeless people. I arrived in the middle of a campaign to force the transit authority to remove a gate they'd erected at a downtown metro station, Farragut West, to stop homeless people sleeping there. Every night, community members would go down to the station; two people would sit in front of the gates to stop them being closed whilst others sang and held banners. Every night, the people blocking the gates were handcuffed and carried off to a police car. Some time the next day they would return to the shelter, tired and hungry, but ready to head off to the station again that night.

I was awestruck: I had never in my life met anyone who had been arrested, and to do it deliberately seemed like the ultimate in self-sacrifice. Community members talked nonchalantly about their many arrests; there was a fashion amongst the younger ones not to remove the yellow plastic wristbands which police put on each prisoner in the lockup, and some people's arms were festooned with these tangible signs of their commitment.

My initial amazement at discovering civil disobedience didn't last long. It seemed to make absolute sense: the people in power were doing terrible things, and it was our responsibility to resist them. Living at CCNV, it was impossible to ignore the effects of government policies on housing, health and welfare. Perhaps taking direct action to raise the profile of the issue was as important as picking up the pieces.

Having come to spend three weeks at CCNV, I ended up staying nearly two years, mostly working in the infirmary, a 24-bed unit in the basement of the shelter where we cared for people with often serious – and largely untreated – physical and mental health conditions. We were the first port of call for many people who should have been in hospital, but were not welcome at the private hospitals and preferred not to brave the single overstretched and overcrowded public hospital in the city.

It was a chaotic, at times overwhelming, place to work, but at the same time there was something about the place which made me want to stay – the wonderful dedicated people I met, the sense of community, a kind of Blitz spirit which kept the place running in the face of almost impossible demands. The emotional strain of caring for so many very sick people was exacerbated by the physical failings of the building itself. On several occasions, pipes burst on the floor above us, and raw sewage poured down into the infirmary. To say it was a challenging place to work doesn't really begin to describe it.

After about a year at CCNV – and perhaps thinking that a day in the cells might be easier than a day in the infirmary – I was arrested for the first time, for taking part in a blockade of Pennsylvania Avenue in protest against cuts in the city housing budget.

Although it was a pretty insignificant action – we carried furniture into the street, then stood holding hands around it as rain fell and traffic hooted – it marked a shift in my life, a step across the line. It was scary, but at the same time exhilarating. Although I didn't know many of the other people being arrested, I felt a real solidarity as each of us in turn was handcuffed and loaded into the police van. As we waited to be arrested we sang: "Down by the riverside" and "We shall not be moved". I felt strong and proud and powerful. It felt like the start of something, although I wasn't quite sure what.

My curiosity about what happened after you were carted off was soon satisfied: we were taken to a foul underground bunker, DC central lockup, and put into tiny, filthy cells. We were fed baloney sandwiches and doughnuts with weak coffee and left to spend the night listening to the howling, crying, screaming and puking of the mentally ill, the addicts withdrawing from drugs, the generally desperate people found in prisons everywhere. It was a place of the most appalling pain and desolation, a place for people thrown away by society, there to be processed and labelled and then sent to another place suitable for such nonpeople.

Those of us arrested at the protest were all taken to court the next day and released on bail. I went back to the shelter, proudly wearing my plastic wristband, which I kept on for

7

some weeks. I still have it; my name, written in strangely beautiful script, is fading now, but I treasure it as a symbol of my first tiny steps into resistance.

In the end, after a couple of years, I had to leave CCNV. Whilst I felt a strong loyalty to the place, and to many of the incredible people who lived this life permanently, life there had simply become too much for me. Everyone worked seventy hour weeks, we all lived in the shelter so it was very difficult to get any personal space, and the stresses of dealing day after day with so much need and trauma led to a lot of very dysfunctional relationships between community members, which were rarely addressed. I'd had enough.

I couldn't leave DC though: I was on probation for some offence or other and my probation officer was threatening to have me locked up if I left town (in retrospect, it may have been an empty threat but at the time, to my inexperienced self, it seemed real enough). A friend suggested I go instead to Dorothy Day House, a Catholic Worker community in the north of the city.

I'd never heard of the Catholic Worker, and was slightly concerned about the religious aspect, but it seemed my only option, so I packed my bags and headed north. It turned out to be a small community of very lovely and committed people, sharing their lives with homeless and refugee families. They all lived in a huge Victorian house on the corner of a block in one of the rougher parts of town. When I arrived, I realised that I had previously been arrested and spent the night in the lockup with several of them, so my initial concern was immediately laid to rest. Everyone seemed very welcoming, and I felt immediately that this was a place where I would be happy.

The Catholic Worker movement was started in New York in the 1930s, at the time of the Great Depression, by Dorothy Day, a journalist and devout Catholic convert, and Peter Maurin, an itinerant and eccentric French worker-scholar. They initially put out a newspaper, *The Catholic Worker* (still going strong over 80 years later), which held a strongly pacifist position. Later, houses of hospitality were started, together with farms where people could work the land communally. Community members lived together with the people they served, in voluntary poverty. Resisting the war machine was an important part of the work of many communities, and remains so today.

Nobody is paid for their work and most communities don't accept government funding; money comes from donations and communal work. In the US today there are over 200 Catholic Worker communities, supporting some of the most vulnerable and outcast members of society: homeless people, refugees, prisoners and their families, people with AIDS. It is a truly inspiring movement and one which has now spread to many other countries, including the UK.

At Dorothy Day House, I was introduced to the delights of early morning dumpster-diving at the wholesale vegetable market, twice-weekly cooking of vast pots of food to take onto the streets, and regular peace actions, at the White House, Pentagon, Department of Energy or other similar sites. When you live in Washington DC, you never have to go far to find somewhere to protest. By now, it felt completely normal to be taking part in protests, watching other people be arrested (having been arrested four times I was becoming a little more circumspect, aware that I was risking deportation), sitting around for hours in court waiting for people to be released, spending time with people who had spent months or years in jail.

I loved being at Dorothy Day House, but eventually, my much-renewed visa ran out, and I had to come home. I'd been in the US for nearly three years – three years which had radically changed my outlook on life, and have shaped my life ever since. I was no longer able to look away from terrible things being done by my government, or from the victims of British policies at home and abroad. I now saw it as my responsibility to speak out, to protest, to refuse to be complicit by silence in the face of injustice.

I moved almost immediately to London, to start a nursing course. It was January 1991, and Britain and the US were about to go to war in Iraq. For months in DC we had been protesting, showing our opposition to the military buildup and the drumbeat of war which had started the previous summer. That August, I had been arrested with other members of Dorothy Day at the White House, for demonstrating without a permit, thus breaking my self-imposed moratorium on civil disobedience. The judge at trial had muttered something about deportation, but did nothing to make it happen.

On the morning of 17 January, I woke up and turned on the television to see images of missiles hurtling through the black skies above Baghdad and explosions lighting up the streets. Despite all the protests around the world, we had failed to stop this bloody war. It was the first day of my nursing course but I found it almost impossible to concentrate. The war was the only thing on my mind, but none of the other students appeared to care; nobody was talking about it, nobody was going to any of the protests. The fact that our country was busy killing people in a brutal war in the Middle East was simply not an issue. I felt very isolated, and knew that I urgently needed to find people who felt like I did about it, but didn't know where to look for them.

Shortly before the ground war commenced in February, I went down to Whitehall for what had been billed as the "Eleventh Hour" action. I didn't know anyone there, but it felt like a necessary response to the appalling crimes being committed by my government. When everyone sat down outside Downing Street, I didn't hesitate: I sat down too, refused to get up, and soon found myself in Bow Street police station, charged with (and later acquitted of) "disregarding commissioner's directions".

The action had been organised by a group called Gulf War Resisters. A few days later, there was a meeting to support those who had been arrested, and to talk about where to go next with the campaign. The meeting was at the Peace Pledge Union offices near Euston, in a tiny room up several flights of narrow stairs. I went along with some trepidation, but hoping that these would be the people I was looking for: people who were politically engaged, and committed to resistance. In fact, many of the people I met that day would become close friends through decades of activism. I had found my community.

After the war ended, those of us still in Gulf War Resisters made a decision to stay together as a direct action affinity group, and to change our name. After much deliberation, we settled on "ARROW: Active Resistance to the Roots of War". ARROW was where a number of us who would become part of the Seeds of Hope action first met; Emily Johns, Lyn Bliss, Ricarda Steinbrecher and Clare Fearnley were all involved with the group at various stages.

ARROW worked on a number of very serious issues including sanctions on Iraq, arms sales, nuclear weapons, immigration and Northern Ireland, but the gravity of the topics didn't stop us having a lot of fun. We were a spontaneous, anarchic group, with little regard for the conventions of normal behaviour and a tendency to off-the-wall actions.

Our events were creative and often funny, and we were quite happy to mock the people in power. We did what we wanted to do, and paid little heed to police officers coming along to tell us we couldn't do it. Many of us were young and free of responsibilities – a few of us were quite old and similarly carefree – and being arrested really wasn't a big deal. We stood our ground and told the police we weren't going to co-operate. If they wanted to arrest us, that was up to them. It was a tremendously powerful feeling, this refusal to submit to what we felt were illegitimate demands.

On one occasion, we heard that Norman Schwarzkopf – the US commander of coalition forces in the 1991 Gulf War – was coming to Harrods to sign copies of his autobiography, *It Doesn't Take a Hero*. This was too good an opportunity to miss. Emily, Milan Rai – another ARROW member – and I made a banner and headed for Harrods' book department. It was packed, with secret servicemen mingling with eager shoppers. Schwarzkopf arrived, led in, unaccountably, by a brace of bagpipers. Emily and I unfurled our banner – "It doesn't take a hero to kill Iraqi children" – and started shouting, whilst Mil endeavoured to capture the event on film.

Unsurprisingly, our intervention was not well received. Emily and I were picked up bodily and carried down the back stairs. Mil followed, trying to continue filming as a security guard pushed him around and attempted to cover the lens with his hand. We were carried out of an emergency exit and along Brompton Road into the Harrods offices, all the time screaming about being abducted. There we were locked in an office in the basement for some time, until eventually the head of security decided to let us go, aware perhaps that what they were doing was completely unlawful.

Another time, we put the Foreign Office on trial for aiding and abetting genocide in East Timor. We walked straight in to the offices in Whitehall, ignoring demands from security guards that we stop immediately (security was considerably less tight in the pre-9/11 days), and kept going until we were finally halted on a landing. We were asked to leave but declined, and instead sat on the floor and held the trial there. Richard Crump, a wonderful, dogged campaigner well into his 70s, acted as judge, wearing a long white paper wig. Eventually the police were called and we were all escorted out, but we'd made our point.

ARROW was a wonderfully supportive group. We undoubtedly had our arguments and sometimes managed to upset each other, but overall it worked very well. We spent time together socially, and got to know and trust each other in a way which I've seldom found in other groups. You knew that there would always be someone waiting outside the police station when you were released at midnight, always people sitting in the public gallery if you were on trial, always someone to visit you in prison. Whilst I've lost touch with many people from other groups I've been in over the years, ARROW people are still very much part of my life, and the first people I would turn to in a crisis.

I continued in ARROW throughout the three years of my nursing course. It was difficult, but I didn't want to give up activism, and managed with some subterfuge to squeeze in a lot of protesting around the demands of coursework and ward placements. Barely a week went by without a planning meeting, a protest, some direct action or a court date, and looking back I wonder how I managed to do so much at the same time as attending a full-time course.

Halfway through my final year, I served a very brief prison sentence for refusing to pay four fines. I was given a week, but only had to serve four days and came out none the worse for the experience. All would have been well had the local paper – the *Hornsey Journal* – not carried a couple of paragraphs about it, entitled "Peace protest nurse jailed". Unluckily for me, my tutor lived in the area and spotted it.

I was hauled in front of the principal and given a very stern talking to: any more such conduct, she said, and she would not be able to sign my certificate of fitness to practise at the end of the course. Without it, I would not be able to work as a nurse. I pointed out that I had arranged the court date so I would be in prison during the summer holidays, which seemed a responsible thing to do. She didn't see it like that, and I was forced to keep a very low profile for the next six months, taking part in plenty of actions but taking care not to be arrested.

After qualifying in 1994, I worked for a while as a staff nurse at Bart's Hospital before switching to work in various shelters around London. I remained very active with ARROW, which at that time was focusing very much on British Aerospace's deal to sell Hawk aircraft to Indonesia, which was illegally occupying the small country of East Timor.

CHAPTER 2

―――――

"YOU HAVE TO LEAVE YOUR CONSCIENCE AT THE DOOR"

When a friend first told me about East Timor in 1989, I listened carefully to the story of the Indonesian invasion, to the terrible tales of indiscriminate murder, mass executions, forced resettlement and concentration camps, and was shocked that I had never even heard the name of the country before, although I liked to think of myself as politically aware. I had no idea of the impact that this tiny country on the other side of the world would have on my life in the years to come.

When Indonesia invaded the small former Portuguese colony of East Timor in December 1975, it marked the beginning of an era of unimaginable horror in which a third of the population – 200,000 people – would die, murdered by the occupying forces or starved to death by being forced off their land. The brutal occupation would continue for almost a quarter of a century, actively supported by the major western powers.

Britain had been complicit with Indonesia even before

the invasion started. In October 1975, five journalists – two Britons, two Australians and a New Zealander – were killed inside East Timor by Indonesian troops. The Australian military were monitoring Indonesian signals traffic and knew that the journalists were murdered in cold blood by Indonesian forces. This information was passed on to the intelligence networks of friendly countries, notably Britain and the United States. The British government therefore knew that Indonesian troops were already in East Timor, clearly preparing for a full-scale invasion. Had the west protested loudly enough then, it is likely that the Indonesians would have backed off, and the tragic events in East Timor since December 1975 could have been averted. But Britain did not protest. The Indonesian government was free to go ahead with what Noam Chomsky has described as "one of the greatest bloodlettings in modern history compared to total population."* It was, quite simply, genocide.

Between 1975 and 1978, the UN passed six resolutions ordering Indonesia to withdraw, but when they were ignored there was a resounding silence. The US Ambassador to the UN, Patrick Moynihan, later explained, "The [US] Department of State desired that the United Nations prove utterly ineffective in whatever measures it undertook. This task was given to me, and I carried it forward with not inconsiderable success."**

As soon as the invasion began, the army instituted a

---

* Chomsky, "East Timor Questions and Answers", *Z* Magazine, October 1999.
** Quoted in Chomsky, "East Timor Retrospective", *Le Monde Diplomatique*, October 1999.

programme of widespread and indiscriminate massacres, whole villages often being felled at once. Women and girls were raped, often in front of their families, before being murdered. Torture was commonplace. Favourite methods included electric shock, beatings, burning, immersion in water and pulling out fingernails. The person being tortured didn't have to be suspected of anything; being Timorese was enough.

Many people were forced out of their homes and resettled in "strategic villages" surrounded by troops. The aim was to keep people from providing support to the resistance fighters in the mountains, and to this end their movements were severely curtailed, with anyone wandering far from the village likely to be shot. Whereas previously each family would have had a large plot of land, and been self-sufficient in food, now each was allocated only a tiny area. Even that could not be cultivated adequately as people were forced to work for the military on construction schemes, or to cultivate cash crops for export. Very soon, extensive malnutrition started to appear, followed swiftly by mass starvation.

East Timor was very cut off from the outside world; few people were allowed to leave, and foreign journalists were not allowed to enter, and for years very little news got out. In 1989, the Indonesian President, Suharto, visited East Timor and declared it open to foreign tourists and investors. The resistance took full advantage of this – despite the personal risks – and organised a demonstration for the visit of Pope John Paul II to Dili, the capital of East Timor, in October of that year. At the end of the mass the Pope was celebrating, people rushed forwards, shouting liberation slogans. The Pope was hustled off, but the event was reported the next day in the *New York Times*, causing great embarrassment to the Indonesian government.

It was around this time that I first heard about East Timor. I was living in Washington DC at the Dorothy Day Catholic Worker community and life was busy: scavenging food, cooking meals to take out on the streets, running a food pantry, tending to the needs of the homeless and refugee families we shared our lives with. There were vigils and protests and demonstrations to go to, court support to offer, prisoners to visit. There wasn't time to worry about every situation of injustice; I filed East Timor mentally in the section of my brain reserved for "far-away countries where terrible things are happening; not much I can do".

It wasn't until three years later, in 1992, that the issue of East Timor came alive for me, when I learned that Britain was preparing to sell Hawk aircraft to Indonesia. When the invasion had begun in 1975, thousands of people had fled from the coast to the mountains, and a network of small, independent cells developed to bring supplies and information to resistance fighters. The resistance movement of Fretilin had great support throughout the country, whilst its armed wing, Falantil, continued to fight the occupying forces although massively outnumbered and outgunned. They had the advantage of knowing the mountains as the Indonesians did not, and often launched successful attacks on army posts and patrols.

Surprised at their inability to quell the resistance, the

Indonesian military soon realised that what they needed in the mountainous terrain were small, agile, ground-attack aircraft. The west had been reliably complicit so far by simply being silent; now it was time to ask for more practical assistance. The first ground-attack aircraft came from the United States – sold by the so-called "human rights administration" of President Jimmy Carter – but in 1978 Britain got in on the act when the Labour government under Callaghan issued licences for the export of 20 Hawks.

Human rights considerations were ignored. Indonesia was a huge country in a strategically important area of the world: this was the era of the Cold War, and its proximity to China made it an important ally. In addition, the west was keen to get its hands on the country's abundance of natural resources. The Indonesian government was military-dominated and authoritarian, tolerating very little dissent: these were the perfect conditions for western investment in the country. Why pick a fight over some tiny country that nobody had ever heard of?

In 1992, Britain was negotiating a deal to supply Indonesia with another 24 Hawks, a deal which – together with contracts to supply Scorpion tanks – would bring the dubious honour of becoming the genocidal Indonesian regime's largest weapons supplier. This was no longer simply atrocities in a far-off land: this was atrocities being committed with British weapons, with the full support of the British government. It was time to take action.

❖

In September 1992 – over three years before we disarmed the Hawk – I wrote my first letter to British Aerospace. A reply came back swiftly from John Weston, the Chair of the defence sector (and later Chief Executive). He said, "The British government purchases its defence equipment to provide security for its citizens in the country's interest. If this is the case, and surely this is not unreasonable, then our friends and allies around the world should also be able to provide security for their people."

Indonesia was described by Amnesty International at that time as "casual about mass murder"; for John Weston to describe it as a "friend and ally" was extraordinary. When I challenged this, he changed tack and in his next letter stated, "It is not companies that can or should dictate policy on the sale of defence equipment overseas. It is for the government to decide whether a potential sale is compatible with our political, strategic and security interests."

This was what we were to hear over and over again during the next few years: British Aerospace steadfastly refused to accept that they had any responsibility for the end use of their weapons. In any case, they said, the Hawk was a training aircraft, not suitable for use in East Timor. This was quite simply a lie: their own sales literature trumpeted the Hawk as a "highly potent" ground-attack aircraft. A British Aerospace press release boasted of all the different weapons this supposed "trainer" could carry: rockets, free-fall bombs, cluster bombs, fire bombs, missiles – all to customer requirements.

Campaigners had for many years been saying that Hawks from the 1978 deal were being used to bomb mountain villages in East Timor. Indonesian military sources suggested that these Hawks were modified from trainers to attack aircraft soon after their arrival in the country. The Hawks were sold at the height of the genocide, when the slaughter was more intense than ever. Justifying these sales, the then British Foreign Secretary David Owen stated, "We believe that such fighting as still continues is on a very small scale."* He must have known that this was very far from the case and that selling the planes would only strengthen the hand of the Indonesian military.

It seemed inevitable that the Hawks under negotiation in 1992 would be used for the same illegal purpose. Whilst British Aerospace and the British government were playing down the attack role, the Indonesian government was not nearly so coy. "The Hawks," BJ Habibie, the Technology Minister, stated, "will be used not only to train pilots but for ground attack."**

I learnt about the second Hawk deal from Chris Cole, a friend from ARROW. For several years, Chris had been running a campaign against British Aerospace, and had become enormously knowledgeable about their sales of weapons to undemocratic regimes and military dictatorships. He had once been told by an unusually forthright British Aerospace director, "In this game, you sometimes have to leave your conscience at the door."

Never one to leave his own conscience at the door, Chris had embarked on a campaign of direct action against British Aerospace, targeting arms fairs, meetings and production

---

* Quoted in Mark Curtis, *Web of Deceit,* Vintage 2003.
** Quoted by Reuters, 7 April 1993.

sites. On 6 January 1993, he carried out the second British Ploughshares action (the first such action in Britain was by Stephen Hancock and Mike Hutchinson on 21 March 1990, at USAF Upper Heyford). He broke into a British Aerospace factory in Stevenage and disarmed nosecones for military aircraft including Hawks. I was part of Chris's Ploughshares support group, along with Emily, and the experience gave us both a good insight into the challenges of carrying out such a high-risk action.

At Chris's trial in Luton later that year, Judge Stephen Sedley told the jury to use their "conscience, common sense and humanity" to reach a verdict, noting that if what Chris was saying about East Timor was true, it might amount to genocide. Some of the jurors clearly took this to heart, as the jury was unable to reach a unanimous or a majority verdict and was discharged. Later, Chris was retried, convicted, and sentenced to eight months in prison, but his first trial was an indication that taking direct action to prevent crime was potentially defensible.

ARROW was in the vanguard of organising civil disobedience against the Hawk deal. One of our first events was at British Aerospace in Stevenage in March 1993, a couple of months after Chris had carried out his Ploughshares action there. Fifty of us gathered in the town centre and made our way towards the site, holding banners and passing out leaflets about the Hawk deal. Outside the factory, some people planted daffodil bulbs in the lawn, whilst others dug a grave to symbolise those who had been killed in East Timor. Security guards looked on impassively; one of them was methodically taking everyone's photograph, but they made no attempt to stop us.

Later three of us managed to squirm under a fence into the site, where we ran round for a few minutes dodging some rather cross police officers. We were arrested and spent the rest of the day in the cells before being released without charge. It was a small and largely symbolic action, but it reinforced my belief – based on experience from other actions – that security measures are very often more psychological than physical.

The following year, we organised another trespass at the same site as part of a national day of action against the Hawk deal. This time a number of us made it onto a roof, some via a carelessly unguarded ladder, and others up a handy drainpipe. We stayed up there all day, displaying our banners to the passing traffic. It was great fun, but also very empowering: we were going to do what we wanted, and nobody, least of all British Aerospace, was going to stop us.

In London in 1994, ARROW made stencils of pointing fingers with the message "No Hawks to Indonesia". Late one night, we crept around central London, spraypainting on the pavement, closer and closer to British Aerospace's offices. We finished with an accusatory finger pointing right at the front door. If we'd been caught, the worst we could expect was a fine. In East Timor, meanwhile, people sprayed graffiti – "Long Live East Timor", "Integration, No!" – on walls, knowing that if they were caught, they would be facing arrest, torture and even death. It certainly put the risks we were taking into context.

Football tournament protest at BAe Warton in 1994.

Campaigners were a constant thorn in the side of British Aerospace, disrupting their AGMs, standing for hours outside their sites passing out leaflets, gatecrashing their receptions for foreign dignitaries and appearing as unwelcome visitors at the various airshows they sponsored. The company must have come to dread public events, where it could almost be guaranteed that somebody would show up like the spectre at the feast to object to their complicity in genocide.

In the summer, we held peace camps in a field near the British Aerospace site at Warton in Lancashire where the Hawks were assembled. We were watched day and night by a spy situated in a house opposite and tailed by security guards whenever we left the site. We held vigils and events including a football tournament on the runway ("Playing fields not killing fields") to which we invited workers to field teams.

Sadly, the only ones to turn up were the security guards.

At one camp, three of us climbed over the fence into the site in the middle of the night, and wandered around peering into buildings. We were soon spotted, and told to get into a van to be driven out. We did so, and were then subjected to a terrifying high-speed drive through the countryside, being thrown around in the back of the seatless van, with the security guards ignoring our pleas to be let out. Eventually we were dumped out miles from Warton and left to find our own way home. We made a complaint to the police, and the guards were arrested on suspicion of kidnap, but – predictably – were never charged with any offence.

Other actions were targeted at the government. There were monthly vigils outside the Foreign Office in London and the Department of Trade and Industry in Manchester, and in town centres around the country. Hundreds of people lobbied their MPs and asked them to sign Early Day Motions condemning the sale of weapons to Indonesia.

The Hawk Walk from Farnborough passes near BAe's London offices, 1994.

In the summer of 1994, ARROW walked from British Aerospace in Farnborough, Surrey, to the Ministry of Defence in London. It was an idyllic few days, wandering through the countryside and along the Thames, meeting up with various peace groups along the way. When we reached the Ministry of Defence, we blockaded the entrance and were very roughly removed by the police, who had no interest in hearing about the Hawk deal or East Timor, and just wanted us out of the way as quickly as possible. It rather summed up the whole issue of arms sales to Indonesia, as far as the government and British Aerospace were concerned: the problem was not that Britain was complicit in genocide, but that campaigners wouldn't just shut up about it.

CHAPTER 3

═══════════

"GET OUT OF THAT FOUNTAIN!"

In November 1994, several ARROW members gathered to watch "Death of a Nation", John Pilger's documentary about East Timor, which included scenes from the Santa Cruz massacre in Dili, the capital of East Timor, on 12 November 1991. This cold-blooded slaughter took place during a peaceful demonstration which had been planned to coincide with the arrival of a Portuguese parliamentary delegation. In the event, the delegation was cancelled when the Indonesians objected to the inclusion of an Australian journalist in the press group. Devastated by what they saw as betrayal by the Portuguese, and feeling that they had nothing to lose, the student protesters decided to go ahead anyway.

Early in the morning, a procession of thousands entered the Santa Cruz cemetery where prayers were to be said for Sebastião Gomes, a young man killed a few days earlier by the Indonesian military. Photographs from that day show crowds of young people carrying banners in Portuguese and English proclaiming East Timor's right to self-determination.

Red, yellow and black Timorese flags fly over the heads of the demonstrators, who were no doubt aware of the risk they were taking in participating in such an act of defiance. As the crowd surrounded the chapel, the shouted demands for freedom and self-determination turned to silence as people paid their respects to the dead man. Young girls scattered petals on the dusty ground. The silence was suddenly shattered by the sound of gunfire, as Indonesian soldiers stationed around the cemetery opened fire without warning.

Many such massacres had happened since the invasion, but most went unreported and unmourned by the outside world. This one was to be different. Two US journalists, Amy Goodman and Allen Nairn, were present, and managed to report the story, although badly beaten by Indonesian soldiers. A British filmmaker, Max Stahl, managed – at great risk to himself – to capture some of the terrible scenes of slaughter on film and smuggle them out of the country. Describing the scene, Max wrote afterwards:

A young man badly wounded, but still not dead, lay across the entrance. Others had tripped and fallen in the dirt. A solid wedge of people were stuck in the entrance, pressed from behind by [those] desperate to escape the hail of bullets. Then the wedge broke, and the people poured screaming through the gap, trampling over the bodies, the wounded and the whole alike.*

Many of those who survived long enough to reach hospital

* *Independent on Sunday,* 17 November 1991.

were killed in a second massacre in which the injured were crushed by army vehicles, stoned to death or forced to swallow insecticide. Recriminations went on for some days afterwards, with the army rounding up and killing anyone they suspected of involvement in the demonstration. The army claimed that the "incident", as they called it, resulted in nineteen deaths; they later revised this to fifty. A Portuguese inquiry settled on 271 dead, 250 missing and 382 wounded.

Despite international condemnation of this terrible massacre, the Indonesian military were unrepentant. Referring to the army's response that day – and exposing as a lie their claim that the killing was due to a few soldiers acting without authority – the regional commander Major-General Mantiri stated, "We don't regret anything. What happened was quite proper. They were opposing us, demonstrating, even yelling things against the government. To me that is identical with rebellion, so that is why we took firm action."*

One positive outcome from that dreadful day was that it led to the formation of solidarity movements in countries including Portugal, Australia and the US. Shortly after the killings, students in Portugal chartered a boat, the Lusitania Expresso, and set sail for East Timor, accompanied by journalists and the former Portuguese president. In East Timor, the boat's arrival was anticipated with great excitement, with activists planning a demonstration for the day it was due to dock. Perhaps predictably, it was intercepted by the Indonesian military and turned back, but the voyage had achieved its goal of bringing international attention to

---

* *Editor* (Jakarta), 4 July 1992.

the situation in East Timor.

In Britain, there had been groups working on the issue of East Timor for many years – notably Tapol, the Indonesia human rights campaign, and BCET, the British Coalition for East Timor – and they were able to step up their work and draw in more support in the aftermath of the massacre. They would later join the large coalition of peace and justice groups formed to work together against the Hawk deal.

In the USA, the East Timor Action Network was founded shortly after the Dili massacre, and immediately set to work to change US foreign policy on Indonesia. Such international solidarity was crucial in forcing the issue of East Timor onto the public agenda, with people around the world putting pressure on their governments to address the situation.

It was with the terrible events of Santa Cruz in mind that seven of us from ARROW got off the train in the Surrey town of Farnborough on a cold, wet November day in 1994, on the third anniversary of the Dili massacre. From the station, we made our way to British Aerospace's offices, in an anonymous, new-build business park on the edge of the town. It was all very neat and tidy and normal: there was nothing to suggest that these respectable premises were being used to aid and abet genocide on the other side of the world.

In front of the offices was a large blue pool with fountains shooting water several feet into the air. Some years earlier, during the run-up to the Gulf war, I had been part of an action in Washington DC where people had poured red dye into the fountains in front of the White House. Inspired by this, our plan was for Emily to tip red dye in the water, whilst I climbed into the pool and painted the message "Fountains of blood – British Aerospace Hawks = East Timor deaths" on the back wall.

We obviously didn't look like British Aerospace clients and as we approached, a security guard came out and eyed us suspiciously. There was no time to lose: I jumped into the water whilst Emily pulled out a bag of potassium permanganate and emptied it into the fountain, then started spraypainting bloody footprints on the surrounding paving slabs.

"Get out of that fountain! Get out! Get out!" The security guard was yelling at the top of his voice but couldn't get to me without climbing into the water. I carried on painting whilst the others started leafleting the crowd of workers who had come to see what all the excitement was about. Another security guard tried to snatch our leaflets back, precipitating an argument with one disgruntled member of staff.

"You've got no right to take that from me," he said, taking back the leaflet which the guard had just grabbed from him.

"These people are trespassing," the guard replied crossly.

"Well, you've got a right to remove them, and I've got a right to read what they've got to say," the worker insisted, walking off triumphantly with the screwed up leaflet.

Eventually, soaked and frozen, I climbed out of the fountain, which by now had turned deep pink. The police had been called and Emily and I were arrested by an Australian officer who knew about the situation in East Timor but had very little sympathy for the people there. We were held all day, then charged with criminal damage and released.

At our trial a few months later, we tried to talk about the atrocities in East Timor, about British Aerospace's lack of accountability in selling weapons to Indonesia. The magistrates were unmoved. They told us that they didn't want to hear any political speeches, and convicted us in very short order. It was frustrating, but predictable.

Afterwards, we went into the nearby police station and asked them to investigate British Aerospace for complicity in genocide. A few weeks later we received a two-line reply, saying that there was no evidence that the company was doing anything illegal. Clearly no investigation had taken place. Nobody, it seemed, would take the issue seriously.

After our trial for disarming the Hawk, various newspaper editorials and commentators asked why we couldn't have just held a peaceful demonstration: why did we have to go to the extreme lengths of smashing up a plane? I found myself shouting at the newspaper: "We did! We did that! We did it again and again and it had no effect! Weren't you paying attention?" Along with thousands of people around the country, we had written letters, lobbied MPs, held vigils, talked to workers, organised public meetings, signed petitions, marched and demonstrated.

But ultimately, everything we and thousands of others did to try to stop the sale was ignored. The British government insisted that they were "engaging" with Indonesia about East Timor but saw no reason to stop the Hawk deal. As for British

Aerospace, the Hawk sales were worth £500m, and made a large contribution to overall profits, which after several bad years were finally rising. What possible reason could there be for them to reconsider the deal?

After several years of campaigning, it was becoming increasingly clear that the deal was unlikely to be stopped by conventional means. Perhaps it was time to consider more forceful action.

CHAPTER 4

"HERE AND NOW, YOU AND ME"

"They shall beat their swords into ploughshares and their spears into pruning hooks. Nation shall not lift up sword against nation, neither shall they learn war any more. But everyone will sit in peace and freedom under their vine or fig tree."

These words, from the biblical prophets Isaiah and Micah, have been the inspiration for more than 300 people in eight different countries to take up hammers and start enacting the prophesy, beating on weapons systems to render them harmless.

When a group of US peace activists entered the General Electric plant in King of Prussia, Pennsylvania, in September 1980 to hammer on nosecones for nuclear missiles, they inspired a long line of similar disarmament actions not just in the United States, but also in Sweden, Britain, the Netherlands, Germany, Australia, Ireland and New Zealand.

By the time we took our place in the Ploughshares history books as the 56th such action, weapons ranging from

Trident submarines to weapons computers, B-52 bombers to automatic rifles, had been disarmed. Virtually all activists had been prosecuted, and all had been convicted, usually after trials in which they were barred from bringing any kind of moral or legal defence. Most had received prison sentences, for periods ranging from a few weeks up to eighteen years.

Although Ploughshares activists take their inspiration from a biblical verse, not all have been Christians. In the United States Christianity is perhaps the most common motivating factor, but in Europe activists have tended to come from a much wider variety of faith backgrounds, or none at all. Common to all, however, is a desire to enflesh the beautiful visions of Isaiah and Micah, in which weapons are transformed into socially useful objects, and people can live in peace and unafraid.

❖

My introduction to the Ploughshares movement came in 1989, when I was living at the Catholic Worker in Washington DC. It was all new to me and I was fascinated by the idea of people taking hammers to weapons. In many ways it seemed such a futile gesture; how could a hammer have any impact on a weapon such as Trident, powerful beyond imagination? How could people think that their tiny acts would make any difference? And yet at the same time there was something incredibly humbling about the idea, a kind of inspired madness that would make people risk years in prison, not for personal gain but in order to bring about a more just and hopeful world.

I was struck most by the certainty these activists had that

their actions, however small, were important – not for any media value, or even measurable change, but that they were important in themselves simply as acts of faith. There was such a strong conviction that things could change, but only if we each take personal responsibility to bring about that change.

Jean Holladay, a US woman who participated in three Ploughshares actions and served long periods in prison, sums up this duty for each of us to work for peace:

If nuclear disarmament is to be a reality in our time, it will not happen merely by political decrees. It will occur because people want peace with such a passion that risks are gladly accepted. While actions each person chooses to take for peace may vary, the moral responsibility to resist the unprecedented nuclear peril exists for all of us – to resist in such a way that our whole lives become means of transformation and healing. *

When I first met people who had carried out Ploughshares actions and talked casually and openly about the disarmament and their time in jail, I was completely in awe. My own experience of civil disobedience was limited to a few minor arrests, and the idea of risking years in prison was something I simply couldn't envisage. I decided that people who did such things were somehow special, fearless, different. Since I wasn't like that, I could relax in the knowledge that it wasn't my responsibility to take such action.

* Don Mason and Catherine Robinson (eds), *Challenge to the New God*, Gooday Publishing, 1988.

Gradually, over the following year of living with and meeting people who had done Ploughshares actions, an uncomfortable realisation dawned on me. They weren't special – they were just ordinary people, with ordinary fears and weaknesses. What was extraordinary about them was their unshakeable belief that these small acts of disarmament were important, in fact had an importance that went far beyond the physical damage to the weapon. And more, that disarmament was not just something to be thought about in the abstract, but something to be carried out literally, despite the personal consequences.

Ploughshares is not an organisation; it has no formal structure, no membership, no creed, no board of directors to decree whether a particular action meets the Ploughshares criteria. If you undertake a nonviolent and accountable disarmament of a weapon, you can call it a Ploughshares action.

All actions have at their centre the use of hand tools to disarm weapons; usually this means hammers, although people have used other tools – notably sledgehammers and even pneumatic drills – on missile silo lids where hammers might have little effect. Some might ask, why use a hammer at all? If the aim is to disarm a weapon, why not use something more powerful and effective?

I like the simplicity of hammers; you don't need any special skills or training, hammers are widely available, and what better instrument could there be to beat a sword into a ploughshare? The other issue is that we are only ordinary people; we are not trying to project ourselves as somehow superhuman, able to completely disarm a weapon with one blow. The aim for me was to do what I could do as an act of genuine disarmament, but also an act of faith, and hope that our example would inspire others to continue the disarmament where we left off.

Perhaps the most striking aspect of Ploughshares for those unfamiliar with the movement is that of accountability. Despite the apparently high security of military bases and factories, many activists have shared our experience of being undetected for several hours, giving ample opportunity to escape. Why not run away, and live to disarm another weapon?

I didn't want to escape after our action because I was clear in my own mind that – whatever the criminal justice system might think – we hadn't committed a crime. In addition, I believe that one of the main problems in our political system is lack of accountability. The government had granted licences to sell weapons to a military dictatorship, British Aerospace could make and sell the weapons, and yet nobody would be answerable for the deaths those weapons would cause. Ploughshares sets an example and says that we should all be accountable for our actions. We are willing to face the consequences of what we have done, and we expect nothing less of governments and corporations.

In prison, we received a letter from a woman who asked why we had disarmed the Hawk, what it was about Ploughshares that inspired us. In her reply, Lotta said, "If we want peace, we must make peace, here and now, you and me. I love the people-power and people-responsibility of

Ploughshares actions, their gentleness and strength. Their putting the military or arms producers on trial, their laying ourselves vulnerable to the 'justice' system – expecting a just verdict from the jury and staying there even through an unjust verdict, their challenging everyone to act." For me, this sums it all up; if we want peace, we must make peace, here and now, you and me.

"Why don't we do a women's Ploughshares action?"

The question hung in the chilly November air as we huddled in the icy dormitory. We were in a workshop on women and Ploughshares at a weekend peace gathering near Oxford in late 1994, and our discussions had moved rapidly from theory to thoughts about action.

"How would we do it?" someone else asked, and suddenly ideas started flooding out in a fantasy quite unconstrained by any thought of possible consequences. We laughed as we talked about what we'd take with us, what our message would be, how we wanted it to be different from other Ploughshares actions, how to project it as a women's action.

It was fun to discuss the idea of a women's Ploughshares action in the abstract, but why couldn't we make it a reality? Of the women in that first discussion group, six were keen to pursue the idea after the gathering. Two subsequently dropped out, which left four: Lyn Bliss, Lotta Kronlid, Jo Blackman and me. (At this time, Jo still used her married surname "Wilson", but she later chose to return to being called "Blackman".)

Lyn and I had known each other for some years; we

had been part of ARROW from its inception in 1991 and had spent a lot of time together standing outside various government departments, arms companies or military bases. Unlike me, Lyn had grown up in a political family and had been a campaigner since her teens on a number of peace and environmental issues. She lived in Luton, and had been very involved in support for Chris's first Ploughshares trial in the town the previous year. Lyn had been data manager at the London School of Hygiene and Tropical Medicine for ten years, working on a study of leprosy and TB in Malawi, but was taking a three year break to home educate her eight-year-old daughter Carrie.

One of the people Lyn and I had first met at Chris's trial was Jo, who had come down from Liverpool to support him and had subsequently become involved in the Hawk campaign in the north-west. Jo was an independent councillor on Knowsley council on Merseyside, having been elected after a huge amount of campaigning in what had always been a solid Labour seat. She had been involved in community work in the area for many years, particularly with tenants and youth groups.

The fourth woman was Lotta, whom we'd met for the first time at the Ploughshares gathering. She was Swedish but had been living in Oxford for a couple of years – she had initially come over to see friends and had ended up staying, doing gardening and cleaning work to support herself. Lotta had been introduced to Ploughshares through her work with a syndicalist trade union in Sweden, where there had been four actions to date. She was interested in the differences between the Ploughshares movement in Sweden and Britain, and keen to explore the idea of a women's action.

As the sky darkened and our discussions continued long into that chilly afternoon, I felt increasingly excited. Until then, I had never seriously considered doing a Ploughshares action myself, although I'd been involved in the movement for some years and had supported other activists through the process. Now, suddenly, a women's Ploughshares action felt absolutely the right thing to do.

The gathering ended with a circle in which everyone announced which weapon they'd like to disarm. Many people chose a Trident submarine, whilst others opted for nuclear-capable bombers or even landmines. Jo and I, however, were unequivocal: "An Indonesian Hawk," we both said. Lyn and Lotta were less certain of their choice of weapon, but when it came to their turns we exchanged smiles. For all four of us, the decision was clear: we were going to do it.

CHAPTER 5

═══════════

A CONSPIRACY OF HOPE

In March 1995, Jo, Lyn and I arrived at Lotta's house in Oxford for our first meeting. It had been delayed several times already, and I was looking forward to finally initiating our Ploughshares group. There was a sense of excitement when at last we got together. It felt as if something incredibly important, which could change all our lives for several years, was about to be born.

The birth pangs turned out to be long and at times very painful, lasting longer than any of us had expected. Perhaps we should have realised this during that first weekend, when we set ourselves the task of making a list of things we wanted to discuss over the coming months. In the end this stretched to 36 different topics. We laughed at the length of the list, and wondered whether we were being hopelessly optimistic to think that we could be ready by the autumn, only six or seven months away.

The final date depended on the readiness of the Hawks for export. However, since we didn't then know when the delivery was due, we wanted to be prepared as soon as possible so that we could act at very short notice if necessary. At the same time, we didn't want to go ahead unless we were completely ready; what we were planning to do was likely to put several of us behind bars for some time, and it could be disastrous if we were not properly prepared for the implications of that.

One of the issues we discussed at some length that weekend, and at several subsequent meetings, was our fears. Many were common to most of us: fear of a long prison sentence (whether for disarming or for conspiracy), fears around the action itself, such as a violent reaction from security guards, fears about how our families would react.

Others were more individual. Lotta worried about being deported to Sweden, and what that would mean in terms of the life and friendships she had established in her two years in England. Jo worried that a Ploughshares action might cause tensions and splits between various peace movement groups.

Lyn's particular concerns about being involved related a lot to her eight-year-old daughter Carrie, and how she would cope if Lyn was sent to prison – particularly since it would mean Carrie would have to go back to school as Lyn would not be able to continue her home education. Of the four of us, Lyn had by far the most responsibilities; as well as home education, she still did some work from home for the London School of Hygiene and Tropical Medicine, and from September she also looked after her grandson – born at the time of our first meeting – two days a week. Fortunately, Lyn was extremely organised and utterly reliable – a quality that I really valued, especially when we were in prison and she was responsible for co-ordinating visits and liaising with our family members.

My main worry was losing my sense of purpose and direction if we were given a long prison sentence. I was also concerned about being struck off the nursing register for bringing the profession into disrepute, a kind of catch-all offence which would almost certainly include what we were contemplating. But naming and discussing our fears – and knowing that other people had similar worries – helped enormously in coming to terms with them, and became something we returned to frequently during the process.

By the end of that first weekend, we'd come up with a plan of how we'd like the group to function. We were all sure that we needed more women involved; even at that early stage, Lotta, Jo and I had all decided that we wanted to hammer, and clearly Lyn could not do all the support work on her own.

We discussed various women we could approach, and made a list of those we would invite to the next meeting. Anyone who wanted to join the group would be asked to make a commitment to attending one full weekend meeting a month until the action took place, and to continue to support afterwards. In order to feel safe in the group, we needed to know that everyone was committed to it for the whole period; we wanted to avoid any feelings of insecurity which might be caused by people dropping in and out.

We each went away that weekend and asked various women if they would like to join the group. Several said that they were interested but were not able to make the level of commitment at that point. When we came together for the next meeting, it was still just the four of us.

However, Ricarda Steinbrecher – whom Lyn and I knew from ARROW – had said that she would come, and would bring Angie Zelter, a friend of hers whom none of us had met before. Ricarda was German but she and I had a lot in common in terms of our political background: she too had spent time in the USA when she was younger, and had been arrested a number of times during her work with the Resource Centre for Nonviolence in Santa Cruz, California. When she joined the group she was working on a PhD in genetics, which she was awarded whilst we were in prison.

Ricarda and I had both taken part in an ARROW action in 1992 at the naming ceremony for the first British Trident nuclear-armed submarine, in Barrow-in-Furness. Diana, princess of Wales, was there to crack the bottle of champagne against its hull, and we got very close to her car with our banners before being dragged away by police. I managed to avoid arrest, but Ricarda was less lucky and ended up spending the day in a cell. Ricarda often had a bit of a twinkle in her eye, a sort of naughtiness about disobeying authority which was great fun. She was a great lover of sweeties and had stashes of them around her house, very useful when we were in long meetings and feeling exhausted.

We were looking forward to Ricarda and Angie's arrival, but there was no sign of them that Friday night. We couldn't get hold of them, and wondered whether they'd changed their minds. A little concerned, but determined to get going, we started working through the long agenda we'd drawn up.

On Saturday morning, Ricarda phoned, saying that she

and Angie were on their way, and wanting to know if it was all right for her to bring her partner, Rowan Tilly. We weren't about to turn down an extra body – although we were a little apprehensive about meeting two new people – and a few hours later they all turned up.

It was the first time I'd met Angie; she had been involved in campaigning on peace and the environment for many years but our paths hadn't crossed. At the time she was working on the issue of logging of old-growth forests. This involved some unusual and inspired campaigns, including the setting up of a group called CRISP-O, the Citizens' Recovery of Indigenous Peoples Stolen Property Organisation. CRISP-O members would enter shops which sold unlawfully logged tropical hardwood products, remove them – in an act of "ethical shoplifting" – and deliver them to the nearest police station.

I loved the idea of people walking into police stations and placing toilet seats on the counter, announcing that they were returning stolen property. The campaign was very Angie; it was slightly off the wall, but somehow it was also completely right. It was typical of her ability to think very far outside the usual campaigning methods, and her willingness to do things which other people would avoid for fear of the consequences.

We spent much of that first weekend getting to know each other. The sessions we'd planned included life-sharing, in which we each in turn talked about our backgrounds, why we had decided to be part of the group, and what we hoped to get out of it. It was fascinating to hear everyone's stories, and to realise that even for those of us who'd been friends for years, there was a lot we didn't know about each other.

What emerged from those first, perhaps slightly reserved, disclosures, was that six of us were fully committed to being part of the action. Four of us – Angie, Lotta, Jo and I – wanted to be part of the actual disarmament. Lyn wanted to support, whilst Ricarda knew that she wanted to be in the group, but wasn't certain at that time which role she wanted to play. Later, she decided that she would be in the support group rather than being a disarmer; her father in Germany had become very unwell and it wasn't a good time for her to risk a long prison sentence.

Rowan was the only one who at the time was unsure of her commitment. She was happy to admit that the main reason she was there was because of Ricarda, and said she would need time to think before she made her decision. She was, like the rest of us, an activist, involved, like Angie, in campaigns against logging. She had spent time at Greenham Common women's peace camp, but the Ploughshares movement was quite new to her.

In the end, Rowan decided she wanted to commit, and would join the support group; she was particularly interested in the methodology of Ploughshares, and wanted to find out more about it and whether it was transferable to the environmental movement. She explained that she would probably only do support work for a limited period – and part time – after the action. Little did she know that the group was going to take over much of her life for the best part of a year after we disarmed the Hawk.

So we were seven, and remained so until August, when it became clear that we needed more help with the support work and managed to recruit three more women. Jen Parker was the student organiser for Campaign Against Arms Trade (CAAT), in which capacity she had been involved in nonviolent direct action against the Hawk deal. She had previously spent time at women's peace camps at the Sellafield nuclear reprocessing plant and at Menwith Hill, a US spy base in Yorkshire. Jen brought a lot of energy to the group, and her knowledge of what was happening in the wider Hawk campaign was invaluable.

I asked Emily Johns, my friend from ARROW – with whom I'd been arrested several times – to be part of the group, and also to be my particular support person. Emily had been involved in the peace movement for many years; she was a wonderful artist, and her artwork graced most of the materials the group produced. She had a baby son, Arkady, born in late 1994, who sometimes came with her to meetings. Emily is one of those people that everyone is drawn to; her optimistic nature is a good counter to my tendency to assume the worst, and I knew that she would be a solid and

ARROW rooftop occupation of the BAe factory in Stevenage, 1994.

dependable friend in the time ahead.

I also invited Clare Fearnley, a teacher with dyslexic adults as well as homeless people and refugees, to join the group at that time. I knew her through ARROW – she had taken part in various actions including the rooftop occupation at British Aerospace's site in Stevenage the previous year. She'd managed to scale the drainpipe, whilst I took the easy route up the ladder. A woman who could fearlessly climb up drainpipes seemed like the kind of person it would be great to have in a Ploughshares group, and so it proved to be.

A noticeable feature of the first sixteen years of the Ploughshares movement had been the numerical dominance of men. Two-thirds of all activists had been men and ten groups had been men-only, as compared with only one group – before ours – consisting only of women. Even that was not conceived as a women's group but became so when the man in the group dropped out after an unsuccessful first attempt at disarmament. In addition, one woman, Katya Komisaruk, had carried out an action by herself, the White Rose action, in which she disarmed the Navstar missile guidance system at a military base in California. The two British Ploughshares actions before ours had both been carried out by men.

Beyond the idea of challenging the dominance of men in the Ploughshares movement, I very much liked the idea of women's solidarity, of taking action with a group of strong women, of being powerful and bold together. I had also had the experience too often of being part of an organising group for an event, then having the police show up on the day and ask the nearest man if he was in charge. Nobody was going to make that mistake in our group.

And I liked the idea of a group of women disarming these bloody weapons, these weapons that were – by and large – designed by men, licensed by men, sold by men into a world in which power was overwhelmingly wielded by men. We were going to reject all that, and instead wield our own power: the power of solidarity and nonviolence.

In addition, I had always been somewhat uncomfortable with the "hero" element of Ploughshares actions. The hammerers – more often than not men – go off and do the heroic thing, go to prison, and have their bravery fêted. Meanwhile, those who supported them to be able to take those risks can go largely unrecognised. I knew of several cases in the US where people with very young children had done Ploughshares actions, leaving their partners at home with the children. There didn't seem to be much acknowledgement that being at home with children could be very hard too, albeit in a different way from going to prison.

This is clearly a gender issue: women are much more likely than men to be primary carers, whether for children or elderly relatives, and far less able to suddenly drop those responsibilities. Even for those who don't actually do the hammering there can be a conflict between caring roles and the commitment and time needed to be part of a Ploughshares group.

The issue of taking account of the caring roles of some of the women in the group was something we struggled to deal well with. It was perhaps only after it was all over that others of us realised how unsupported Lyn and Emily, both with young children, had felt at times. For me, it illustrates how any group can develop an ethos where some people's needs are overlooked: just because we were a women's group didn't mean we were immune from insensitive behaviour.

But I hoped that as a women's group, we'd be able – as far as was possible – to subvert the idea that the hammerers are all-important, whilst those doing the work behind the scenes – whether writing newsletters, organising prison visits or caring for children – can be overlooked. Realistically we knew that the public and media focus would most likely be on the hammerers, but we wanted to make it clear publicly that this was a group effort. We all had different roles, but each one of us was important to the whole.

Our preparation lasted ten months. We met at someone's house for a full weekend every month, to spend hours in long and sometimes convoluted discussions. We always tried to timetable in some fun time too, but we seemed to be forever running late, and the walks or games we'd planned were usually the first things to be ditched.

We'd always start on the Friday evening with a session where each of us in turn would have a chance to say how we were feeling, both personally and about the process. It was a good way of checking in, of knowing where each of us was emotionally, of understanding if there was something going on in someone's life which would affect how she would be that weekend. After that, we'd have supper, then go into the first scheduled session – we always worked from very tightly timetabled agendas, drawn up by each of us in turn. On Saturday we'd work from 9am to 7pm, and on Sunday from 9am to 5.30pm. The long hours were unavoidable; since we all lived so far apart, these weekends were the only chance we had to talk, so we had to pack in as much as possible.

There was so much to cover. Early on in the process, we spent a lot of time discussing philosophical questions: militarism, patriarchy, co-operation with authority, secrecy and openness, when is it right to break the law, the symbolism of Ploughshares, our hopes for the action. We weren't aiming to come to consensus, but to give ourselves a chance to explore the issues and to think more deeply about our own positions and how the positions we held affected the action we were planning.

Later on, we focused more on practical matters. Here, there was even more to think about, and we took turns keeping minutes so we were clear about what decisions we had reached. The actual action itself obviously required a great deal of discussion: where were the Hawks, what was the security like, how would we break in, what tools would we need, how much damage would we do, what would we take with us? One weekend, we met with a sympathetic lawyer who was able to answer all our many questions about legal issues: would we be likely to get bail, what were the possible charges, what were the various steps in the legal process, would the support group be at risk of conspiracy charges, what would be the best defence, should we appeal if we got a long sentence?

We talked about contingency plans, about support for the supporters, about being in prison. Lotta drew up and shared a plan for involving her Swedish activists friends. We discussed presswork and made a list of difficult questions that the media might ask. We talked about prison visiting and trial support and drawing other people into the campaign. We put together a list of all the things we wanted to say in the booklet and video we would make to leave at the site of the action. We drafted press releases, planned recces, talked about fundraising, roleplayed police interviews. It might not be true to say our preparation was completely exhaustive – it's impossible to think of everything, as we discovered later- but I think we did as much as we could possibly have done in the time available.

It was not a process for the fainthearted. The weekends were very intense; sometimes we'd go on until late at night, ploughing through the agenda, reluctant to stop as we knew there wouldn't be time to reschedule whatever it was we were discussing. And although I often came home from meetings exhausted and needing several days to recover, I also had an excited feeling that something important was slowly being chiselled out.

Quite late on in the planning process, we decided that we would attempt the disarmament in two waves, Lotta, Jo and I going first, and Angie following on. Angie was involved in presenting a case to Norwich Magistrates Court, asking the court to issue a warrant for the arrest of Ian Lang, the Secretary of State for Trade and Industry. By issuing export licences for the Hawks, Angie would say, he was in breach of British law; namely, that he was aiding and abetting genocide in East Timor.

Knowing that we were all likely to be in prison for some time, Angie wanted to get that process finished beforehand. There was, however, another important reason for her to stay on the outside. If Jo, Lotta and I were unable to disarm the Hawks, she would be able to make a second – secret – attempt at a later date. If, however, we did disarm one or more planes, Angie would then be open about her intention to carry on further disarmament and would invite others to join the campaign. We hoped that this strategy would maximise the chances of the action being a success.

At one meeting, we discussed what to call our group. The problem was how to express everything we wanted to say about the action without ending up with a name that was far too long. We wanted to say something about East Timor, about Hawks, about it being a women's action. We wanted it to be inspiring and easily understandable. Trying to reach consensus with so many of us proved difficult, and we went through dozens of possibilities, some of them sensible (Hawk Ploughshares, East Timor Ploughshares), others decidedly less so (Hawk Resister Sisters, anyone?) In the end we decided that to encompass everything, we needed a name with a sort of subheader, and came up with "Seeds of Hope East Timor Ploughshares: Women disarming for life and justice". It was a bit of a mouthful, but we could all live with it, and in the end we just became known as "Seeds of Hope".

Our venues varied from the space and beauty of Angie's north Norfolk home, where we had meetings in the garden and tried to make time to go down to the beach and swim, to the somewhat more cramped facilities of Jo's flat in a tower block in one of the poorest parts of Liverpool. We had a travel pool, so that the costs of getting to meetings could be shared between us on the basis of what each of us could afford, and also shared food costs, with the host being responsible for buying the food and everyone sharing the cooking.

During one planning meeting at Angie's house in Norfolk in the summer, we made a banner together, a big purple sheet bearing the words "Women disarming for life and justice", along with a Hawk, broken in half with a hammer. We gathered in Angie's barn and stitched the banner together, each adding symbols which were important to us. Lotta, a gardener, had sewn seeds and shoots. Lyn had added white poppies for peace. Rowan had carefully sewn on a huge silver web to symbolise the interconnectedness of life. Jo added a crocodile, to represent the legend that the island of Timor sprang from the body of a crocodile. Angie attached musical instruments. My contribution was a bicycle, to represent both a socially-useful object and the conversion theme of the action – swords into ploughshares, Hawks into bicycles.

When we'd finished, Angie hung the banner on the wall of the barn. It was beautiful. I hoped that we'd soon be hanging it on a disarmed Hawk.

CHAPTER 6

"DIDN'T YOU SEE IT?"

I'm not scared of cows, but having a large herd bearing down on us was too much. Jo ran at them, shouting and waving her arms, and they backed off into the darkness. Not for long though; within a few minutes they had returned, snuffling and blowing and putting their huge bodies right in our line of sight. Wriggling out of my sleeping bag, I joined the fray. "Move!" I shouted, as loudly as I dared – we were close to British Aerospace's fenceline and our voices carried a long way in the still night. They stared curiously at me, jaws rotating and ears flicking, and eventually ambled off to another part of the field.

This was our first recce, on 2 November 1995; it's recorded in my diary as "night out". By this time, our group had discussed many of the more philosophical questions around the action, and we were spending most of our time on practical preparations. The limited information available to us suggested that the Hawks would be leaving early the following year. Before we could carry out the action we needed to know more about the site, particularly about the security systems.

I had moved to Manchester in April 1995, to join another group, Stop the Hawk Deal, which was operating out of the basement of the Quaker centre. Being in Manchester meant that I was much closer to the British Aerospace factory at Warton in Lancashire where the Hawks were being made, and could spend a lot of time there, taking part in campaign events and getting to know the site. Jo and I were the only ones living anywhere near Warton – albeit three hours away – so it fell to us to do the necessary investigations of the site.

Jo and I devised a code for discussing these "nights out" over the phone; we were always going to meet Anne Montgomery in Preston. Anne was an American nun I had met during my time in the US. She took part in the very first Ploughshares action in 1980, and carried out a further five actions before her death in 2012. Had anyone actually been tapping our phones, they might have come to the conclusion that she was a key figure in this criminal enterprise.

Our night out had required a long journey on public transport, culminating with the last bus from Preston to Warton. Although we'd walked the route to the site many times in daylight, at night everything looked different and we had to stop several times and wander around looking for the right path. As we passed a house set alone outside the village, a security light came on and a dog started barking. We switched off our torches and scuttled onwards in the dark as fast as we could.

Finally we reached the site and set ourselves up in a field just beyond the perimeter fence, from where we had a good view of the hangar in which we thought the Hawks were kept. We'd brought a groundsheet and Jo had a sleeping bag, but I hadn't anticipated how cold it would get, and was soon feeling decidedly chilly. On subsequent visits we were far better prepared, bringing sleeping bags and many extra clothes. By our last visit, we had become so bold that we even brought a tent.

We each had binoculars, and Jo had a notebook in which to write down our findings. It all felt very cloak-and-dagger, and after some slight apprehension the first time, I came to quite enjoy our recces – not the cold and discomfort, but the sneaking around in the dark, watching, making notes, always with that slight frisson of doing something forbidden.

We seemed to have found the perfect observation point, with a full view of the hangar and a little protection from the cold wind in the form of a scrubby hedge. But within an hour the cows were upon us, completely obstructing the view. We moved much closer to the fence, where we were in quite an exposed spot, but we'd had no sign that British Aerospace was aware of our presence so it seemed safe enough.

We'd brought lots of food that first night, as well as a flask of soup, and even a tiny bottle of whisky, which was perhaps a mistake since the point of the exercise was to stay awake and alert. Lying on our backs munching our sandwiches, we stared up at the stars and reflected on how beautiful the sky was when seen from the darkness of the countryside. My tummy comfortably full, I soon drifted off to sleep.

Unfortunately, Jo fell asleep too – we were both supposed to stay awake – and by the time I woke it was four o'clock and we'd slept through half the night. We laughed about spending the night asleep in a field of cows when we were supposed to be carrying out serious observation work. However, we'd learnt a lesson for subsequent visits, when we always took it in turns to watch and to sleep, thus ensuring that we missed nothing.

❖

Around the time of that first recce, in November 1995, I wrote to British Aerospace to ask whether Jo, Lotta, Angie and I could meet with Dick Evans, the Chief Executive, to discuss our concerns. Surprisingly (not least because at the time I was on bail for pouring fake blood over a Hawk at a British Aerospace display) we were offered a meeting, not with Dick Evans, but with Locksley Ryan, the Director of Communications.

Mr Ryan met us in a smart London hotel near the British Aerospace offices in Victoria, a venue he was perhaps more comfortable with than we were. He arrived with two other public relations men and they took us to a conference room, where a large table was set with blotters, notepads and pencils. A waiter came in and offered us tea. It all felt rather odd, especially since we had come straight from spending a weekend conspiring to disarm some of their planes.

We started in immediately on the questions we'd brought.

"Do you think it's right to sell weapons to oppressive regimes?" I asked.

"It's difficult to make judgements on other people's information," Mr Ryan replied. "I don't have any reason to feel personally that we're doing anything wrong. If there was any concrete evidence of repression then the UK government would tell us about it."

His faith in the government was touching. He went on to explain why British Aerospace had to rely on the government to decide where they could sell their weapons.

"The principle," he explained, "is that we are a business which makes particular products and relies on a bureaucratic process to assess whether or not the guidelines are being followed. We don't have the resources to make our own decisions."

We pointed out that it wasn't necessary to have a lot of resources to know that Indonesia was committing gross violations of human rights in East Timor. By selling weapons to the regime, British Aerospace was condoning those abuses.

Mr Ryan disputed this and it very soon became clear that we had reached stalemate. The British Aerospace men wouldn't accept that their company had any responsibility for the use to which their weapons were put, and we wouldn't accept that they didn't. They claimed to have total confidence in the government's objectivity when assessing applications for export licences.

"So do you think the export guidelines are being followed in the case of Indonesia?" Angie asked finally. The answer was a triumph of skewed logic.

"If we're issued with a licence, then by definition the guidelines are being followed," Mr Ryan said. It seemed not to have occurred to him that they might be issued with a licence precisely because the guidelines were *not* being followed.

61

It sometimes felt as if my whole life had been taken over by the action; if we weren't in a weekend meeting, I'd be in a subgroup meeting, or travelling up to Warton with Jo, or putting together information to use as evidence in court, or scouring bookshops and libraries for more details about Hawks.

There seemed to be no end to it, no demarcation between my ordinary life and the preparation for the action. Even when I wasn't actually working on it, my thoughts turned to it constantly. I wanted to discuss it with everyone I met, to share my fears and excitement, and to bounce ideas off others. However, we'd decided to keep the action very quiet and I had to rein in my urge to tell the world about our plans.

Secrecy has always been a major issue within the Ploughshares movement, because of the fear of conspiracy charges if the authorities can prove that others knew about the action beforehand and did nothing to stop it. Most actions in the United States have been planned in extreme secrecy, even to the extent of not telling people who are very close to those involved and will undoubtedly be affected by what happens.

When I lived in Washington DC, three of the people in the community were preparing for the ANZUS Ploughshares action, in which they disarmed a B-52 warplane shortly before the Gulf War started. The rest of us knew something was up, but were not allowed to know any details. There were frequent furtive meetings, in which they would shut themselves in the office, lower their voices and throw a blanket over the computer screen if one of us chanced to walk in on them.

Whilst understanding why they were going to these lengths, I found the secrecy very difficult to deal with personally as well as quite destructive of the community. The implicit message was that we couldn't be trusted with any details, even if we understood the risks involved and were willing to take them. Not knowing when these three people were suddenly going to disappear, leaving the rest of us to shoulder their responsibilities, left me feeling insecure and upset. An atmosphere of mistrust and mutual suspicion hovered over what was in most other ways a close and supportive community. And whilst it all dissipated after the action, and the community set to work on prison support, I couldn't help wondering whether this extreme secrecy was strictly necessary.

Ploughshares in Sweden, in contrast, tends to be a much more open movement. There seems to be a belief amongst many activists that there is more integrity in acting openly and honestly, and trying to have a dialogue with those whose weapons are the target of the disarmament. Sometimes Swedish activists have even contacted the companies in advance, and told them that they will – at some unspecified date – be disarming some of their weapons. Despite this, actions have still been successful. It would be fair to say, however, that prison sentences in the US have been much more severe than in Sweden, so it is understandable that people are more concerned about conspiracy charges.

Secrecy or openness was the subject of many long and animated discussions for us, until eventually we managed to reach a kind of loose agreement about where we stood. On one hand, being secret meant that the chances of actually carrying out the action were maximised, and the chances of others being charged with conspiracy reduced. At the same time, it meant not being able to be completely honest with our families and friends. In addition, having to be careful not to mention our plans in any but the closest circles could cultivate an inherent suspiciousness which we recognised might be destructive.

For me, the overwhelming priority was to get to the planes and disarm them; other considerations were secondary. Although I was somewhat uncomfortable with secrecy and the problems it could engender, I felt that a degree of stealth was a price worth paying in order to be able to disarm the Hawks and prevent them leaving for Indonesia. At the same time, though, I wanted to be able to discuss our plans – in broad terms – with close friends and family. I wanted them to feel that I trusted them not to share the information inappropriately, and I was also anxious not to just disappear from their lives, without a chance to explain or say goodbye.

Others in the group felt that they would like to be more open – although not to the extent of informing British Aerospace of our plans – in order to be more inclusive of other people. They didn't want other people in the campaign to feel upset and excluded when they only found out afterwards what we'd been planning for so long. And being very secret would be a big emotional strain, having to always edge around conversations to avoid tricky questions.

In the end, after much debate, we agreed that we could tell the broad details of the action to close friends and family more or less on a "need-to-know" basis. We would keep the group informed of who we had talked to, and would stress to anyone who was told that this was not a topic for discussion with others. We would also not tell anyone what the date or target of the action was, although anyone who knew about the long-standing involvement of several members of the group in the campaign against the Hawk deal could probably have guessed.

However, even the relatively high level of secrecy we chose wasn't enough for everyone. After spending a weekend with us, one potential new member said that she couldn't join the group, in large part because she felt we were not secret enough and were putting ourselves at risk of conspiracy charges. We were sad that she felt that way, as it would have been great to have had her in the group, but we were agreed that we didn't want to increase the secrecy level any further.

At times, trying to be secret became almost farcical. On one occasion, shortly before the action, Angie, Jo, Lotta and I were meeting at a friend's flat in London. It was absolutely freezing, with the only heating being from a gas fire in the living room. Unfortunately – for reasons known only to the owner of the flat – the living room contained no fewer than five telephones, all apparently connected. We were cautious about talking near telephones, believing – rightly or wrongly – that they could be modified to act as microphones, and had taken to unplugging them whenever possible. These ones, however, were the old-fashioned kind which couldn't be unplugged. Being far too cold to go into another room, we compromised by putting a blanket over them and talking very quietly.

Working on the assumption that anyone's phone could

be tapped, we devised endless codes to convey information between us. Some were so complicated that rather than spreading information, we were merely spreading confusion. Occasionally I'd slip up, forget the code, and make some unguarded comment on the phone which I'd then spend days agonising about. We each chose a codename for use in the minutes of our meetings. "Gorilla", "wombat", "spider", "cat", "virus": looking at the minutes now, almost twenty years later, I can no longer remember who was who, apart from Emily's baby son Arkady, who was Bee. Whether this amateur subterfuge would have confused the police for long is questionable, but at the time it felt important. I rather liked the codenames in the same way I liked sneaking around in the dark at Warton; it was fun, like playing spies but with a serious purpose.

It's easy to laugh at the lengths we went to, and the absurd codes we came up with in case anyone was listening in to our conversations or got their hands on our notes. Weren't we being ridiculously paranoid? Well, perhaps not.

It came out in 2003 – through a *Sunday Times* investigation – that Campaign Against Arms Trade (CAAT), Stop the Hawk Deal and various other groups had been spied on for years by a private company employed by British Aerospace. They had infiltrated people into several groups and even the campaigns co-ordinator for CAAT, Martin Hogbin, turned out to be a spy. He had been feeding vast amounts of information back to his employer, Evelyn le Chêne, who ran a company called Threat Response International which specialised in spying on activists.

Whilst the scale of the infiltration was shocking, I wasn't too surprised at the mere fact of it. I'd had my suspicions already about a man called Ken who kept popping up at Stop the Hawk Deal events around Manchester. He was very vague about his background and appeared to be keener to get to know details of our lives than to educate himself on the Hawk deal, about which he seemed to know little. I once found him in our office, peering into the filing cabinet; he had no reason to be there and quickly made some excuse and left. I tried to set aside my concerns: we were such a small group, it seemed absurd that anyone might want to spy on us. But I was right: like Martin, "Ken" was a spy, along with "Alan" who infiltrated an arms trade group in Hull, a photographer called Paul Mercer who had attended a number of our events, and several others. We were well and truly under surveillance.

It turned out that several of us in Seeds of Hope featured in the thousands of pages of information sent to British Aerospace. The level of detail was ludicrous, and quite often simply wrong, as if the spies had been making things up in order to justify their wage packets. At one point, the informant (I assume "Ken") stated – incorrectly – that I had moved out of Manchester, his sole evidence being that my spare bicycle helmet (I didn't even possess a spare bicycle helmet) was no longer in the office. I don't know where they found these spies, but "Ken" was more Inspector Clouseau than George Smiley.

I like to think about British Aerospace's reaction when they found out we'd hammered on one of their Hawks. They had been paying vast amounts to Evelyn le Chêne in order to find out every last detail of protests and protesters against the

Hawk deal. They'd even been watching some of us in Seeds of Hope. Yet we had slipped in behind their backs and carried out an extremely audacious action without them noticing.

In November 1995, I gave up my flat in Manchester and moved in with Jo in Liverpool: it made no sense to have an unnecessary empty property to worry about if we ended up in prison. Jo and I – and sometimes Lotta – started visiting Warton frequently during the day, as well as at night. Our daytime visits had a single purpose: to find out where the Indonesian Hawks were kept. The site is enormous, a vast airfield with a multitude of hangars. It was possible we'd only have a few minutes to reach the Hawks before we were noticed, so it was vital to know exactly where we were going.

During the peace camp at Warton earlier that year, Jo and I had climbed over a fence into the site one evening, but were soon spotted by security guards and put into a car to be driven out. Sitting in the back seat, I noticed a map of the site on the floor. I nudged Jo, pointed with my eyes at the map and made a questioning face. Jo understood immediately, and leaned forward between the seats to engage the guards in conversation whilst I surreptitiously folded up the map – a tricky exercise as it was very large and laminated – and shoved it under my jumper. It proved to be very useful.

When Jo and I had wandered around the site on another occasion, we had peeped into all the buildings and had seen Hawks in one of the hangars by the back gate. We knew by the serial numbers that they were not destined for Indonesia, but it was a good place to start looking.

In fact, it turned out during the trial that Indonesian Hawks were not usually kept in that hangar at all. The one we disarmed was there just for a few days because it had developed a problem with its electronics and required special tests. However, the fact that we had known that this plane was in that hangar on that day was taken by British Aerospace as evidence that we'd had inside information. The suggestion that we knew because we'd spent days and days sitting in a ditch watching the site was clearly too ridiculous to contemplate.

From the limited information available to us, we knew that the Hawks were due to be delivered to Indonesia in January, although we didn't know the exact date. A decision had already been made, based on our recces, that a Sunday would be the best night to do the action, as there was less activity on the site than on other nights. We set a date: 22 January.

In the week running up to that date, Jo and I went up to Warton several times, hoping to see an Indonesian Hawk. Each time, we'd come home after a long, cold day of watching, to report to the rest of the group that we hadn't seen one.

The final recce brought no joy. We still weren't sure where they were keeping the Hawks, but were due to do the action that weekend. This raised a big issue within the group: some people felt that we should postpone for a week, to allow more time for recces, so we could be absolutely sure where the planes were. Others wanted to go ahead, feeling that we'd made all our plans and just had to hope for the best at that point, whilst a third group was happy with either decision.

It has to be remembered that we were all under a huge

amount of pressure at this point. We were about to do something which we'd been planning for nearly a year, which could put some of us behind bars for several years, with everyone in the group at risk of conspiracy charges. The potential for a relatively small issue to become a big one was never far away.

The huge stress of the situation was too much: a big conflict arose between those wanting to go ahead, and those wanting to wait. There was upset and anger and a loss of trust between us. At the last minute, it looked as if the action we'd spent so long preparing for was about to be derailed.

We couldn't let that happen: we had to find a way to somehow hold it all together, and to be able to carry on with the action. To that end, we had an emergency meeting of all ten of us in London. Over the course of a couple of days, we talked and argued and cried, and somehow managed to reach a decision. It was a very difficult time for everyone, and the fact that we were able to get through it is testament to each person's commitment to our shared vision of disarmament.

The decision was made to move the date back to the following Sunday. Jo and I would continue to do recces, and if we still hadn't seen a Hawk by then, we'd go ahead anyway. It was a trade-off between the desire of some people in the group to be absolutely certain of the whereabouts of the Hawks, and the reality that, if we waited too long, they might leave before we got there.

Jo and I went up to Warton several times after that emergency meeting. It was laborious, tiring work; the journey took three hours each way, and often we set off in the early hours and didn't get home until very late. On our earlier recces, we had arrived in the daytime and lurked in the lane at the back of the site, which was a dead end used mostly by workers, with the occasional planespotter or walker. We tried to look inconspicuous, busying ourselves with a map if anyone appeared, or diving into the hedge if there was time.

Once, however, we had arrived to find two cars parked in the lane, with men standing by them with binoculars. We thought they were security officers rather than planespotters as they were wearing suits and driving Rovers: all British Aerospace's company cars at that time were Rovers, a legacy from the days when they owned the company. We had stayed for a while, closely scrutinised by these men, before deciding that we were just too obvious and giving up for the day. It was clear that a new tactic was needed.

What we came up with was each sitting in a separate spot in a field behind the site, from where we could see the doors of all three hangars. However, the only way to get there without being seen was to arrive while it was still dark. This meant staying overnight in Preston in order to catch the 6am bus, which arrived in Warton before the long winter night came to an end.

We could cut through fields for most of the way to the site but at one point we had to walk about a hundred yards on the road. I led the way the first time, sprinting as fast as I dared down the icy lane. Just before I reached the field, I heard a car coming up behind me, and I only just managed to squeeze under a barbed wire fence and flatten myself on the ground before its headlights swept over me. Jo quickly followed, and we lay on the frozen ground in the darkness, panting and laughing. It all seemed rather melodramatic and I wondered whether we were taking ourselves just a bit too seriously.

Once in position, we had to stay there until darkness fell again, so we could leave without being seen. That meant sitting alone for the whole day, unable to move around in case we missed something or were spotted, with nothing to do except keep a constant eye on the site in front of us.

From my ditch I could hear the beeping noise which signalled the opening of the hangar doors, and each time I would grab my binoculars and peer across the fields, hoping that this time I'd see the right plane. Time after time I would be disappointed; it would be a Tornado, a non-Indonesian Hawk, or just one of the little buggies which are used to pull planes around. Finally, after hours of watching and seeing nothing, it would be dark enough to leave without being spotted. We'd set off on the long journey home, cold, exhausted and dreading having to come back and do it all again. But that was what needed to be done, and a couple of days later, we'd be back.

Our third recce was another freezing day, with an icy wind and frequent showers of sleet. I was tired and miserable and very soon chilled to the bone, and wanted to be anywhere but alone in a wet ditch in Lancashire. Days and days of watching had led me to despair of ever seeing one of these planes. I'd even started wondering whether we'd got completely the wrong idea and the planes were in fact kept on the other side of the site.

We sat and sat. I could see Jo from my position, but she

was too far away to communicate with and we'd agreed not to cross the field between us during the day as it would expose us to view. I couldn't move around to keep warm and within half an hour my fingers and feet were frozen. The hangar doors were opening and closing constantly, and each time I heard the warning noise I'd peer out of the ditch, hoping desperately that this time it would be an Indonesian Hawk.

By about noon, I was desperate to go home. We'd agreed that, because we were both so tired, we'd give up and creep away if we saw nothing by two o'clock, and I was counting down the minutes until I could be released from this icy tomb. I heard the doors again, and wearily picked up my binoculars.

The nose of the plane came out. It was undoubtedly a Hawk, a strange apple-green one. "Come on, come on," I was muttering, as it moved slowly out of the huge doors. I leaned forward, resting my elbows on the top of the ditch to steady the binoculars. The vital thing was the serial number. Finally the plane came all the way out and I could just make out the number in black on the tail. ZH 955. I blinked and looked again, screwing up my eyes to make sure I'd read it correctly. ZH 955 – there was no mistake. It was an Indonesian Hawk.

I wanted to yell and shout and jump up and down. Days and days of watching and waiting had finally paid off. We knew where they were keeping an Indonesian Hawk! We could go home! I frantically gathered my scattered belongings and stuffed them into my rucksack. From her vantage point, Jo could also see the large hangar – albeit not as well as I could – and we'd agreed that if we saw a Hawk, she would come over to me, to save extra trips across the exposed field. I thought she'd also be packing up, but she was still in the same position, not moving at all.

Impatiently, I slithered out of the ditch and ran along the hedge, keeping my head down low, until I was opposite Jo but still some distance away. Still she didn't move. Finally I could wait no longer, and started whistling as loudly as I dared. She turned and looked at me and I made frantic beckoning motions.

"What is it?" she asked as she approached.

"Didn't you see it? An Indonesian Hawk coming out of the big hangar?"

It turned out she'd been looking at another hangar and had missed the Hawk, but on hearing the news she broke into a huge grin. We grabbed each other, laughing and hugging. This was the moment we'd been waiting for: we knew where a Hawk was. Everything was set. We were ready to go.

CHAPTER 7

TYING UP LOOSE ENDS

For weeks before the action, I had been saying my good-byes to friends and family. I had visited old friends whom I hadn't seen for many months and explained to them that I might not be around for a while. Most of them knew enough about my lifestyle not to ask too many questions, and were content with the explanation that I was likely to be in prison for some time, and that all would be revealed to them very soon. It felt rather like having a terminal illness, this desire to leave relationships in good order and tie up the loose ends of one's life.

On New Year's Eve 1995, the group shared a final ritual together. After this, we did not expect to meet all together until well after the action; we were ready to go, and were simply waiting for the right moment. The ritual was to confirm our commitment to each other and to the action and to mark an end to the preparation we had been doing for nearly a year, and a start of the next stage of our work together.

We spread out the banner and sat on the floor around it. Everyone had brought an item that was of special significance to her; these were passed round and their meaning explained. Among other things there was a stick picked up from the riverbank outside the British Aerospace site, a paper chain of dolls, a glass of water, a paper ball, a peace crane and a photograph of a young woman injured in the Santa Cruz massacre in East Timor, which Jo would later leave on the wing of the disarmed Hawk.

We had a meditation on the theme of fear, violence and despair, in which each of us wrote on a piece of paper what these words meant to us. This was for each of us alone, not to be shared with the group. The papers were then burnt. Next we did another meditation – this time on the theme of hope – whilst holding a handful of seeds we had brought with us. The ash from the burnt paper was mixed with the seeds, and we each took a little of the mixture, to be scattered wherever we felt appropriate.

Finally, after some readings, drumming, singing and silence, we had a blessing ceremony for the hammers. Lotta and I already had ours, but Angie and Jo were presented with theirs for the first time, beautifully carved by Rowan and Ricarda. Sitting there holding my hammer, thinking about what we were planning to do and the likely consequences, the action suddenly felt much closer. I had spent months coming to terms with my fears, and now I was ready to go ahead; the fears were still there, but the imperative to act was stronger.

The night before the action, I rang my parents for the last time. We had been together a few weeks earlier, over Christmas, and

I had told them then that I would shortly be embarking on something which might put me in prison for a considerable length of time.

Over the years, my parents had become accustomed to the idea of having a daughter who was frequently arrested, even put in prison. I know they would have preferred me not to do such things, but they had never tried to stop me. Speaking to them that night, I wanted to tell them that this might be the last time I would speak to them from outside prison for some time. But I held back, worried as ever about our phone being tapped. I had been vague about my movements over the next few weeks, and hoped that this would be enough to give my parents the hint that the action was imminent. We exchanged the usual pleasantries and family news, then said goodbye as normal.

That night, I reread the booklet we had prepared to leave at the site, to remind myself of the importance of what we were doing. It included the history of the Indonesian invasion and eyewitness accounts of the brutalities that followed. Timorese voices – so rarely heard – would explain far better than we could the nature of the regime to which Britain was selling weapons. We chose the words of Mr Siong, who was in the capital, Dili, when the invasion began and described the scene at the harbour:

People came in groups of two or three or four, stood on the wharf and were shot. One group after the other coming and coming, killed and thrown into the sea.... Some are shot and fall into the sea at once, but if they fall on the wharf we have

to tie the pipe to them. We are trembling, we are nearly gone
mad, but we don't know what to do, just do whatever the
Indonesians want. *

We added statements of Timorese who had seen Hawks –
sold by Britain to Indonesia in 1978 – bombing villages in
the mountains, and information about international law, the
Hawk deal and the attack capabilities of the planes. Finally,
Jo, Lotta and Angie and I each put in our own personal
statements of conscience.

Reading the accounts of atrocities carried out by the
Indonesian military made me ashamed and angry that our
supposedly "civilised" country could be involved in aiding
and abetting such inhumanity. I felt very sure that whatever
happened to us in the next few days, weeks, months, even
years, as a result of our action, what we were about to do was
absolutely the right thing.

---

* Michele Turner, *Telling East Timor: Personal Testimonies 1942–1992*, New
South Wales University Press, 1992.

CHAPTER 8

───────────

"I'VE FOUND A WAY IN!"

It had been an odd kind of day, most of it spent at Jo's flat in Kirkby, near Liverpool, in last-minute preparations. Lotta, Jo and I had packed our bags ready for prison, defrosted the fridge, run round several times to Jo's neighbour to leave valuable items for safekeeping, and made a strange meal out of all the perishable food in the flat.

Busy as we were that day, my thoughts were never far from what lay ahead of us. I felt a strange mixture of euphoria that the day we had been preparing for so long had come at last, sadness at what we were leaving behind, and fear at the unknown into which we were about to step.

Many sites where Ploughshares actions have taken place – military bases, manufacturing plants - have been very remote, and activists have had no option but to be dropped off by car. However, we had decided that taking the bus would be safer as the road to the site was a dead end, and there would be little reason for driving down there late at night. If British Aerospace did know we were coming, we would play straight into their hands and our driver would almost certainly be charged with conspiracy.

To get from Kirkby to Preston – the nearest town to the British Aerospace site – took two buses and a train. It was very late when we arrived; the town centre was almost deserted but I nonetheless felt very noticeable as we trudged from the station with our huge bags. We had an hour to wait for the last bus. The only place still open was a pizza restaurant, its warm red lights beckoning enticingly as we stood outside in the cold night. Not wanting to be hanging around in a freezing bus station, we decided to go in to pass the time.

The restaurant had double doors, and as Lotta struggled through them her heavy bag of tools swung against the glass with a loud metallic crash which echoed around the room and caused all the diners to look up in surprise. In confusion, we hastened to a table in the corner, ordered hot drinks and tried to look inconspicuous.

It was a strangely surreal experience; here we were, sitting in a pizza restaurant, surrounded by people going about their normal lives, and we were about to launch ourselves into something which was likely to put us behind bars for several years. None of us wanted to talk much: there was nothing much left to say. I stared out of the window at the empty streets and tears dropped slowly into my tea.

The final bus ride didn't take long, and soon we were climbing off in Warton. Lotta and I got off a stop before Jo, and we walked through the village separately, thinking it might be less suspicious if we weren't all together. We had torches but didn't want to draw attention to ourselves, so we skulked along in the moonlight. We passed along a road lined with houses, then dived down a narrow footpath behind a row of cottages. I'd walked this path so many times that even in the dark I knew exactly where there was a concrete post lying on the path, and was able to warn Lotta to avoid it.

The route we had always taken at night went straight through the middle of a boatyard. There was no way of avoiding it, as it occupied a narrow shelf of land between the river on one side and a high bank on the other. This hadn't been a problem before, as the boatyard had been deserted every time we crept through late at night. This time, however, a light was on and a man was working outside: there was no way through without passing within a few feet of him. It seemed very odd to be repairing a boat in the freezing cold at nearly midnight, and for a second the thought flashed through my mind that perhaps he was a spy for British Aerospace, in position to catch us as we came past. I quickly tried to put this ludicrous idea out of my mind.

The man hadn't seen us, and Lotta and I tiptoed back into the darkness to wait for Jo. When she arrived, we had a whispered conversation about what to do. We quickly dismissed the idea of taking a different route: the only other way to the site was back through the village and then down the road which ran along the eastern end of the runway. We would almost certainly be spotted. There was only one option: to climb the bank, which from where I was standing looked almost vertical.

The bank was made of loose earth, anchored by wet brambles which grabbed at our legs and hands as we scrambled upwards in the pitch dark beneath the trees. Our heavy bags made progress very slow, and often we would slip and slide a few feet before being able to regain a foothold. Finally we reached the top, puffing and gasping, and climbed over a barbed wire fence onto the path.

From there the route was simple; we had plotted it out to the last yard and even with our torches off Jo and I knew precisely where we should branch off from the path and across a field, which gates to climb, where was the best place to squeeze under the fences, where the farm buildings were. On one of our earlier trips, a dog had started barking in a nearby farmhouse as we passed, so we had modified the route and now stayed well away from any kind of habitation.

We knew from our many recces that on other nights of the week there were often people working in the hangar all night, but on Sundays the lights were always off, and the only people on the site were the security patrols. This time, however, as we got closer we saw that the lights were on.

I was suddenly thrown into panic; perhaps, despite all our carefully coded phone calls and cryptic letters, British Aerospace were onto us. We huddled together in the dark for a quick discussion. There were two options: we could carry on and hope for the best, or we could return home and come back the following Sunday.

We knew that the Hawks were due to be delivered to Indonesia any day. It was too risky to leave it a whole week. Besides that, we were as prepared as we were ever going to be. We'd said our goodbyes, packed our bags, and prepared ourselves emotionally as well as practically for doing the action that night. We would go ahead as planned, and hope for the best.

❖

We were close to the fence by now, and looking for a suitable spot with a little cover, where we could wait until it was time to go in. Our plan was to watch from outside the site for two security patrols to go by before we entered, so we'd know roughly how frequent they were and wouldn't be taken by surprise whilst cutting the fence.

Suddenly we heard the noise of an engine, and a searchlight swept over the frozen fields towards us. I dived into a ditch whilst Jo and Lotta flattened themselves on the ground. I hardly dared breathe as the bright beam came closer and closer to where we were lying. It passed over us then was gone, and we were once again plunged into a cold darkness relieved only by a little moonlight and the distant floodlights around the huge hangar. I had a moment's panic; we had never seen a searchlight in any of our night time visits to the site. Were British Aerospace lying in wait for us, having discovered our plans? Or was it merely coincidence?

Several weeks earlier, I had taken part in a vigil outside the site, with a few friends from the Stop the Hawk Deal group. A small army of security guards had watched us suspiciously from behind the gates, shut and locked as soon as we hove into sight. Later, I walked around the perimeter fence, and was trailed the whole way by plain-clothes guards driving a few feet behind me.

It was with that day in mind that I was feeling decidedly

worried about the level of security we were likely to encounter, and the powerful searchlight did nothing to reduce my fears. However, the security vehicle drove on, and I gradually calmed down, reassured that we had not been found out.

It was a freezing night; there had been heavy snow a few days before and much of it was still lying. In the last days before the action, as the snow fell ever deeper around Jo's flat, I'd stared despondently out at the whitening landscape around us and worried about whether we'd make it to Warton at all, reliant as we were on public transport.

There was another worry: we might be more easily spotted against snow as we crept across the fields to the site. We had planned to wear dark clothes on the walk, then before we entered the site to change into blue boiler suits of the kind worn by British Aerospace mechanics. This was so that, at a glance and from a distance, we might be taken for workers rather than intruders.

The advent of the snow sparked long discussions about whether it would be better to wear white for maximum concealment. In the event, enough of the snow had melted for us to decide to carry on with our original plan. In any case, it was unlikely that anyone would be out in the fields at midnight on an icy January night.

We passed the time outside the fence watching the hangar through binoculars, looking for any signs of movement, and jumping around trying to keep warm. We didn't talk much, each deep in our own thoughts about what was ahead of us – not just the next few hours, but possibly the next few years. I tried to focus my mind on why we were there; I'd spent nearly a year thinking about prison and coming to terms with my fears of it, and now I wanted to concentrate on the action at hand.

Finally, the sound of an engine broke the silence and another patrol drove into sight. We flattened ourselves against the sides of the newly-dug ditch in which we were standing; the lights passed over our heads and were gone. The time had come. We stood in a circle, held hands and had a minute's silence. Images came flooding into my mind; young people, covered in blood, screaming in terror as Indonesian soldiers opened fire on them in the Santa Cruz cemetery in Dili after a peaceful procession. A young boy standing in front of a banner showing the East Timorese resistance leader, Xanana Gusmao. Both of the boy's arms are raised; one fist is clenched in a gesture of defiance, whilst with his other hand he is making a victory sign. His face is set, determined. Shortly after the picture was taken, he was shot by the Indonesian military, one more casualty in a bloody occupation which had claimed the lives of a third of the Timorese population.

I thought also of the promotional video we had recently watched about Hawk aircraft. Along with much gloating over the attack capability of the plane – the narrator almost salivating as he declares that the Hawk "packs a healthy wallop" – there are shots of a Hawk flying in low and firing a missile into a tank, which explodes in a ball of fire. Although it was obviously a scene created for the camera, it was impossible to watch it without thinking about the outcome if the target was a house in East Timor. Standing in that ditch, many thousands of miles from East Timor, I felt a great connection with the people who would be at the receiving end of these

British weapons, and a great sense that what we were about to do was right and necessary.

For several weeks I had been having panic attacks. They would swoop on me out of nowhere; walking down the street, not even thinking about the action, my legs would suddenly turn to jelly, my heart would start pounding and great waves of panic would engulf me. I'd have to sit down and take some deep breaths to calm myself. These episodes made me worried about how I would cope on the night: if I could react like that beforehand, how much worse would it be in the actual event?

But now I felt very calm and focused. We'd spent nearly a year in planning, and had talked through every last detail of what we were to do, right down to the configuration in which we'd cut the fence and who would wield each tool as we broke into the hangar. I think we all needed reassurance that we could carry off this disarmament, and such detailed planning offered a sense of security; there were to be, we hoped, no surprises.

We finished the minute's silence, gave each other a last hug, and headed for the fence. Lotta and I were carrying boltcutters, Jo had the Japanese peace cranes we'd made to tie on the fence as a symbol of our peaceful intentions.

Lotta and I worked on cutting an arch-shaped hole in the fence, whilst Jo tied the peace cranes nearby, her frozen fingers struggling with the string. We were confident the fence wasn't alarmed: Jo and I had made a small cut in it during one of our night time recces some weeks earlier, before giving it a vigorous shake and scuttling behind a bush to watch for any reaction. Nothing had happened.

(After the trial, a British Aerospace worker in an unguarded moment told us that there was in fact a movement sensor on the site but it was set off so often by rabbits that it was generally ignored. Perhaps that night the security guards were sitting in their office wondering vaguely about the three extremely large rabbits hopping around.)

It seemed to take ages to cut the fence; our hands were cold and we were made clumsy by the urgency of the situation. Finally the last strand gave way. I scrambled through the hole and grabbed the bags which Lotta and Jo passed to me before squeezing through themselves.

From where we had got in, it was only about fifty yards to the nearest entrance, a fire door on the corner of the building. However, we had to walk through chest-high grass, which was dry and frozen, and crunched and snapped as we passed. There was otherwise complete silence and the noise of the grass seemed incredibly loud. But there was nobody to hear us, and soon we were clambering up the bank onto the road around the hangar.

The fire door was right in front of us. We planned to smash the glass, then reach through and push the exit bar from the inside. Having no idea how strong the glass would be, we'd taken no chances and come equipped ("armed" as the prosecutor would later put it with no sense of irony) with an enormously heavy iron bar, a weight from inside a sash window. It had been ceremoniously presented to us a few weeks earlier by Ricarda and Rowan who were replacing their windows. Not wanting it to appear to be an offensive weapon, they had carefully painted "Women disarming for life and justice" on it.

There was a camera over the fire door, and security lights on each corner of the hangar. Standing there in the glare of the lights I felt very exposed and vulnerable. Surely they must have noticed us? What if we were caught now?

We'd talked a great deal about what we could do to make the action a success even if we didn't manage to disarm the Hawks. To that end, we carried with us personal statements and a video we had made to leave at the site to explain what we had come to do. We even had business cards with our names and "Seeds of Hope East Timor Ploughshares" inscribed on them. Nobody would be left in any doubt as to what our intentions were.

But despite all that, I knew that I'd be desperately disappointed if we failed to hammer on the planes. And more than any personal feelings, the fact was that we were trying to prevent these Hawks from leaving for Indonesia; it was absolutely vital that we were able to carry out the action as planned.

The glass smashed easily, and Lotta put her hand through the window, feeling about for the bar inside. "I can't find it!" she whispered. "Can you break the other panel?" I smashed the other panel of glass. "I still can't feel it," she said, her voice tense. "Let's try the crowbars!"

In desperation, and expecting a heavy hand on our shoulders at any minute, we set to with the crowbars, but the gap between the two doors was too thin for them. Things weren't looking good: it would be terrible to be caught now, so near and yet so far from our target.

While Lotta and I wrestled with the door, Jo ran off round the corner to see if we could get in anywhere else. A couple of minutes later she was back. "I've found a way in!" she said.

There were small doors set into the big folding metal shutters which opened to let the planes in and out of the hangar, but in our planning we'd dismissed these as being too difficult to crack. However, Jo had almost got one open with her crowbar; a little extra pressure from Lotta and me, and the whole lock popped off. We were in.

CHAPTER 9

═══════════

"DID YOU DAMAGE THE PLANE?"

The lights in the hangar were on low, bathing all the planes inside in an eerie green light. We were interested in only one of them: an Indonesian Hawk. By this time, Jo and I were experts on how to identify Hawks. We'd spent hours browsing military aircraft magazines and planespotters' guides. We knew how to tell a Hawk 60 from a Hawk 100 and a Hawk 100 from a Hawk 200. We knew which serial numbers had been allocated to the Indonesian order of 24 Hawks. British Aerospace were also making the planes for other countries, including Saudi Arabia and, whilst that regime committed plenty of its own human rights abuses, we needed to keep the issue very clear, and not hammer on the wrong planes.

But there, standing right in front of us, was the apple green Hawk ground-attack plane which Jo and I had seen being taken out of the hangar two days earlier. The lettering on its tail – ZH 955 – told us that it was destined for the Indonesian military, one of the world's most brutal regimes. This was one of the actual weapons they planned to use to perpetrate murder in East Timor.

I'd expected it to be much bigger. For so long it had loomed large in my imagination, filling my thoughts, screaming into my dreams, overwhelming me with its power and violence. And yet now that we were standing in front of it, the Hawk seemed so small, so vulnerable – so easy to disarm.

By this time we'd been inside the site for about ten minutes. We'd cut through a fence, smashed two panes of glass, and forced a door, all under the eye of security cameras. Discovery must be imminent: we had to work fast.

I had a heavy lump hammer which I'd bought a few months earlier to chip mortar off old bricks when I was rebuilding a wall. I'd decorated it with the words from the biblical book of Isaiah which have inspired so many disarmament actions: "They shall beat their swords into ploughshares and their spears into pruning hooks". On the handle I'd painted "Choose life!", a reference to another biblical line, from Deuteronomy: "I put before you life and death, blessing and curse. Therefore, choose life". For me, this action was all about choosing life: choosing to say yes to a disarmed world and no to weapons of destruction; to say yes to nonviolence and no to violence; to say yes to accountability for our actions and no to the abdication of responsibility shown by British Aerospace and the British government.

Jo had a smaller hammer which had been a gift from friends, and Lotta had two hammers, which had both been used in previous Ploughshares actions. One of the beautiful things about Ploughshares actions is that anyone can do them. You don't need to be a technical genius or an engineer, you don't need to be physically strong, you don't need any expensive equipment or special skills. All you need is a hammer and a functioning arm. We each had both of those things. We started hammering.

The Hawk turned out to be surprisingly fragile. At best, I had thought, we might be able to make a few dents in the fuselage. This was, after all, a weapon capable of mass destruction; how could our little hammers make much impact on it?

Molly Rush, one of the women who participated in the very first Ploughshares action in 1980, describes this same belief that these weapons are somehow inviolable:

One thing I hadn't realised until I was actually hammering on those things was the mystique I had personally put on those weapons. I had really assumed they would be impervious and I could hammer as much as I wanted and nothing would happen. I had this wild idea that, since they could travel beyond the atmosphere and come back and withstand the temperature, how in the world could my hammer do any harm?*

She soon found out that her hammer was quite sufficient to render the nosecones she was disarming totally unusable. The reality of DIY disarmament – as we soon discovered – is that a few well-placed hammer blows can make most weapons,

---

* Don Mason and Catherine Robinson (eds), *Challenge to the New God,* Gooday Publishing, 1988.

carefully and expensively forged to precise proportions, quite useless. Our first tentative blows dented the fuselage; a little more force with subsequent strikes and our hammers burst right through the metal outer skin, leaving large puncture holes in the sides of the plane.

Anxious as we were to choreograph the action to the last degree, we'd agreed our roles in advance. Lotta was to hammer on the bomb targeting and release controls in the cockpit. Jo would start on the nose, whilst I was to make a token blow before running round the hangar to see if there were any more Indonesian Hawks. If there were, I would start on them and the others would join me once they'd disarmed the first one.

The noise of metal striking metal as we hammered was deafening. The crashing and banging echoed round the huge hangar, and it seemed impossible that nobody had noticed we were there. After a few blows, I headed off to check out the rest of the planes. There were several Tornados, a few I couldn't identify, and three more Hawks, but none of them with Indonesian serial numbers.

The media later described our hammering as a "frenzied attack", but it was very far from that. It was purposeful, calm and deliberate. To me, it felt like a job of work; we'd been planning it for nearly a year, and now I wanted to make sure I did it properly.

My main emotion as I hammered was relief; something we'd spent so long thinking about, preparing for, worrying about, was completed. We'd done our part, and what happened from now on was up to the authorities. Handing that responsibility over was a very liberating experience; in the moments after we disarmed the plane, I felt an almost indescribable sense of freedom and happiness.

Lotta continued to hammer whilst Jo and I attached banners to the plane: the purple "Women disarming for life and justice" banner the group had made the previous summer, and a "BAe kills: swords into ploughshares" banner made by my friends in Washington DC for a vigil at British Aerospace's US offices during Chris's ploughshares trial a few years earlier.

We had each brought a packet of seeds and ashes from our New Year's Eve ritual, and we scattered them over the wings of the plane. I added a photograph of my baby niece, Skye. I wanted to say that ordinary children, just like her, were going to be killed with this weapon, and we couldn't ignore that reality just because we didn't know them personally.

We left copies of the video and booklet we'd made in the pilot's seat, which by now was covered with shards of glass from the shattered screens. We hoped that they would be seen by British Aerospace management, and after that by the police, and – if we went to trial – the jury, and that this would help them understand the reasons for our action. Leaving them in the cockpit was also a symbolic appeal to the pilot not to fly the plane to Indonesia.

By the time we'd strung up the banners, we'd been in the hangar for about twenty minutes, and there was still no sign of any security guards. But they would surely arrive soon; how could they not have noticed we were there?

We waited and waited. We sang a song, we talked, we ate

some of the food we'd brought with us. Suddenly we heard the noise of an engine nearby. Lotta ran over to the door of the hangar and looked out. "They're coming!" she shouted.

❖

This was the moment we'd been thinking about for so long: the moment of discovery. We had role-played this situation many times, in case the guards were angry that we had damaged "their" plane, or thought we'd put their jobs at risk. We had sneaked around Angie's barn, pretending to be hammering, whilst others playing security guards had suddenly turned up, angry and ready for violence.

We had agreed that as soon as we saw any sign of guards approaching, we would put down our tools and sit with our hands open in front of us so that we were as unthreatening as possible. At Lotta's shout we all sat down on the steps leading up to the cockpit of the Hawk, hands outstretched, hearts thumping. My legs were shaking almost uncontrollably and I pressed my hands down hard on my thighs to keep them still.

The engine noise grew louder, and soon we could see headlights through the far door of the hangar. The vehicle drove down the side of the building, nearer and nearer to where we were sitting. As the driver approached, he turned towards us; we could see his face quite clearly through the narrow windows in the shutter doors. But he looked away and carried on driving, and soon we saw the vehicle's tail lights disappearing across the runway.

This was really strange: how could he not have seen us? Lotta suggested we prop the door open to make ourselves more visible. She took a crowbar and put it up against the door, letting in a draught of icy air, and we continued hammering.

Soon we heard the noise of an engine again, and after a minute saw headlights on the runway. We ran out and waved, jumping up and down as we did so. The vehicle seemed to change direction and head straight for us so we hastened back inside, sure that we had been seen and wanting to be sitting by the plane when we were found.

The headlights came closer and closer. This was really it. I took some deep breaths and squeezed a bit closer to Jo. But suddenly the lights turned from white to red. The car was driving away.

In our planning, we thought we'd covered every conceivable eventuality. Unable to break into the building? Discovered immediately? Someone in the hangar? No Hawk in the hangar? The plane sitting outside on the tarmac? We'd discussed all of these situations and more but the one possibility we hadn't discussed was that of not being able to let British Aerospace know we were there. It hadn't been so unlikely that we didn't need to discuss it; it had been so unlikely we hadn't even thought of it.

I was desperately thirsty. On one side of the hangar was a door which I thought might lead to a washroom with a sink. Walking towards it, I spotted a small office which looked out across the floor of the hangar. On a desk near the door was a telephone. Of course: that was what we needed.

We hadn't brought a mobile phone – in 1996 they barely existed – and we hadn't considered the possibility of having time to find a landline and make some calls. We had a quick discussion of whom to call. First of all would be Angie to let her know that we'd disarmed the plane. She'd be able to inform the support group and then swing into action herself, informing people about what had happened, and preparing for further disarmament.

Angie was still at home when we called. She knew that the police would start looking for her as soon as they watched the video or read the booklet, and realised she was a conspirator in the action. However, she had quite a lot of experience of her local police, and wasn't expecting them to be very quick off the mark in their pursuit of her. She said she wouldn't stay at home much longer, but in any case her house was very remote and she could easily make off through the woods if the police approached.

Lotta was keen to ring her friends and family in Sweden. She had told several friends that she was going to do a Ploughshares action, although hadn't revealed any details. The phone woke Kajsa in Gothenburg, and at first, half asleep as she was, she didn't understand what Lotta was talking about. Suddenly she understood and Jo and I could hear the squeals of delight on the other end of the phone.

Still undiscovered, we then hit upon the idea of ringing a press agency, telling them what we'd done, and asking them to ring British Aerospace for a comment. That way not only would the security guards know we were there, but we might also make the news.

Jo made the call, and got through to a very sleepy journalist who knew nothing about East Timor and couldn't grasp what Jo was saying. She patiently explained the situation over and over again and ended up talking the journalist through the entire history of the Indonesian occupation in order to explain why we had just disarmed the Hawk.

"No, a Hawk. It's an attack plane. They're being sold to Indonesia and would be used in East Timor – "

"No, it's not part of Indonesia – "

"A Hawk. Britain is selling 24 of them to Indonesia. We've just disarmed one of them – "

"No, with hammers – "

Eventually Jo got the story across, and then we thought of one more person to ring. The Australian journalist John Pilger had been instrumental in bringing the situation in East Timor to the attention of the west. His documentary "Death of a Nation" had alerted many people for the first time to the atrocities going on there, and he had been vocal in his opposition to the Hawk deal. Would he mind being woken in the middle of the night? We decided he wouldn't.

While Jo was on the phone, Lotta was watching just outside the hangar door. Suddenly she dashed in and shouted across to me.

"They're coming!"

"Jo! Jo! Move it!", I yelled.

Putting the phone down, Jo shot out of the office and joined us by the door. Peering out, we could see the headlights of a security vehicle, and it was definitely heading our way. For the third time that night, we sat down on the steps and waited. This time, it seemed, was for real.

A Landrover stopped by the open door and two men got out, both dressed in dark uniforms and carrying torches. As they came through the door we said hello and smiled at them, but they didn't respond. One started walking around the hangar, whilst the other stood and looked at us silently for a few seconds before turning away and speaking quietly into his radio. After a minute he turned back to us and asked us to come with him to the car.

Friends in the US had told me about being forced to lie face down with a gun pointing at their heads when they'd disarmed a B-52 warplane. Clearly that wasn't going to happen at British Aerospace, but I'd expected a strong reaction when we were discovered. But this man's face was emotionless, his voice flat; there was nothing to indicate his feelings towards us. Picking up our bags, we followed him outside and climbed into the back of the Landrover.

"Did you damage the plane?" he asked over his shoulder as we drove off.

"We disarmed it," Lotta said.

"Did you damage any other planes?"

"No." After that he said nothing more, and we drove along in silence.

Jo and I had trespassed at Warton many times. Each time we were caught, we'd be driven to the main gate and released outside the site with a warning not to come back. As we headed across the runway this time, it felt no different and I started to wonder if we were just going to be let out as usual. Perhaps the lapse in security was so serious that British Aerospace would rather not be shown up by a trial?

However, it was not to be. We stopped inside the front gate where the security guard got out, leaving us sitting alone. A few moments later he returned and told us to follow him into the gatehouse.

We were taken into a back room and made to sit at a small table. A cup of recently abandoned tea stood steaming on a nearby bench. Another security guard appeared; Jo and I knew him, and we greeted him cheerfully. Normally he was friendly and chatty, but this time he barely acknowledged us, although he did tell another officer to make us a cup of tea.

Over the next few minutes more security guards arrived, each sticking their head round the door and having a look at us before disappearing. Several of them said hello to us, in a manner that was more puzzled than angry.

Everything was so bizarre that I was finding it difficult to take it all in. We'd breached all of British Aerospace's expensive security systems, disarmed one of their precious aeroplanes, and as a result – I assumed – were going to be the cause of more than a little embarrassment once the story got out. Now here we were sitting in a nice warm room being plied with company tea. It was all a bit odd.

Suddenly the room filled up with policemen. Six of them, which seemed excessive, but perhaps not much else was happening in the wilds of Lancashire that night so they'd all piled in for a bit of entertainment. We knew one of them from our peace camp at Warton the previous summer. Concerned for our safety, he had told us not to hesitate to ring the police if we had any trouble. He recognised us immediately, and smiled, saying, "Not you again!"

Finally a senior officer cleared his throat and announced, "This young man's got something to say to you." A young officer stepped forward and carefully recited his lines. "I am arresting you on suspicion of criminal damage. You do not have to say anything unless you wish to do so but it may harm your defence if you do not mention when questioned something you intend to rely on in court. Anything you say may be given in evidence."

Thus cautioned, we were led out to the waiting police van and put in the back with three officers. As we drove through the deserted lanes, not knowing what was to come but feeling relieved and happy, we held hands tightly and grinned into the blackness. We'd done it.

CHAPTER 10

═══════════════

"THIS ISN'T SOME KIND OF ADVENTURE,
YOU KNOW"

At around 5.30am, Lotta, Jo and I were led into Lytham police station, seven miles from Warton, each with an elbow gripped by a police officer. I had been arrested dozens of times before, but never for such a serious offence, and I was feeling quite apprehensive about our reception.

I was the first one to be dealt with. I was taken in front of a custody sergeant who asked my police officer what I'd been arrested for, then took my details and confiscated most of my belongings, although after some argument I was allowed to keep a book. He was coldly efficient, filling in the necessary forms but making no small talk or comment beyond what was strictly necessary. He assigned me to a cell, then moved on to book Lotta in.

The cell was about twelve feet by eight, painted in a murky shade of orange and lit by a dull striplight suspended from the high ceiling. Along one side was a wide wooden bench – smooth and shiny from years of polishing by the seats of prisoners' trousers – with two thin blue plastic mattresses.

The only other furniture was a metal toilet in the corner, which had no screen and could not be flushed from inside the cell. It was far from the most pleasant accommodation, but at least it was clean, unlike many police cells I'd spent time in.

Soon I was joined by Lotta and then Jo, who reported that the custody sergeant had lightened up somewhat and had been amused by the fact that each of us was carrying almost exactly the same things: clothes, books, pens, paper, stamps, food, a torch, a copy of the video and booklet we'd made, and £25 in cash.

We'd devised a complicated plan in the event of the police not allowing us to make phone calls, as had happened to Chris when he was arrested for his Ploughshares action. It involved Rowan ringing the police station and claiming that we had left her a letter, with instructions not to open it before 29 January. On opening it, she would say, she'd found details of our action, and a request that she ring Lytham police station to see if we were in custody. This elaborate story would, we hoped, explain how Rowan came to know about what we'd done and minimise any risk of conspiracy charges. In the event it wasn't necessary because we had been able to ring Angie from the hangar, thus providing a simple cover story for the rest of the group.

In the event, the police let us use the phone almost whenever we wanted, and it was great to be able to contact the support group every day, to have a chat and catch up on the news. On the evening of the first day, Jo rang Lyn, who said the support group had managed to generate a lot of local media coverage of our action as well as some national interest.

There had been a vigil at Warton that afternoon and lots of people were coming to court the next morning. They were all frantically busy, doing presswork, organising people to come to court, contacting our friends and family, putting together a newsletter and arranging public meetings, including one in Preston which Angie would speak at before heading off to attempt some further disarmament.

Meanwhile, we were lounging in our cell, with nothing more demanding to occupy us than deciding whether to play whist or rummy with the pack of cards which Jo had managed to wheedle out of the police. For the time being, at least, I was perfectly content.

In our preparation, we had talked extensively about, and roleplayed, police interviews. We expected to be questioned at length, and had decided that though we wouldn't talk about what we had done, we could if we wished talk about the Hawk deal and East Timor. We were concerned that if we admitted everything in our interviews, the prosecution at trial might use this evidence as a substitute for showing our video. If we admitted nothing, we thought, the prosecution might be forced to show the video, with the footage of the four of us talking about what we planned to do and why.

In retrospect, perhaps we could have talked more freely to the police. However, our previous experience of police interviews had led Angie and me to the conclusion that it usually isn't in our interest to answer questions. The police will always claim the interview is for our benefit, to give us a chance to be heard, but in reality they're the ones who stand to gain the most. We were concerned too that if we started answering questions about the action, it might be harder to refuse to answer questions about who else had been involved in the planning, which was something we definitely didn't want to discuss.

In fact, we needn't have worried about hours of grilling underneath a bare lightbulb. Perhaps the officer in charge thought he'd got the case against us wrapped up, because our interviews were at best cursory, each taking less than fifteen minutes. The detectives investigating the case had decided that Angie had driven us to the site, taken part in the action and then left, and were keen to get us to admit this. They were sceptical when I told them we'd got the bus to Warton, but their doubt turned to sheepishness when I pointed out that my bus ticket was in the property they had confiscated, and the issue wasn't referred to again.

Later that day, a prisoner in the next cell shouted to us.

"What are you in for?"

"Hammering on an aeroplane at British Aerospace," we shouted back.

His cell was near the custody office, and he'd overheard some of the officers discussing our case.

"They're saying you did two or three millions pounds of damage," he informed us, a certain disbelief evident in his voice.

How much damage – disarmament – to cause had been a subject of much discussion before the action. In fact, this was an ongoing debate within the Ploughshares movement, loosely – and rather inaccurately – referred to as "minimum versus maximum damage", or "effective versus symbolic disarmament".

In the United States, at least, the debate seems to polarise to some extent – and this is my own analysis – around the degree of religiosity of the participants. Those who identify very strongly as Christians have seemed to tend towards the view that the important thing is what might be called the witness aspect of the action, or the willingness to put oneself at personal risk in order to bring about a more just world. At its extreme, this position dictates that one should stop after a single blow. Others have argued more pragmatically, saying that if the intention is to disarm, we should do just that, and do as much damage as possible in the time available.

This is no doubt one of those debates that could go on indefinitely, but for our purposes we wanted to reach a decision which we were all happy with. Opinions varied greatly, and were often in flux, with several of us changing our minds as we heard other people's arguments. Some of the group thought we should do as much damage as possible, which would not only make it harder for any planes we'd disarmed to be mended quickly, but also might mean that we'd have a better defence. Others preferred the disarmament to be symbolic. We discussed the idea of not doing too much damage, but instead leaving open the possibility that other people might take responsibility for continuing the work.

Some in the group were uncertain of where they stood. I was one of these – in fact the minutes of one meeting record me as "swinging wildly" (which was more or less what the prosecutor later accused us all of doing with our hammers). I wanted to prevent any planes we disarmed from leaving for

Indonesia, of course, but at the same time I was concerned that if we did a vast amount of damage, we might end up with a huge sentence. I recognised, however, that disarmament is a very inaccurate art; we might do almost no damage and still receive an enormous sentence, or we might do an awful lot and only get quite a short time in prison.

Finally we reached some kind of consensus: we would do what might be called a "midway" amount of damage. We wouldn't completely wreck any planes we found, but we would do enough to make it a real, rather than symbolic, act of disarmament. If we found more than one plane, we would attempt to hammer on each one in order to cause maximum disruption to the whole Hawk deal. In the event, we actually did more damage – in purely monetary terms – than almost any other Ploughshares action before or since.

Once I'd had time to absorb the news shouted out by the other prisoner at Lytham, I actually felt fine about it. Monetary value was largely irrelevant since British Aerospace could claim as much or as little as they wanted, and there'd be little we could do to dispute it. It just illustrated what hugely expensive and wasteful things weapons are, I thought. It occurred to me that we could be facing a very long sentence – perhaps five years – but I pushed the idea out of my mind. It was less than twenty-four hours since we'd been arrested, and anything could happen in the coming months.

Later that evening, we were all charged with criminal damage and burglary, which is defined as "entering as a trespasser with the intention of committing an illegal act". We'd never considered that we might face a burglary charge, and I had a sudden moment of unease, thinking that I really didn't want to have that on my record. After Angie was arrested the following week, burglary was dropped and a joint charge of conspiracy added, which came as a relief even though legally it was more serious. When we were charged we were asked if we had any comment to make, and we each said something about Britain's complicity in genocide in East Timor.

Our first night in custody passed slowly. The cell was hot and airless, I had a raging headache, and couldn't sleep because of the events of the last twenty four hours running constantly through my head. There was just enough light in the cell to read, but it meant holding the book inches from my nose and squinting hard. Forcing my addled brain to plough through *Crime and Punishment* under such conditions served only to irritate my aching head still further.

"Wakey, wakey, ladies! Off to court this morning!" The custody sergeant – in a considerably better mood than the previous day – grinned at us through the hatch in the door and proffered plastic cups of tea, followed by plates of cold beans on toast. He told us we had a couple of hours to get ready.

I'd been expecting a trip in a police van, but it turned out that our cell was actually right underneath the magistrates court – we were often scolded for laughing loudly and disturbing the gravitas above us – and the only journey we'd be making was up a flight of steps which led directly into the dock.

As we went up the stairs, I could see an ornate plasterwork ceiling above us, and then stained glass windows and a raised bench where the magistrates were sitting. We popped up like rabbits out of a hat into the dock, which was like an island in the middle of the court, high above the surrounding seats, with very little room for three of us and a couple of policemen.

It felt like being in a church; we were in the pulpit, and the magistrates were sitting on the altar, all of us assembled to worship at the high court of law. The court was packed. Friends jostled for space with reporters, police, and several besuited men I assumed to be from British Aerospace. We turned and grinned inanely at the people we knew, before being told in a sharp whisper to face the magistrates, who were glaring at us sternly from their bench.

Strangely, all the characters in this drama were women: the three of us in the dock, the three magistrates, and the prosecutor. I looked hopefully for signs of female solidarity, but got the distinct impression that the magistrates and prosecutor felt we were a disgrace to womanhood rather than a shining example of women acting nobly in the cause of justice.

It was a very short hearing, with the sole purpose of deciding whether we should be released. "The defendants are accused of a very serious offence and have refused to give their dates of birth," the prosecutor said sternly. "I would therefore ask for them to be remanded in custody for a further two days in order that the police can verify their identities by fingerprint checks."

We were allowed to respond to the prosecutor's request. "We should be released," Jo declared, "because we haven't committed a crime. We were acting to prevent the crime of genocide in East Timor."

"I would like to invite you to drop the charges against us and ask the prosecution to investigate British Aerospace for breaches of the Genocide Act," I added.

"It's important that we're released so we can carry on with our work of crime prevention. There is still a crime going on," Lotta put in for good measure.

Our appeals were not well received. The chief magistrate glared at us. "I don't want to hear any political speeches," she said coldly, before remanding us in custody for a further two days. This was referred to by the police, with unintended irony, as a "two-day lie down". We were escorted back to the cells to the sound of applause from our friends on the public benches.

Since I'd assumed we'd be remanded in custody, I wasn't at all downhearted after the hearing. On the contrary, it had lifted my spirits to see our friends in court and to stand up in the dock and claim what we had done. I'd expected that we'd be sent straight to prison rather than spending more time in police cells, but wasn't at all unhappy about the prospect of an extra two days at Lytham, basic though the conditions were. I was extremely apprehensive about going to prison and although I knew it was going to happen sooner or later, having it put off for a while was no hardship.

The police on the whole were helpful and pleasant, but almost all of them seemed to think we had no idea what serious trouble we were in. Shortly after our first court appearance, an inspector came to break the news – which he clearly thought would come as a shock to us – that we were likely to be remanded in custody at our next hearing and sent to prison to await trial. We explained that being remanded in custody was exactly what we'd expected and prepared for, but he just kept on about how hard it would be in prison for women like us.

Later, Sergeant Lee – in charge of our case – came and talked to us through the hatch in the door. He was even more condescending, telling us sternly, "This isn't some kind of adventure, you know." He clearly thought we were naïve young women who had taken this action on a whim, and would very soon come to regret it. The duty solicitor also assumed that we must be shocked that we were likely to be remanded in custody. He thought our only concern must be how to get out on bail, and was keen to represent us at the next court hearing in order to maximise our chances of release. He seemed slightly offended when we assured him that we were confident about speaking for ourselves.

Accepting bail – or not – had been something we'd talked about a great deal before the action. It was unlikely, but there was an outside chance that at least some of us might be offered bail with strict conditions, such as staying away from Warton and abiding by a curfew. Most of us felt unease at the idea of accepting bail conditions, and, realistically, there was a good chance we would be convicted and given a jail sentence, so we might as well serve what time we could before trial. Remand prisoners had more privileges than convicted prisoners – such as daily, rather than fortnightly, visits – so it made sense to take advantage of that.

A further complication was that since I was already on bail for a similar offence – pouring fake blood over a Hawk at a British Aerospace display the previous year – it was almost certain that I would be remanded in custody, but there was a small chance that Lotta and Jo – and possibly Angie – might be granted bail. We had already decided that we all wanted to be in the same position, whether that was on bail or in custody, both for solidarity and to enable us to prepare our defence together.

In the event, being offered bail was never going to happen. When we came to court for the second time, the prosecutor once again objected to our release. "We have verified the identities of the defendants," she said, "but I would ask for them to be remanded in custody on the grounds that the main perpetrator of the alleged offence, Angie Zelter, is still at large. If the defendants are released, they may interfere with police enquiries."

This was patently ridiculous; Angie had been sitting at home for a whole day after we were arrested, and the police had made no attempt to come and get her. In any case, signing an open statement of intent to disarm the Hawks, and being interviewed on a video which was to be left at the scene of the crime, were hardly the actions of someone out to avoid being arrested. However, shocked at the idea that such a dangerous criminal was at large, at liberty to strike again, the magistrates nodded gravely and remanded us in custody for a week. This time, there were to be no more police cells. We were on our way to prison.

CHAPTER 11

━━━━━━━━

"THEY CALL IT GRISLY RISLEY"

Our planning for prison had been extensive and detailed. There were only twelve women's prisons in England, and it didn't take much research to find out that we would almost certainly end up in Risley, the main remand centre for women in the north west. Jo and I had rung the prison on numerous occasions, posing as friends of inmates, to find out what personal possessions were allowed.

It was a little nerve-wracking; I don't like telephones at the best of times, and worried about what I'd say if asked to give the name of the prisoner on whose behalf I was phoning. I wondered whether to say, "Well, actually it's me. I'm likely to be in your prison next week and I'd just like to know what I'm allowed to bring with me."

The information we gained by such subterfuge was at best only marginally useful. As we soon discovered, every officer had their own interpretation of the rules. Whether a prisoner actually received items sent in to her depended not so much on the nature of the item as on the whims of the officer opening the mail. It was enormously frustrating – especially if you were waiting anxiously for a particular item which when it arrived was ceremonially brought to you so that you could be told that you couldn't have it – but that was the nature of prison.

The practicalities of prison preparation were perhaps the easy part. We packed up books and clothes we wanted to be brought in and left them with friends; found out about the prisons to which we might be sent if we were convicted and sentenced; talked to peace movement friends about prison life; and made tapes of our favourite music. I visited the optician and the dentist, not wishing to trust my eyes and teeth to prison health care services. We sorted out our domestic arrangements, to ensure that houses would be looked after and bills paid if we were away for a long time.

Far more difficult, however, was emotional preparation for prison. Every previous Ploughshares action – over fifty of them – had ended in a conviction, and virtually all activists had undergone some measure of imprisonment. Even though we felt we had a good defence in law, we knew that it was quite possible that we would not be allowed to use it. In any case, it was very likely that we would be remanded in custody to await trial.

Prison therefore seemed more or less inevitable, but the big unknown was how long we might be there. Sentences in the United States had ranged from a few weeks up to eighteen years. The two previous Ploughshares actions in Britain had ended in sentences of fifteen and eight months, but we didn't want to rely on that as a guide. One thing all activists know is that anything can happen – never truer than in our case, as it turned out.

Angie had been to prison many times before; besides numerous short sentences in Britain, she had spent two months in a Malaysian jail for protesting against logging in the rainforests. Going into that, she said, they didn't know what the penalty might be; as far as they were concerned, it could be anything up to life imprisonment. The idea of life imprisonment in a foreign jail, thousands of miles from friends and family, made me shudder. We talked about Angie's experience and joked that at the worst they could only give us ten years – how bad could that be?

My previous experience of prison was limited to the four days I had served in Holloway – the women's prison in London – three years earlier. Whilst I hadn't been unduly traumatised by it, I had found many aspects of prison life unpleasant and intimidating. The worst part – and the thing I was worrying about most this time – was the noise, the never-ending shouting and blaring music which made reading, writing, sleeping and even thinking so difficult.

In Holloway, two of my cellmates had had a radio which they played at full blast until late into the night. I couldn't bear it and buried my head under the covers, put my fingers in my ears, even tried using soft white bread as earplugs, but nothing would block out the noise. Requesting them to turn it down had no effect at all, and in the end I just put my head under my pillow and cried with frustration.

This episode bothered me greatly as we prepared for prison; if a few nights of noise was such torture, how would I cope with months, even years of it? But I was determined to carry out the action, so there was little point agonising over such things. I would just have to trust that somehow I would learn to cope with whatever was thrown at me – which, I was well aware, might be far worse than excessive noise.

Jo and Lotta had never been to prison before – indeed, neither of them had even been arrested before. Whilst we were in Risley, we were visited by four Ploughshares activists from the US and Australia who were in Britain for a conference. Art Laffin, a veteran of two Ploughshares actions and numerous periods in prison, was astounded that Jo and Lotta had taken part in the action. "In the US," he said, "they wouldn't be allowed to do an action until they had more experience."

For us, though, we were each prepared to go ahead not because of our previous experience of being arrested and imprisoned, but because of the long and detailed preparation process we went through together. It's easy enough to learn from someone else what happens when you're arrested, and until you've spent a long period in prison – which none of us had – you can't know how you're going to cope with it. So for all of us to a greater or lesser extent, it was a step into the unknown.

However, even all our extensive preparation didn't prepare us for the reception when we finally reached Risley. Until then, life behind bars had been relatively easy, almost fun in a strange kind of way. We'd spent four days at Lytham police station, where we had perhaps had built up a false sense of security based on our cosy, intimate little world there. As we were soon to find out, being a prisoner in a police cell is an entirely different experience from actually being in prison.

"They call it grisly Risley, you know," remarked a young police constable as he stood in Lytham police station custody office struggling to fasten handcuffs around our wrists. "You won't like it – it's no holiday camp."

Jo told him that we didn't expect it to be a holiday camp, and I remembered how three years earlier, the police officer accompanying me to Holloway prison had remarked, "It's like Butlins there, you know." It seemed that many police officers could only think of prisons in terms of holiday camps; either they were like them (bad), or not like them (good).

We were led out of the police station and into a waiting van. It was a long drive to Risley, but I was in no hurry to get there; I'd quite happily have ridden in the van all night. Most of the time the three of us sat in silence, but the three police officers accompanying us took great delight in telling us how terrible Risley would be: the food, the other prisoners, the prison officers. Ever since our arrest we'd had to put up with a stream of police officers telling us that we didn't know what we'd got ourselves into, and this was their last opportunity to let us know how naïve we were.

It was almost dark by the time we saw the huge walls of Risley looming out of the flat landscape. The driver spoke briefly to the gatekeeper, then the massive gate swung open. We were in prison.

I took a deep breath as the door to the reception wing was unlocked and we were hurried into the bright glare inside. "Three from Lytham," announced one of the police officers as he undid our handcuffs.

I was aware of many eyes fixed upon us; cold stares from the two prison officers at the desk, and curious looks from the crowd of women sitting on plastic chairs nearby. I immediately stared down at the floor, not knowing whether to return the looks – what did prison etiquette dictate?

"Stand up straight!"

One of the officers yelled at Lotta, who had momentarily rested her elbows on the high reception desk. Shocked, she stood straight as the officer proceeded to explain to us that we wouldn't be allowed to keep any of the belongings we had so carefully packed in preparation for prison.

"You know they can't have them. You should have left them at the station," she scolded the police officers.

Jo stepped forward.

"But we have – " she began, wanting to explain that we needed our belongings – our clothes, legal papers, pens, books. She had barely opened her mouth when the officer turned on her.

"Don't speak when you're not spoken to!" she screeched. "You can't have them and that's that. You're in prison now and we make the rules, not you."

Jo was stunned into silence, and I shrank into the corner, biting my lip and trying to blink away my rising tears. I didn't want the police officers to see that I was upset; a misplaced sense of pride made me want to hide my feelings, and not allow them to think that they were right about our naivety and inability to cope with the harshness of prison life.

But I struggled to fight back the tears as it came to my turn to be booked in. Any trace of our humanity was swept away as the staff shouted to each other, "Is that one finished?" and "Have you processed that one yet?" "Processing" was a good term: we were like battery chickens on a conveyor belt, waiting to be weighed, measured, stripped and inspected.

"Needham!" The officer's voice was indistinct over the general hubbub and I didn't react immediately. "Needham! Are you deaf?" I jumped up and hurried over, anxious not to find myself in trouble before I'd even been booked in. She took me into the reception office, a tiny cluttered space with prisoners sitting on hard chairs against the wall, plastic bags of personal possessions at their feet. Most of the room was taken up with a vast desk almost obscured by paper. Propped against the wall behind it was a large board covered in dirty and dog-eared notices.

I only had time to read the demand for payment of tea money, the rather puzzling "Prisoners are not allowed Wonderbras", and a notice insisting that "No prisoner is to be accepted without a body receipt", before the officer started firing questions at me. Name, address, age, occupation, eye colour, next of kin, have you been in prison before, are you on bail for any other offences?

Having answered all the questions, I was weighed and measured and then told to go into a cubicle with another officer and undress. We were strip-searched every time we entered or left the prison, and occasionally at other times too. There was tremendous variation between officers in how it was done. Some would make you take all your clothes off and scrutinise them closely, a look of distaste crossing their face as they handled your underwear. Others would just make you lift your top and drop your trousers, all the time carrying on a conversation with the officers in the next room and barely glancing at you as you stood half naked in front of them.

It was clear that the strip search was less about actually discovering contraband (in Holloway I had met a women who'd smuggled a lighter in between her buttocks), and more about putting the prisoner in her place, showing her straightaway how the land lay. Coming back into prison on later occasions, by which time we were all quite used to the routine, we would talk to new prisoners and explain to them what happened in reception. When we told them they would be strip-searched, their eyes would often widen in terror, and many would start crying at the mere prospect of it.

The final routine is to be seen by the nurse and the doctor. My previous experience of prison was that these "consultations" were minimal to the point of absurdity, going through the motions because that's what's required by the system. On my reception into Holloway, the doctor had asked me two questions: "Are you suicidal?" and "Do you want sleeping tablets?" I was shocked that I was being offered sedatives by a doctor who had spent no more than a minute with me and had no idea of my background nor whether I had a history of addiction. Later that night, when the nurse came wheeling her medicine trolley round the wing, the other women in my cell were no less shocked that I had refused the offer of sleeping tablets. It was apparently virtually unheard of not to be taking them. "You could have given them to us," I was told somewhat accusingly.

This time the medical examination was little different.

"Have you been in prison before?" the doctor asked almost before I sat down in front of him.

"Yes, once, but only for a few – " I was cut short as the doctor continued impatiently.

"Are you in good health?"

"Yes."

"Are you suicidal?"

"No."

"Are you taking any tablets?"

"No."

"Do you use drugs?"

"No."

That was the end of the consultation. The doctor didn't glance up throughout the whole time I was in his office and discharged me with a wave of the hand when I'd answered his few questions.

Reception procedures completed, we were taken into another room and given large plates of curry and rice. The room was already full of prisoners, most of whom seemed to know each other. Our arrival – middle-class accents, looks of bewilderment, clearly first-time inmates – attracted their attention immediately. "What are you in for?" one of them shouted over to us.

In reception there was a big poster, no doubt produced by some well-meaning but ultimately clueless civil servant in the Home Office, which warned new prisoners not to ask others what they're in for. The implication was that people could get very upset, and perhaps angry, at being asked such a sensitive question. However, anybody who's been in prison knows that the very first question everyone asks each other, almost as a form of greeting, is "What are you in for?" It serves as a common defining factor; we're all in for something, and we might as well admit what it is.

A few months earlier, we had discussed our fears of prison. We came up with a multitude of things, from lack of exercise, health worries and noise, to bullying, apathy and isolation. One of my worries was that other prisoners might resent us for being middle-class and having chosen in some senses to be in prison. So when this young woman demanded to know what we were in for, my heart started pounding. The three of us looked at each other, and finally Jo took the initiative and launched into an abbreviated version of the action. She'd barely started before the woman exclaimed, "Was that you?" She turned to the others and said, "Hey, remember that plane that was smashed up? That was them!"

Having spent the previous four days in police custody, we had little idea of the impact our action had made locally. The Blackpool *Evening Gazette* had put our story on the front page, beneath a headline which screamed, "Vandal attack on British Aerospace war jet". The following day's front page was "British Aerospace jet attack risked lives", with the subheading – in case anyone was left in any doubt – "Vandal protest could have blown warplane plant sky high". The action had been covered extensively on local television and radio news, and there could have been few people in the north-west of England who didn't know about it. Everyone – except us, of course – had heard the news.

Suddenly all attention turned to us, and we were

overwhelmed with a barrage of questions. "How did you get in?" "Why did you do it?" "How much damage did you do?" "Why didn't you run away?" Everyone was talking about it, demanding answers, discussing it amongst themselves. The general consensus after a few minutes was that we must be slightly mad. But the tone of the discussion was friendly; several women even pronounced the action "cool", and my initial fears about how we'd be received began to subside.

Finally it was time to go to the wing. We'd been given small plastic bags of toiletries, and I'd managed to talk the officers into letting me keep a pair of sandals before all the rest of my belongings were spirited back to the police station. But apart from that we had nothing more than the clothes we stood up in. Jo and Lotta didn't even have shoes – the police had seized all our footwear for forensic examination – and had to spend several days walking around in their socks, being yelled at by every passing officer for not having their shoes on.

An officer called our names. "Wilson, Kronlid, Needham. Let's be having you!" Some officers made the effort to learn prisoners' first names, but many referred to us always by surname. After a few weeks in prison I found myself answering "Needham" when asked my name, and I had to make a conscious effort to use my first name too, almost as a way of reminding myself that I was an individual, I wasn't just "Needham, prisoner number VD 0088".

We followed the officer as she led us and several other women out of reception and down a long corridor with yellowing paint flaking onto the scuffed linoleum floor. Between the reception area and the wing were five doors;

we stopped in front of each one and waited for the officer to unlock it with the huge bundle of keys fastened securely to a chain on her belt. As each door was locked behind us, it felt as if we were leaving the outside world a little further behind, and being subsumed more and more firmly into the cold greyness of prison.

The corridors through which we were led were dank and dimly lit; our breath billowed out in clouds, and several women, wearing only scanty dresses, set up a chorus of "Miss, it's freezing in here!" Suddenly the last door swung open and we were hit by glaring lights and the staggeringly loud noise of women laughing, talking, shrieking. We had arrived.

Butler, the main wing at Risley, was newly-built in the typical prison style, with three levels of cells overlooking a large open central area. This made for interesting theatre, especially for those on the top floor who could peer over the balcony and see the whole of prison life being played out beneath them. However, the drawback was the noise; sound echoed round the entire wing, amplified by the concrete and steel surfaces.

I looked upwards and saw crowds of women standing round the railings on the upper two floors, peering down to see who had arrived. Many were yelling greetings to other women who had come in with us. Shouts of "What are you doing back?" and "How did you get on?" just reached us above the din, and a reply of "That bastard judge gave me six months" was met with shrieks of outrage from overhead.

Later we learnt that the three of us had been spotted by women from the third floor, who had heard on the radio that we'd been remanded in custody and had stood waiting to see us as we walked onto the wing. "We picked you out straight away," they told us gleefully.

An officer yelled my name and opened cell number 27.

"In you go," she said breezily.

As the door swung open I was met with a wall of cigarette smoke which almost obscured the dingy glow from the striplight on the ceiling.

"Um, I don't smoke, would it be possible for me to share with a non-smoker?"

The response was sharp. "You're in prison now. You'll go where you're told to go."

I swallowed hard and entered the cell. The heavy steel door swung shut behind me and there was a very final clunk as the lock was turned, and a thud as the officer slammed shut the metal flap covering the window. My cellmate stood looking at me curiously.

"So what are you in for?" she asked.

CHAPTER 12

===

"WHY HAVEN'T YOU BUNKED YOUR BED?"

Heavy smoking notwithstanding, I liked Janet, my new cellmate. We'd spent the evening chatting about our respective crimes – she was in for shoplifting – and I had grilled her at length on prison routine and procedures, about which she seemed to know pretty much everything there was to know. She'd been in Risley many times and for her – as for so many of the women there – prison was a way of life. It wasn't something to dread, more an annoyance to be accepted. At least, she said, it was an opportunity to catch up with old friends whom she rarely saw on the outside.

Janet told me that she was withdrawing from heroin, and though she hadn't felt too bad in the evening, by bedtime she was really suffering. She was ready to turn the light out quite early, much to my relief as I'd been wanting to use the toilet – which had no screen around it – and was embarrassed about using it in front of her. Once the light was out, I also changed into the coarse green prison pyjamas I'd been provided with. They were several sizes too big as women in Risley wore the

126

same pyjamas as the male prisoners. The prison authorities appeared not to think this was inappropriate.

I was exhausted but it soon turned out that I wasn't going to get much sleep. The valium Janet had been given was having little effect on her shakiness, nausea and the general misery of cold turkey. She spent the whole night smoking, muttering, going to the toilet and crashing round the cell. At one point she turned the light on and dragged her mattress onto the floor, waking me up for the fourth or fifth time.

I had lain there in the half-darkness, looking out through the curtainless windows at the glaring security lights illuminating the prison walls, and trying to filter out the smoke by holding the sheet over my nose. Suddenly I was overwhelmed by a feeling of powerlessness; here I was, this was how life was going to be for the foreseeable future – certainly months, possibly years – and there was absolutely nothing I could do about it. Fighting down the waves of panic which were starting to rise up from deep within my belly, I reminded myself of the action, why we had done it, the importance of what we had done. I finally turned over, buried my head in my pillow and fell into a restless sleep.

t was taken off very early, before the rest of the wing woken up, to go to court. She was expecting probation as back that evening having been given a five-month ce, which she accepted with equanimity. "Life's shit on side, life's shit on the inside – what's the difference?" philosophy.

Her departure that morning left me on my own in the cell, feeling apprehensive and vulnerable. The wing was still quiet but I couldn't go back to sleep, and without Janet there, I started worrying about what was going to happen. Should I get dressed now or wait for the official wake-up call which I assumed would be made soon? I didn't want a prison officer to burst in on me when I was half dressed, so decided to get my clothes on, then wait to see what would happen next.

Once dressed, I sat on my bed, trying to read my book but quite unable to concentrate. At about 7am, an officer yelled at the top of his voice, "Wakey, wakey, girls!" Over the next few minutes, the noise gradually increased: crashing of metal against metal as officers banged the window flap in each cell door to wake the occupants, shouting from all sides, radio being turned on, food trolleys trundling below.

The racket was incredible and I wondered if something of the ordinary was happening, but soon realised that th' just how prison was. Even in the dead of night it wa' quiet. There were always a few women having a conversation across the wing, or someone bashi' door to attract the attention of the night officers. ' first thing that strikes you in prison, and one of t' that I found impossible to get used to.

About fifteen minutes after the first wake-' suddenly crashed open and a prison officer

"Why haven't you bunked your bed' Bunked my bed? I had no idea what she

"I don't know what that means," J reasonable answer, and the look of an' subsided, to be replaced by a flicker of a smile, perhaps of amusement at my ignorance.

"You have to strip it and fold all the sheets and blankets on the bottom of the bed," she said. That sounded pretty pointless, so I ventured to ask why we had to do it.

"Because you have to," came the short and very final answer.

I very soon learnt that "Because you have to" was the answer to most questions about the required routine – there didn't have to be a logical reason for anything. We could have been told to stand on our heads all day and "Because you have to" would be considered more than adequate explanation by most of the officers.

Not wanting to rock the boat on my first day, I started hauling the heavy green blankets off the bed and folding them into some semblance of a neat pile. As soon as I'd done that, the officer returned, handed me a broom and told me that all prisoners had to sweep and mop their cells every morning. It was hard to believe; a cursory swish of the broom around my cell produced a huge pile of dirt and cigarette butts, and it was obvious that Janet and her previous cellmate hadn't been too house-proud.

Peering out onto the landing, I could see a mop bucket with three mops. I cautiously ventured out and took one, unsure whether this was allowed or if we were supposed to wait for the officers to bring them to us. I scuttled back to my cell, and had barely whisked the mop over the floor before another officer was at my door, shouting, "Breakfast! Hurry up!"

In Risley, everything had to be done in a hurry. The fact that the prisoners were going nowhere, and had twenty-four hours a day in which to – mostly – do nothing important, was irrelevant. We had to be seen to be moving rapidly at all times, whether we were cleaning our cells, collecting our dinners, walking around the prison, or carrying out any one of the many menial and often pointless activities thought suitable for prisoners. We were harangued constantly by officers coming up behind us, shouting "Hurry up! Hurry up!" as if there were some dire emergency in progress.

We hadn't eaten much the day before and I was more than ready for breakfast. I followed the crowds of women clutching their prison-issue blue plastic mugs, and found myself with Lotta and Jo in a queue outside the servery. We were called in five at a time to fetch our breakfast – cereal, toast and tea. We all registered as vegan when we entered prison, but it took some time for vegan supplies to arrive, so our first, eagerly-awaited, breakfast consisted of dry cereal, dry toast and black tea.

The three of us found a table together and compared notes. Jo and Lotta had slept rather better than I had, but all of us were somewhat shell-shocked by the whole experience of our first night. It had been a harsh and frightening introduction to prison, and perhaps that morning we all had the same, unspoken, question inside us: "Is this how it's going to be from now on?"

CHAPTER 13

"YOUR MATE'S BEEN NICKED!"

As we slowly settled into prison life, we were wondering what was happening with Angie. One day, when we'd been in prison for nearly a week, we were standing in the queue for lunch when one of the other women shouted over to us, "Your mate's been nicked!" She'd heard it on the local news, but was unable to tell us anything more, so we spent several hours in suspense until we were able to make a phone call to the support group and get all the details.

Angie had been arrested on her way to address a public meeting in Preston and I later saw the video which captured her arrest. As she walks through thick snow towards the meeting hall, Sergeant Lee emerges from the blizzard to block her path. "Hello Angie," says the sergeant. "Just a moment before you go any further. I'll just show you my warrant card." Angie looks at the card as the sergeant continues speaking.

"I don't want to appear not to be a gentleman, but I've got to arrest you."

"What for?"

"Conspiracy to commit criminal damage," he replies, as he notices the video camera, pulls off his woolly hat and runs his fingers through his hair. He politely declines Angie's invitation to attend the meeting about our action, and refuses to countenance her request to be allowed to address the gathering before being taken into custody. The last we see of Angie is her disappearing into a police car which then sweeps off into the wintry night.

The police had spent the week since Jo, Lotta and I disarmed the Hawk trying to trace Angie, having decided that she was the main perpetrator of the crime. They had set about tracking her down with some enthusiasm, even to the extent of putting an appeal in the local newspaper asking her to contact them. Flattering though such attention was, Angie had other plans.

Immediately after our arrest, Angie had gone to Norwich magistrates' court to ask for an arrest warrant to be issued against Ian Lang, Secretary of State for Trade and Industry. He was responsible for issuing export licences for the Hawks, and as such, Angie told the court, should be arrested for aiding and abetting genocide. Her request was dismissed. Undeterred, she approached various MPs and campaigning groups to call for an emergency Parliamentary debate on the Hawk deal, and asked MPs to approach the Attorney General to institute proceedings against the Department of Trade and Industry and British Aerospace.

Angie had also made clear her intention to carry on the disarmament which we had started. Unfortunately, her encounter with Sergeant Lee outside the public meeting put paid to her plans of going to British Aerospace that night to do some more hammering, and she soon found herself occupying the same cell that Jo, Lotta and I had spent so much time in the previous week.

She was taken to Lytham police station, where the police found a hammer, boltcutters, a banner, a peace crane, and a packet of seeds in her briefcase – exactly the same items as the other three of us had been found with the previous week. She was charged with conspiracy to commit criminal damage and told that she would have to go in front of a court in order for magistrates to decide whether to let her out on bail.

The next day, Lotta, Jo and I had to return to Lytham for our third court appearance. It was our first taste of travel in a prison van, which turned out to be rather an unpleasant experience. Each prisoner was locked into a tiny metal cubicle about the size of a wardrobe, containing nothing but a plastic seat. There was no seat belt – for safety reasons, we were told, with no hint of irony – and consequently a crash at even a low speed would bring the prisoner's head into probably fatal contact with the metal wall just a couple of feet away. Smoking in the vans was banned, but few security guards enforced this, and our journeys were usually accomplished in a cloud of choking smoke.

It was a brilliant winter's day, with bright sunshine reflecting dazzlingly off fresh snow, and – uncomfortable conditions notwithstanding – it was a real treat to be outside the prison walls. The radio was playing in the van, and we suddenly caught the words "British Aerospace". Straining to hear, it soon became apparent that it was a news item about our action. By craning my neck and looking backwards through the little window in the door of my cubicle, I could just see Jo. We grinned at each other and raised our thumbs.

An hour later, we arrived at Lytham to be greeted by friends of Jo's, who threw snowballs at us as we were escorted from the prison van. Inside the police station we were at last reunited with Angie. It was a strange reunion; we had been together only ten days earlier but so much had happened in between that it took us several hours to tell and then retell our respective stories. The police officers seemed surprised at the raucous laughter emanating from our cell. One of them commented that we were remarkably happy considering our position; he clearly thought that even now we didn't understand how much trouble we were in.

Later that morning, we were taken up to court again. The dock was an even tighter squeeze this time, with the four of us plus two police officers. Other officers were dotted around the court, keeping a stern eye on us and the friends who filled the courtroom.

Whilst being booked into the police station that morning, I had seen the delightfully-named "body receipt" used when prisoners are transferred. In the box labelled "special instructions" somebody had written, "May try to take part in demonstration". This obviously explained the number of police officers in court. I smiled at this; the last thing on my mind at that point was taking part in a demonstration. All I wanted now was a quiet life.

Although Angie had been arrested separately, the magistrates soon decided that we would from then on be treated as four co-defendants. The prosecutor outlined the charges against us, making sure to elaborate the details to make it sound as serious as possible.

"The defendants Kronlid, Needham and Wilson," she explained grimly, "were caught in hangar 358 at the British Aerospace site in Warton. They were sitting on the steps of a Hawk trainer aircraft, surrounded by heavy tools. The Hawk had been extensively damaged. Present estimates put the damage in the region of £2.4m. When asked if they had damaged the plane, Kronlid said that they had de-armed it."

She was being rather economical with the truth, suggesting we had only been arrested by dint of the efficiency of security guards. We had chosen not to have a lawyer, preferring to speak for ourselves, so when it was our turn we corrected her version of events. We also invited her to drop the charges and instead investigate British Aerospace for contravention of the Genocide Act. Angie applied for bail, explaining that the crime of genocide was still going on and she needed to be released in order to continue her work of crime prevention.

"I'm not going to comment on nonsensical bail applications," was the prosecutor's response as she asked for all four of us to be remanded in custody for another four weeks. The magistrates granted her request without even retiring to consider the matter, and we were led back to the cells, cheers from the public benches ringing in our ears.

❖

We spent much of the next two days in the cells, as the police van had broken down and they had no way of getting us back to Risley. The previous week, I had been quite happy to put off going to prison, but now I was keen to get back there rather than spend time in police custody.

At last a van was found. We were loaded in with another prisoner, a middle-aged woman wearing nothing but a nightdress. She said she'd been dragged out of bed in the early hours and had not even been allowed to get dressed before she was arrested. "I haven't even got any knickers on," she declared loudly, glaring at the officer sitting next to her.

It was dark when we arrived, but I could see as soon as the door swung open that the two officers on reception were the same ones who had been so awful to us the previous week. My heart sank and I braced myself for being shouted at and ordered around and treated like a lump of meat.

One of the officers stared at Angie. "Are you a prisoner?" she asked, clearly thrown by her relatively smart clothes and grey hair.

"No, I'm a prison inspector. I'm testing out handcuffs," Angie replied. Horrified, I shrank back and gritted my teeth in preparation for the fury which seemed sure to follow.

But to my amazement, the officer responded by laughing and telling Angie that she wasn't taken in. The other officer smiled and said, "All right girls? How are you today?" as if she were greeting old friends, and asked us if we'd had any tea. They both cracked a few jokes, and even allowed me to keep my book, which was my sole remaining possession after a mix-up at the police station had caused all our belongings to be passed out to a friend. When they found that there was nothing in reception that we could eat, they rang the kitchens and had a special meal sent over for us, and even apologised when it turned out to be cheese salad rather than something vegan.

From that day on, in some dozen or more arrivals at reception, we never had the slightest problem with those officers. Yet each time we were there, we could see them yelling at and intimidating new prisoners, often reducing them to tears. It seemed to be a calculated strategy: terrorise all new prisoners, to let them know who's in charge, but once they've been terrorised once there's no need to do it again unless they're being particularly difficult.

After that, things just got better and better. I managed to get hold of a pen and paper, we were each given a new bag of toiletries and underwear, and when we were taken up to the wing Lotta and I discovered that we were sharing a cell. Jo and Angie had been put in separate double cells with smokers but after a bit of wangling – which we seemed to be able to get away with now that we were no longer new prisoners – managed to secure a cell together next to ours.

There was just time to catch up with a few friends on the wing and to have a quick shower before it was time for lock-up. When the door was finally locked, our heads counted and the flap over the window slammed shut, Lotta and I hugged each other, revelling in our situation. I felt truly rich: a friend, a book, a pen, paper, and a toothbrush. What more could I possibly want?

CHAPTER 14

FOLLOWING THE THREAD

A few days after Angie's arrival in Risley, we were all promoted to single cells on the top floor – the threes. The wing had three floors, with each prisoner's location being determined by how long she'd been in prison and her behaviour. New arrivals, those considered to be suicide risks, and those whose behaviour was below the expected standard were housed on the ground floor – the ones. Good behaviour could mean promotion to the twos, and eventually to the threes, if you managed to avoid any transgression of the written and unwritten rules. Theoretically, each level up brought with it more privileges in terms of time out of cells, access to education and gym, and the amount of money you were allowed to spend in the prison shop.

Each cell contained a narrow metal bed or bunkbed, a table and chair, and a small cabinet. If you were lucky – or good at seizing the opportunity to craftily acquire more furniture – you also had a tiny chest of drawers. At one end of the cell, a couple of feet from the door, was a toilet and washbasin, with a sheet of polished stainless steel to act as a mirror. The total lack of privacy was disturbing; you could be having a wash or sitting on the toilet when an officer – quite likely a man – would without warning fling the door open. It was an unpleasant reminder that once you're a prisoner, you might as well say goodbye to any notion of privacy.

Every time we went to court, we would lose our cells and be allocated new ones when we returned. This was extremely annoying if you'd spent several weeks acquiring a decent cell and furniture and would have to start all over again on your return. I always tried to get a cell on the south-facing side of the wing; being cooped up on the north side in a tiny space without any sunlight made me miserable. The south side had another advantage: it faced outwards and provided a view over the wall to the fields and houses beyond. Perching on the narrow windowsill in the sunshine, watching for the kestrel which often hovered over the meadow next to the wall, I could almost forget I was in prison.

It was also much quieter on the south, as the north side faced across to the men's prison, and every night there were long and loud exchanges which could occasionally be entertaining but were more usually just annoying. There was a tradition of yelling across to the man in the cell corresponding to yours, so the nights would be punctuated by shouts of "Who's in twelve on the twos?" or "Who's in eight on the ones?" These exchanges were known somewhat disparagingly by the prison officers as "window romances", but there was no attempt to stop them.

Within certain limits, we were allowed to decorate our

cells. The four of us received vast numbers of cards, pictures and photographs from well-wishers, which we strung across the room with wool from the art room (the time-tested method of sticking things to the wall with toothpaste having recently been banned). Posters were not allowed; they were a security issue, I was informed by an officer, as prisoners could be digging tunnels at night and covering them up with posters. Digging a hole in the side of a cell thirty feet off the ground didn't seem like such a smart idea to me, but who was I to question the wisdom of prison rules?

Gradually, prison life began to make sense – or at least, as much sense as could ever be made out of it. Once you'd worked out what happened one day, you knew what would happen almost every day, since there was rarely much variation. Although this could get tiresome, it also offered a certain sense of security which I found reassuring. Within the illogicality, constantly-changing rules and arbitrariness of prison life, the daily routine provided a welcome stability. You could wake up each day reassured that the routine would be the same as it had been yesterday, and would be for every day you were unlucky enough to spend in Risley.

The day always started with bunking of beds, followed by sweeping and mopping your cell. This seemed like very over-zealous cleaning, but it wasn't too arduous so it was easier to do it than to object. Angie had told us the story of her time in Styal prison a few years earlier, when she was made to scrub walls with a toothbrush, so perhaps we were getting off lightly. Some officers would inspect the cells closely each morning, looking for signs of dust under the bed or grime on the washbasin, but most contented themselves with a cursory glance.

Cleaning done, we would be called down for breakfast. It never varied much: cereal and toast during the week, porridge and baked beans at the weekend. There was always lots of tea, stewed and lukewarm. During the week we would sit at tables on the landing, but at the weekend we had to eat in our cells, and it soon came to seem quite normal to be eating breakfast just a few feet away from the toilet.

In Risley, prisoners had to put in an application – known in prisonspeak as an "app" – for almost everything: having laundry done, requesting a phone call to a solicitor, going to the prison shop. These routine apps were made in the evening, but if you wanted to make a "governor's app" – for non-routine issues, such as special requests or complaints – you had to do it at breakfast time.

The four of us seemed to make governor's apps almost every day, in stark contrast with most of the other women. Each morning, a senior officer would arrive on the landing with the applications book. Most would blanch slightly on seeing us waiting expectantly. "Not you again," they'd say, only half joking. We had many more apps than other prisoners, in part because we were defending ourselves in court and often had to ask for access to legal facilities, but also because we didn't hesitate to complain about poor conditions and breaches of the prison regulations, whilst most women would just put up with them.

After breakfast, we'd be locked up again for a while, then soon after nine o'clock would be let out for education, gym or work. On our first day in Risley, we'd been seen by the head of education who explained to us what classes were available: textiles, computing, pottery, art, individual study and beauty. Beauty? A friend of ours had gained a qualification in bricklaying during his six months in prison, but that clearly wasn't something we were going to be doing. I did drop in to beauty occasionally though: it was the only way you could cut your nails, as we were otherwise not allowed nail clippers or scissors.

We immediately enrolled in the textiles class which was held in a Portakabin in the prison yard. Any prisoners wanting to do this class had to have security clearance as there were no prison officers present. We were given immediate clearance and the next day, were introduced to the delights of the artroom: buckets of dyes of every colour, a batik wax machine, fabric paints, and all sorts of other interesting resources.

The best thing about textiles, though, was the teacher, a wonderful woman called Ayshe. In only a few days in prison I'd grown used to being patronised, ordered about, called only by my surname, yelled at when I didn't move fast enough and often treated – by many although by no means all of the officers – as somehow less than human. Suddenly here we were, no officers in sight, being called by our first names, asked what we wanted to do and treated as adults.

Ayshe would wander round the room, helping out and making suggestions, all the time laughing and chatting, telling us about her family and what she'd been doing, and making us feel very much at home – at least insofar as one could feel at home in prison. It was a wonderful change from our experience of prison up to that point, and I immediately began to feel that maybe life in Risley wouldn't be so bad after all.

❖

Meals were timed for the convenience of the prison rather than the wishes of the prisoners, and lunch was at 11.30am. We were provided with vegan food, but it was rarely very appetising: endless pasties and mashed potato pies – pastry filled with mashed potato, often served with – surprise! – mashed potato. Raw vegetables were unheard of and almost every meal was accompanied by diced carrots and swedes, boiled to a pulp if not actually burnt. Most prisons used vegetables grown by other prisons, which conjured up images of prisoners toiling over acres and acres of root vegetables, desperately trying to keep up with the demand.

Sometimes we got what we'd christened "the three-starch meal". A large dollop of yellow rice, a scoop of mashed potato and – if you didn't snatch your plate away fast enough – a spoonful of spaghetti hoops, cunningly masquerading as a vegetable. Back upstairs, I would gloomily pick the few microscopic pieces of onion out of the invariably uncooked rice, and eat them together with a forkful or two of mashed potato before depositing the rest in the bin.

After lunch, there was another work or education session, followed by exercise, then teatime at half past four. On most days, there was the possibility of an afternoon visit. Because we were unconvicted prisoners, awaiting trial, we could have visits every day rather than once a fortnight. In the evening we usually had association – a chance to socialise with other women on your landing, watch the television, play pool, take a shower and make telephone calls. One of the officers on our landing sometimes brought in videos for us to watch, and another organised quiz nights. If nothing particular was happening, the officers would just sit on the landing, chatting and playing board games with prisoners. It was usually quite a relaxed time, and you could almost forget that the person with whom you were playing Scrabble, and hotly disputing the existence of a particular word, was an authority figure.

Sometimes the four of us would be visited in the evening by Kay, the Quaker chaplain. Angie, Lotta and Jo had registered as Quakers on arrival in prison, and I was usually allowed to see Kay as well by virtue of being "one of the four", although some officers grumbled that I was trying to have the best of both worlds, going to mass as well as Quaker meetings. Kay provided a sharp contrast with the patronising and rigid attitudes I had experienced from the Catholic and Church of England chaplains, being very supportive of us and going out of her way to smooth our path.

The pool room was a favourite place to hang out after tea. It was where you could hear the latest prison gossip – who was going out with whom, who had a crush on whom, who was being released, who was up in court – all of which I found fascinating. It was also the place to exchange and use drugs, and women would quite openly smoke pot or pass out tablets whilst the officers sat on the other side of the glass door, blissfully unaware of – or perhaps deliberately ignoring – the blatant rule-breaking going on under their noses.

At about seven o'clock, we'd be given "supper", a rather

grand name for a cup of tea and a piece of cake, then it was time to be locked up for the night. The shout of "Let's be having you, girls," would ring out, precipitating a mad rush of women dashing round the landing saying goodnight, cadging cigarettes, making last cups of tea and getting themselves ready for the next twelve hours in solitary confinement.

Finally everyone was locked up. A few minutes later the flap on the cell door would be opened as the officers did their final count, and again at nine o'clock as the night officers did a count, then we were on our own for the night.

For a few hours after lock-up the night air would be filled with the sounds of women shouting to each other or to the male prisoners. Sometimes there would be a lot of banging as women tried to attract the attention of the night officer, or the lonely sound of screaming from the segregation unit. I always found the noise a problem, but was able to block out the worst of it with earplugs. Other women would simply yell out, "Shut the fuck up!" at the tops of their voices, which usually served only to increase the noise.

There was no lights-out time; we had switches in our cells and could keep the light on all night if we wanted. But I found prison exhausting, even when I hadn't been doing anything physical, and by ten o'clock I was usually ready for bed. I tried to do a few exercises each night – a bit of yoga, some stretching, a few press-ups – and then fell into bed, worn out by the exertions of the day.

If the prison was fully staffed, weekdays passed quickly; we were out of our cells frequently during the day, and sometimes I felt as if I could actually have done with a bit more time to myself. At the weekend, however, everything changed. There was no education, no gym, often no association or even exercise. Prison weekends – heralding as they did only a vast stretch of time locked up with nothing to do – were dreaded in the same way that people on the outside dread the advent of Monday mornings. In 1996, there were no televisions in cells and for those who didn't – or, frequently, couldn't – read, the prospect of two solid days staring at the wall must have been appalling.

Sundays brought a little relief in that we could attend a service in the little prison chapel, and I usually took advantage of my nominal Catholicism to go along. Many women went not because of any religious belief but simply as a chance to get out of their cells, talk to friends, bum a cigarette. We were closely monitored by officers all the time: whispering during the sermon was frowned upon, giggling was likely to lead to the guilty party being marched out immediately. This seemed unfair, given the nature of the sermons we were subjected to, which could drive even the most well-behaved of prisoners to uncontrollable laughter.

The Catholic priest seemed to think that all prisoners had the intellectual maturity of five-year-olds, and pitched his sermons accordingly. On one occasion, he illustrated the transfiguration of Christ by talking about frogs. "Now then," he said, leaning towards us with a pitying smile, "who knows what a baby frog is called?" One woman humoured him with an answer, the rest of us staying stubbornly silent in protest. He finished his tale by producing a toy frog from under his cassock with a great flourish, apparently unaware of all the rolling eyes and contemptuous sniggers passing amongst his congregation.

He did once, however, manage to redeem himself in the eyes of his congregation. On Easter Sunday, after a particularly tedious service, he presented each of us with a little chocolate egg. The women who had attended the Church of England service earlier (many of them in the hope of precisely such a reward) had been given not chocolate, but a sticker reading "Christ is risen". Needless to say, this was not that well received.

I didn't like the priest, but I loved the singing. It was led by a perpetually-smiling, red-faced man who played the organ with enormous enthusiasm in a style which wouldn't have been out of place in the Blackpool tower ballroom. The first time I went to church, we sang "Go Tell Everyone", a hymn with the immortal line, "Tell prisoners that they are prisoners no more", which seemed perhaps not the most sensitive choice in the circumstances. We also sang "Down by the riverside", and I immediately thought back to my first arrest, in Washington DC some eight years earlier, where we'd stood in the road and sung that same song. It was as if there was a thread running straight from that wet day on Pennsylvania Avenue to this cramped and dingy chapel in an English prison. All I'd had to do was to follow the thread and it had taken me to the right place.

CHAPTER 15

"WE CAN'T GIVE YOU SPECIAL TREATMENT"

Life in our first few weeks in prison was relatively simple. We went to education every day, we had visits from friends, received stacks of letters, and generally settled fairly easily into the routine of prison life. I felt quite happy and relaxed most of the time, and naively began to think that perhaps prison wasn't going to be too bad after all. Our honeymoon period lasted only briefly, however, and it wasn't long before the stark realities of prison started to hit home.

One thing which soon became an issue was that we were almost never allowed to go out for exercise, despite it being one of the few legal rights accorded to prisoners. We kept asking to go out but it was always too cold, too wet, there weren't enough staff. There was always some excuse.

I hated being stuck indoors all the time. I love to be outside, to walk around and look at the trees and breathe fresh air, and at home would never spend a whole day indoors, however foul the weather. And whilst I'd come to terms with the fact that in prison my access to the outdoors was going to be severely restricted, to have it completely – and unlawfully – denied to us was incredibly frustrating.

After a couple of weeks, we complained to the governor, who claimed to have had no idea that we hadn't been going out, as no other women ever complained. This wasn't strictly true; other women complained long and hard, but only to each other. Most were of the opinion that there was no point complaining officially about anything, because nothing ever changed.

However, our complaints did have some effect and on 17 February we were finally let out into the yard. In my diary for that day, I wrote, "Being let out into the yard today almost felt like being freed completely. I just took off running, taking in great gulps of cold air and revelling in the freedom to move my limbs properly and to run until I was out of breath. Everyone else thought we were mad – one or two of the others did a token circuit, but most just huddled on the benches, making ribald comments as we sweated past."

We thought we'd cracked the problem, but being allowed out for exercise proved to be an ongoing struggle during our entire six months inside. At first we were given only half an hour a day, which the prison insisted was our entitlement until we found the prison rule book and pointed out rule 27: "A prisoner not engaged in outdoor work... shall be given exercise in the open air for not less than one hour in all each day, if weather permits."

The governor had to concede that we were right, but the "if weather permits" rider was used as an excuse for cancelling exercise at the merest hint of what officers liked to call "inclement weather". Some would even cancel it if the ground was still wet from earlier rain. I got into several ultimately pointless arguments with officers who insisted it was raining when it clearly wasn't. The basic problem was that, for many of them, exercise was a privilege (to be fitted in if the sun was shining and they had nothing better to do) rather than a fundamental right.

I found this arbitrariness extremely frustrating. At the weekends we were usually locked up all day and exercise might be the only chance to get out of our cells. The call to go out – if it came – was at the same time each day, and as the minutes ticked away I'd get more and more anxious, worrying that it might not happen. My ears would be straining for the shout – "Put your lights on for exercise!" – which would be the signal to lunge for the call bell, shove on my shoes and stand expectantly at the door like a dog waiting to be taken for a walk.

But often the call wouldn't come; there would be an ominous silence around the wing, and I'd sit on my bed, unable to concentrate on anything except my yearning to go outside. Eventually I'd have to accept that it wasn't going to happen; there'd be no chance of going outside for at least another day. Once I had the temerity to push my call bell and ask the officer who appeared why we couldn't go out, as it patently wasn't raining. "Because I said so," came the all-too-familiar reply, as he slammed the flap in my face. I crept back to my bed, curled up into a ball and cried quietly to myself at the sheer injustice of it all.

The exercise saga dragged on and on. A couple of weeks after we first went out, we were doing our daily jog around the

TOP: Outside BAe's offices in Central London, ARROW (Active Resistance to the Roots of War) members and family (left to right): Faith Kenrick, Emily Johns, John Rety, Gill Allmond, Arkady Johns, David Polden, Carrie Bliss, Susan Johns, Milan Rai, Mark Chapman, Lyn Bliss, Richard Crump, Chris Cole. **ABOVE:** Andrea and Mark Chapman on a Hawk jet at a display in Hyde Park, May 1995. **LEFT:** Directing the public's attention to BAe's London headquarters.   PHOTOS: ARROW

The Seeds of Hope Ploughshares group now.
THIS PAGE (from top left):
Jo Blackman, Lyn Bliss,
Clare Fearnley, Emily Johns,
Lotta Kronlid.

THIS PAGE (from top left):
Andrea Needham, Jen Parker,
Ricarda Steinbrecher PHOTO: HUGH
WARWICK, Rowan Tilly, Angie Zelter.

TOP: The tools, photographs and Seeds of Hope booklet which were taken to the action. **ABOVE:** Hawk jet ZH 955 in the BAe Warton hangar with the Seeds of Hope banner on its nose. **LEFT:** The disarmed ZH 955 control panel. **OPPOSITE PAGE TOP:** The lump hammer that Andrea used to beat swords into ploughshares. **RIGHT:** The banner that was hung on the jet.

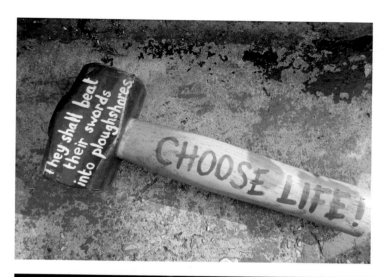

OPPOSITE PAGE TOP: Procession to Liverpool Crown Court. **MIDDLE:** Supporters waiting for the verdict outside the court. **LEFT:** Father Fitz praying on the court plaza. PHOTOS: JAMES MEADEN **THIS PAGE TOP:** Andrea, Angie, Lotta and Jo after the "not guilty" verdict. PHOTO: RICARDA STEINBRECHER **ABOVE:** Jo (centre), her mother (right) and dozens of people dancing outside the court.   PHOTO: JAMES MEADEN

TOP: Andrea, Lotta and Jo outside Risley with prison officer. PHOTO: JULIE CURRALL
ABOVE: Andrea and her daughter Esme, Hastings, 2013. PHOTO: KRYSIA MANSFIELD

yard when an officer shouted over to us.

"Stop running!" he yelled. "It's not allowed." Surprised, we came to a halt in front of him.

"Why not?" I asked. "We've been doing it for ages."

"I don't know why not. I'm just following orders."

The governor, when pressed for an explanation, said that it was because some prisoners were coming off drugs, had slow reflexes, and might not be able to get out of our way as we ran past. A further issue, she said, was that if the officers were watching us running, they might miss incidents of bullying in the yard.

The idea that other women might be staggering around the yard and falling into our path was beyond ridiculous. And whilst it was true that it would be easy to bully someone in the yard, it was not because the officers were distracted by watching the four of us but because they spent the whole time sitting in a corner chatting and largely ignoring what was going on around them.

But the governor had made her mind up. She gave us, for the first time, what would turn out to be an excuse for many more nonsensical prohibitions in the months ahead: she could not be seen to be giving us special treatment. The fact that other women had absolutely no desire to run round the yard was irrelevant; if we were allowed to do it, that would constitute special treatment and as such could not be countenanced.

We had to accept the ban, but took instead to walking briskly around the perimeter of the yard; if we got our full hour of exercise, we could cover three to four miles a day. A few weeks later, we were banned from walking round the perimeter – in case we passed things to women on the hospital wing overlooking the yard, we were told – and our already small circuit shrank even further. The senior officer dismissed our objections with a casual, "It's no big deal," causing Lotta to point out that whilst it was no big deal to her, who could go home at the end of the day and walk wherever she wanted, it was a big deal to us, whose world was already so circumscribed.

Frustrations like this aside, though, it was a joy to be able to go outside. Although the yard was in many ways very stark – bounded on three sides by buildings, and on the fourth by a high fence backed with the huge perimeter wall – the prison authorities had gone to some trouble to make the place pleasant. There were flower beds, a few benches and a patch of grass to stretch out on in summer.

The other women would watch us as we walked, and often called us over to tell new inmates about our action. We were nicknamed "the bombers" and sometimes a few of the women would stick their arms out and wheel around us as we walked, laughing and making aeroplane noises. In the usual run of burglaries, shoplifting, robberies and drugs offences, our crime stood out and was the subject of endless – but always good-humoured – interest.

One day the Virgin Mary appeared in the yard. She definitely hadn't been there the day before, and yet there she was, standing serenely in the corner, a vision in blue and yellow. Upon closer inspection she turned out to be a plaster cast rather than a heavenly vision, which came as a great disappointment to those of us waiting expectantly for some divine intervention on our behalf. It looked as if we'd just have to wait a bit longer.

❖

The exercise saga was far from the only problem. On our first day in Risley, we had been taken – like every new prisoner – to see the governor. She told us that we would shortly be able to move to Windsor, the "privilege" wing for women who are well-behaved and drug-free. She said there was a waiting list, but if we applied at once we should be accepted within a few weeks.

We didn't apply immediately, uncomfortable with the idea of being in a place for "good" prisoners, with better conditions than on the main wing. However, we soon came to realise how difficult it was going to be to prepare our defence whilst living on Butler wing. We were not allowed in each other's cells, so the only place to work was on the landing during association, where the noise was deafening and the interruptions constant. On Windsor, we'd be allowed in each other's cells and the atmosphere was much quieter. We decided to apply.

Jo and Lotta went to Windsor first, a few weeks after we arrived in Risley. Angie and I were told that we'd be moved when there was room. At the time, Angie was on the threes whilst I was languishing on the twos, waiting to move up. Prisoners on different landings were not allowed to mix, so Angie and I could do no more than wave at each other over the railings. The four of us were now in three different places, meaning that there was absolutely no opportunity of getting on with any trial preparation together.

We'd heard that standards of cleanliness on Windsor were much higher than on Butler. This was proven to be true when Lotta and Jo arrived in the artroom on their second day there to tell us that they'd both been given warnings – just a short step from being put on report – about the state of their cells.

Their crimes were dreadful indeed: Jo had been found to have water-marks on the inside of her stainless steel sink, and Lotta had been discovered harbouring a piece of waste paper in her waste bin. Lotta also reported that one of the officers had stormed into her cell, thrust up the lid of the toilet, peered down it and then stormed out, without saying a word. It all sounded quite mad.

However, there were compensations. As well as the luxury of being able to hang out in each other's cells, there were baths, duvets, a non-smoking television room and toast-making facilities. Compared to Butler, it sounded like the Hilton.

A week after Jo and Lotta had been moved, all four of us were summoned to see the governor. She wanted to discuss various issues with us including diet and mail, but didn't raise the question of Windsor. I decided to take the initiative.

"Do you have any idea when we might be able to move to Windsor?" I asked. "Only it's impossible for us to work on our defence whilst we're split up like this."

"You and Angie are behind several other women in the queue," the governor replied sternly. "You'll just have to wait your turn."

This was rather odd; we'd applied at exactly the same time as Jo and Lotta, so it made no sense that now several other women were ahead of us. The governor went on to say that in fact we might not be able to go to Windsor at all, because of concerns that we might present a security risk. She said that the prison had instructions – she refused to say from where – that we had to be held in conditions of higher security than other prisoners because of our political motivations.

The first hint of this had arisen when Lotta was being interviewed for Windsor. She had been told that there was concern that we might be a disruptive element because we might try to "further our cause" whilst there. Now the governor was saying to us that if there were a sit-down protest on Windsor – which only we could organise, she implied – she would be in hot water. The meeting concluded with her saying that she would discuss the issue with the head of security and let us know the outcome.

Clearly the head of security thought we were dangerous characters: the following day Lotta and Jo were both expelled from Windsor. They'd been told that, in consultation with the Home Office, it had been decided that it was too risky to allow us on a wing with a low officer-to-prisoner ratio. There was also talk about our being an escape risk; we had managed to break into a very-high-security site, so there were concerns that we might be able to break out of Risley.

This was obviously nonsense, and the governor finally came out with the real reason: "You've embarrassed the government once," she said, "and we don't want to give you the opportunity to do it again." We were, therefore, to be banned from Windsor.

For me, it wasn't too much of a blow. Having never experienced the delights of Windsor, I hadn't lost anything, and many women who'd been there told tales of bullying, unfriendliness and the complete fixation with cleaning which made the place sound rather less tempting. It seemed strange though to be treated so blatantly politically. We thought of ourselves as political prisoners, but we had – perhaps naïvely – not considered that the prison authorities might see us that way too, or at least not to this degree.

However, we had to accept it, and as compensation we were told that we would all but put on the threes, so for me it would actually be a promotion. Later that day, Lotta and Jo moved back from Windsor, and I was moved up from the twos. The problems with noise and being able to meet to prepare for trial wouldn't go away, but at least we were all together again.

Two days later we were once again summoned to see the governor. This time she was with the head of security, and dropped a real bombshell.

"Because of the charges against you," she said, "you will no longer be allowed to attend art classes in the portakabin. We have instructions from Head Office that you are a security risk."

"You fit certain criteria," the head of security added, as if that explained everything.

"What criteria?" Lotta asked.

"I can't say," he replied mysteriously.

"Administratively you cause us a lot of work because of certain requirements," the governor went on, refusing to be drawn as to what "certain requirements" might mean. "What you did was very serious. Because of the implications of your offence, you have to have more security. If you escaped, we'd be in trouble."

This was patently ridiculous. I thought about the two-inch-thick steel doors, high fences, razor wire and thirty-foot wall. Nothing short of a helicopter would have got us out, and in any case, if we were so anxious to escape, why hadn't we run away after the action rather than telling British Aerospace we were there? Why hadn't Angie gone into hiding rather than attending a meeting at which she knew the police would be waiting to arrest her?

But there was no persuading them, and we were thenceforth banned from art. This really was a blow; I enjoyed our daily art classes so much, and to be suddenly exiled was very hard. As if this weren't bad enough, the head of security had to add insult to injury by telling us how lucky we were to be in Risley.

"Normally you'd be doing time behind the door," he said (meaning spending all one's time locked in a cell). "You get extra privileges here which you wouldn't get at other prisons." The governor meanwhile dragged out the usual old chestnut, which was starting to look distinctly tired.

"We can't give you special treatment," she explained. "Other women would get jealous."

"We're not asking for special treatment," Jo said. "But by saying that we can't go to education you're not even giving us equal treatment."

"That's because you're in for a serious offence," was the governor's reply.

The conversation was going nowhere. They would justify

any and every discriminatory aspect of our treatment by referring to the seriousness of our offence. We'd found out the real reason: we'd embarrassed the government once, and they didn't want to give us any opportunity to do it again. As if to underline this, the head of security asked us as we got up to leave, "Why do you think the Train Robbers got such long sentences?" When we didn't deign to reply, he answered for us. "Because it was a national embarrassment," he said.

No longer being able to attend the classes I'd enjoyed so much was really tough, but perhaps worse was the feeling of insecurity it engendered. The prison authorities had been told by the Home Office (and also, as the governor later admitted, by Special Branch, the arm of the police responsible for national security) that we were a security risk, and were now reviewing all aspects of our confinement. Having banned us from running, from Windsor wing and from art, what would be next? Would we be banned from gym, from church, from exercise, from education?

The other possibility was that we might be moved to separate landings, even separate prisons, so that we couldn't get together to do the organising which we were clearly intent on. The four of us started discussing how we would deal with being separated, which would make legal preparation next to impossible.

In conjunction with the support group, we made plans which would include asking everyone we knew, and everyone on the mailing list, to bombard the prison and their MPs with letters of protest. The support group would make a huge fuss about it on the outside, and if that failed to achieve any result, at least two of us would consider going on hunger strike. If they thought we were a problem now, just let them see what we were capable of if they tried to split us up.

A few weeks after the Windsor incident, a number of women were sitting on the landing one evening discussing the worst aspects of prison life. "Laundry," said one woman. "We haven't had any in six weeks." This was true, and was beyond a joke given the tiny amount of clothing we were allowed to possess.

"The worst thing is the bang-up," said someone else. "We only got association twice last week, and they cancelled education every day. I'm going off my head sitting on my own in that cell 24/7."

"And you can't even get to the library, so there's fuck-all to do," added another woman. Other complaints included the arbitrariness of exercise, the appalling lack of stock in the prison shop and the terrible food, which one woman pronounced "Not fit for pigs."

Thinking that it would be useful to pass these complaints on to the governor, Angie started making a list. It was all done openly; the gripes were completely legitimate and there was no reason to be secretive. Jo took the list to type up in education, aiming to bring it back to the other women for approval before handing it to the governor. I was only marginally involved in this whole process, sitting on the edge of the group offering occasional suggestions. Lotta wasn't even present.

A few days later, Jo had typed the list and it was being

looked over by the other women when an officer approached and asked what it was about. He was shown the list, which he promptly tore up. Fortunately, Jo had a spare copy and it was agreed that it would be handed to the governor the next day.

The following afternoon, I was lying on my bed, listening to the radio and enjoying the warm sun coming through the narrow window. Suddenly the door was flung open and three officers marched in. "We're turning you over," one of them announced. Being "turned over" or "spun" is prisonspeak for a cell search for contraband. It involves being strip-searched then taken out whilst the officers sift through all your property with a fine-tooth comb, usually leaving your carefully-arranged cell looking as if a tornado has hit.

"Have you got anything in your possession that you shouldn't have?" one of the officers asked. I admitted to having a few books of Jo's – borrowing of property being strictly forbidden – but they weren't interested in that. Clearly they had something else in mind, although I had no idea what it might be.

Grabbing a blanket off the bed, one of them held it up in front of her and ordered me to take my clothes off. This was presumably a token attempt to preserve my decency by shielding me from people walking past the open door of the cell, but as all three officers were peering over the top of the blanket at me as I undressed, it did nothing to reduce the indignity of the situation.

Satisfied that I wasn't concealing whatever it was they were looking for in my underwear, I was told to put my clothes back on, then hustled out and locked in the adjoining cell.

Lotta's cell was next to mine and I called out to her through the window.

"I'm being turned over!" I yelled.

"So am I. I think they're doing all of us!" she shouted back. That was no surprise; by this point, nothing they did could have surprised us, and targeting us for a spin seemed perfectly sensible given how dangerous they apparently thought we were. Usually being turned over was a pleasure reserved for those suspected of having drugs, but obviously that wasn't what they were looking for this time.

After half an hour I was allowed back in my cell; nothing had been found. I was fortunate that the officers had left the place in a reasonable state, such that a few minutes of tidying up remedied the disorder. Jo had not been so lucky. We met up at education later that afternoon, and she was terribly upset. The officers searching her cell had left it in the most terrible mess, with every last one of her possessions, including all her carefully filed papers, heaped in a huge pile on the bed. They had also removed a number of documents, including personal letters from close friends.

There seemed to be no appreciation of how distressing it could be to be suddenly subject to such a search. I felt as if I'd been burgled; it was a violation of my personal space, my personal possessions and even my body. It was done with no explanation, little sensitivity, and no attempt to lessen the humiliating nature of it.

The search was successful in the eyes of the prison in that they found what they were looking for: the list of complaints, found in a pile of papers in Jo's cell. The idea of simply asking where it was, rather than using twelve officers to turn our cells upside down, clearly hadn't occurred to anyone. Had she been asked, Jo would have been happy to hand it over – she was about to give it to the governor anyway – but in prison nothing is ever that simple. As the governor said to us one day, "I can't afford to trust any prisoners, and that includes you."

Even though by this point we were aware of the complete irrationality of the prison system, we could never have foreseen the results this innocent list of complaints would produce. Jo and Angie were taken in front of the governor and accused of prison mutiny ("conduct which is intended to further a common purpose of overthrowing lawful authority"). This is a very serious offence, usually treated as a criminal charge with a possible ten-year sentence.

Of course, it was perfectly obvious that openly writing a list of complaints could not by the furthest stretch of the imagination amount to mutiny, but the overall head of the prison was anxious for us to be split up before we caused real trouble. We were kept in suspense for about a week, not knowing whether we would be shipped off to different prisons. It was a very difficult time; not only were we worried by the idea of being split up, we were also working flat out to prepare as much as possible of our defence in case we were separated.

Eventually we were told that the head of the prison had initially decided to split us up, but had changed his mind. We were definitely on our final warning, however, and any more such behaviour would mean our immediate separation.

It was an enormous relief, but I was left with a great sense of disquiet. The prison was unable to consider our behaviour objectively; because our "offence" was political, anything we did – however innocent – could be interpreted as a threat. It was all a bit strange; we'd had no idea when we entered prison that we were such dangerous women, and now we seemed to be getting more dangerous by the minute. Where would it all end?

CHAPTER 16

════════════

"A CAREFULLY-CRAFTED PIECE OF PROPAGANDA"

In March, we were taken back to the magistrates' court at Lytham for a committal hearing, the process by which more serious cases are transferred to the Crown Court. Some of the evidence is read, witnesses can be called, and the case is formally moved to the higher court.

We had asked for the site manager at British Aerospace to be called as a witness. He had clearly not been in a court before, and his voice trembled slightly as he took the oath. The prosecutor was the first to question him.

"Would anyone be allowed to come onto the British Aerospace site or enter a hangar without authority?" he asked. "No," the manager replied.

"Are there any circumstances in which permission would be given for this sort of damage to an aircraft?"

"Absolutely not," answered the manager, glancing at us in a not-entirely-friendly way. He went on to talk about the damage we had caused – then estimated at £2.4m – and stated categorically that the Hawk was a training aircraft.

When it was her turn, Angie asked him to which country the Hawk was due to be exported. He frowned, and turned to the magistrates as if to appeal to them to declare the question irrelevant. The chief magistrate told him to answer, and he admitted that it was destined for Indonesia.

"Are you aware of the likely use to which Indonesia would put the aircraft?" Angie continued. He claimed not to be.

"Are you aware that Indonesia invaded East Timor twenty years ago and..." Angie was stopped by the clerk who informed her that the line of questioning was irrelevant.

"Can I explain the relevance?" Angie asked the magistrates. "No," they said. They also didn't allow any questions about international law or lawful excuse for damaging property. There were to be no politics in their courtroom.

One of the key planks of the prosecutor's case on the charge of conspiracy was the video we'd made with the help of filmmaker friends, Zoe Broughton and Jamie Hartzell. The video had been Angie and Ricarda's idea, but had been seized on eagerly by the whole group as it seemed such a clear way of communicating all the issues involved – the situation in East Timor, western complicity, the Hawk deal, breaches of international law. The purpose of the video was for us to use it as our statement to the police, who would then pass it to the prosecution as evidence against us. We hoped that by including everything we wanted to say, we would be able to convey our motivation to the jury even if we were stopped from talking about East Timor ourselves.

To that end, it included interviews with the four of us about why we'd decided to disarm the Hawks, intercut with

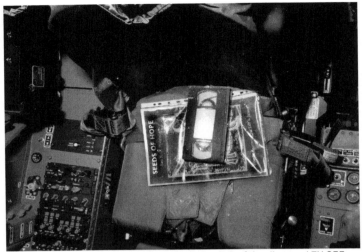

The Seeds of Hope video and booklet in the cockpit of the disarmed ZH 955.

footage of the Santa Cruz massacre. There was also part of a promotional video about the Hawk, with the narrator salivating over its attack capabilities, and clips from "Death of a Nation", John Pilger's documentary about East Timor.

The prosecutor had obviously watched the whole video, and was anxious that the magistrates saw only the "relevant" part; that is, us stating that we intend to disarm the Hawks. He didn't want them to see footage of people being killed in East Timor, or evidence that the Hawk was not, in fact, a training aircraft. Friends attending court reported that he spent quite some time before we came in trying to set the video recorder to avoid those scenes. This proved impossible and in the end he was forced to show the video in its entirety. Before he switched it on, he warned the magistrates about its contents. "What you are about to see," he said gravely, "is a carefully-crafted piece of propaganda. It was made by the defendants and illustrates their state of mind. I must warn you that it is partial and should be viewed in that light."

So British Aerospace's evidence was fact whilst ours was propaganda. Despite the warning, though, the video had a remarkable effect upon the magistrates. They sat there motionless as images flashed by of terrified young people running for their lives as soldiers opened fire on them. The courtroom was filled with the sound of gunfire and screaming.

The courtroom was completely silent for a few seconds after the final image of a young woman looking straight into the camera and pleading, "Please cut your commercial relations with Indonesia, if you are really human." Then the magistrates said they'd go out to discuss our argument that there was "no case to answer" because we were acting to prevent the crime of genocide in East Timor. If they had accepted this, the charges would have been dismissed and we would have been free. A few minutes later they returned, and announced that there was a case to answer, and we should be put on trial. This came as no surprise but what was remarkable was the change in their attitude towards us. Whereas before they had been stern, unsmiling, scolding us for making "political" statements, now they sat and looked interested and open to what we had to say. If the video had the same effect on the jury, I thought, we would be halfway to acquittal.

They transferred the case to Preston, the nearest Crown Court. This was somewhat alarming: Preston was only a few miles from Warton and was British Aerospace's company town. Many people there would have friends and family working at Warton, and there had been a lot of prejudicial reporting of our case locally. It seemed impossible that we could have a fair trial in Preston, and at a later hearing a judge agreed it should be moved to another town.

As we left the dock, friends rushed forwards and thrust white roses into our hands. A police officer grabbed them, saying we were not allowed to be passed anything. Jo, however, managed not only to keep hold of hers – we have a photo of her leaving the police station that afternoon, still clutching it – but also to get it through prison reception and back to her cell, a quite amazing feat.

In my diary for 5 May, I wrote, "I look back on our early days in Risley and think that we didn't realise how easy things were then." This was at the end of a week when we'd been locked up almost all day, every day. Staff shortages and overcrowding meant that education, association and exercise were cancelled almost daily. We were virtually being held in solitary confinement, let out only to collect our meals and taken them back to our cells. Sometimes the four of us barely saw each other for days on end, even though we were on the same landing. Our contact was restricted to a few words in the meal queue or a quick conversation if we were allowed out briefly for exercise.

We'd never be told until teatime if we were to have association that evening. The deciding factor was what the officers said when they unlocked us for tea. If they just said, "Tea!" all was well; we'd be out later. The dreaded words "Tea and back to your room" meant we'd be locked up until the following morning.

I found the long hours locked up alone very difficult. There was no shortage of things to do: work connected with trial, dozens of letters to answer, articles to write (officially banned, but we disguised them to look like letters), my diary to keep up to date. The work kept me busy in the morning, but by mid-afternoon I'd had enough: my eyes would be aching, my head throbbing, my whole being itching for some human contact. At that point I couldn't do any more work; even writing letters became too much of a chore and I'd be reduced to lying on my bed listening to the radio or reading cheap thrillers from the library. The weighty tomes I'd asked friends to send in would sit unopened; I simply didn't have the energy for them.

It was hard, really hard, but it could have been much worse. For some years, I had been writing to a prisoner on death row in Arizona. We were able to continue our correspondence while I was in prison, and comparing conditions it was clear that mine were really not so bad. LeRoy had been in solitary confinement for over twenty years; he had no contact with other prisoners at all, apart from shouted conversations, and was let out only a few times a week to shower or exercise. In relative terms, our conditions were easy, but I nonetheless found the long hours locked up alone really hard to tolerate.

I'd been used to spending quite a lot of time on my own on the outside, but that was very different. Here there were few distractions, and it was hard to stop all my fears about the future crowding in on me. Would prison always be like this? Would I get used to it after a year or so? What if I didn't? I hoped fervently that I would never have to find out.

When our contact was restricted by so much time locked up alone, the support of people outside became especially important. Letters from all over the world reminded us that people were thinking of us and that there was life outside our tiny universe of prison.

Anne, living at Menwith Hill women's peace camp in Yorkshire, wrote several times a week, always on beautiful cards, describing the ins and outs of peace camp life and the flora and fauna all around the site. In June, she wrote, "Soft rain, but very mild; the white froth of hedge parsley almost glows against the grey sky". I could almost smell it, and longed to be there with her.

Jill wrote from Wales, beautifully poetic letters which I read and reread, lying on my bed in my hard grey cell, dreaming of the hills. In May, she wrote, "Up here on the edge of the Cambrian mountains spring is late, the wind is cold, and the slugs are so happy I can hear them humming in the hedges in a satisfied tummyfull sort of way". I missed nature so much, but experiencing it vicariously like this was some small compensation.

Family members, old friends, more recent acquaintances or complete strangers – every day we'd each receive a huge pile of letters. I'd hoard them for the quiet hours after lunch, when I could lie on my bed and greedily read and reread these messages from the outside world.

Before we disarmed the Hawk, we'd wondered whether people in East Timor would hear about our action. We thought the word would get through somehow, but to our amazement we found that it had in fact been reported in the *Jakarta Post* (we were described as "fanatic supporters" of the East Timorese resistance). As a result, many people in East Timor heard about it, as did those being held prisoner in Indonesian jails.

One Timorese prisoner, serving a long sentence for nonviolent resistance to the Indonesian occupation, wrote: "In my opinion this is the most efficient way to help stop the Indonesian army from killing our people and destroying our land." I would always return to letters like that when I was feeling low, to remind myself of how important our action had been. They gave me a great feeling of solidarity with other imprisoned activists and reminded me that our situation really wasn't so bad in comparison with what they were enduring.

During this time, the support group was working non-stop on the outside. I was aware that whilst we were getting all the attention, they were doing most of the hard work. Organising prison visits, putting out a regular newsletter, contacting journalists, writing articles, making links with other campaigns, making sure we had everything we needed, speaking at public meetings, liaising with lawyers, supporting us when we were in court; it was a massive job.

Rowan and Ricarda were using their home address and phone number as contact points for press and supporters after the action. For the first month, the phone hardly stopped ringing and every day would bring another big pile of post from people wanting to be sent more information, to buy a video or to be added to the mailing list. By the time of our trial, there were 1,500 people on the database. This was before widespread use of email, and newsletters had to be laboriously written, laid out, printed and stuffed into envelopes to be stamped and addressed.

The support group continued to meet every month whilst the four of us were in prison. These meetings were reportedly difficult at times; the stresses of running the campaign and supporting us meant that sometimes tensions could erupt into conflict. Communication with us in prison was hard, and there were times when disagreements arose over what we had said about a particular issue. That they managed to hold the group together, and continue to run the campaign and provide us with all the support we needed, is testament to the strength of all the women in the group.

Several of the support group were also involved in the ongoing Hawk campaign. In April, Lyn went to a meeting in Parliament with José Ramos Horta, the CNRM (East Timorese resistance) representative to the UN. He described some of the atrocities being committed in his country, and asked why Britain was continuing to sell arms to Indonesia. Ann Clwyd, a Labour MP who'd been very outspoken on the issue, reported that she'd been told by Labour's shadow defence secretary that there were no plans to institute an arms embargo if Labour came to power the following year. Since there was neither an EU or a UN embargo, there was no need for Britain to impose one.

The day after Ramos Horta's visit was the British Aerospace AGM, held at a conference centre in London. Jen, Lyn and Ricarda all went along and took part in a die-in outside the meeting. Inside, someone had thrown an egg at British Aerospace's board, which sparked a great deal of discussion in the evaluation meeting afterwards. Was it nonviolent to throw an egg? Probably not, but compared with the crimes the board were facilitating on behalf of their company, it seemed fairly insignificant.

One important role, taken on by Jen, was to keep us updated on campaign news. One day, Jo arrived in education in a state of great excitement. "Guess what?" she said. "The Indonesians don't want that Hawk – they want a new one!" Jen had written to say that an anonymous source had reported that the Indonesian air force had rejected the Hawk we'd disarmed – supposedly on the grounds that it was jinxed – and were demanding a new one. We never found out if it was true, but it certainly lifted my spirits.

In June, Jen sent us a press cutting about a demonstration at Warton, where over a hundred people had climbed over the fence onto the runway. The report said that, "Police were called to the base after reports of suspicious activity." It was interesting that the police were so biddable; we'd been telling them for years that there was suspicious – not to say criminal – activity going on at British Aerospace, and they'd never bothered to investigate.

One of Lyn's roles was co-ordinating prison visits. By April, visits had begun to take on a much greater significance as they could be the only chance all day to get out of our cells. We were allowed a visit every day, except Sunday, with up to three people at a time. Jo, being relatively local, had a lot of visitors. The rest of us had fewer, but enough to make us feel that we weren't completely cut off from the outside world.

If we felt rather unvisited, we only had to say the word and Lyn would round up willing volunteers to come and see us. Visitors did not have to book with the prison, so she developed her own booking system. This meant that people didn't arrive from far away only to find that someone else had turned up before them and used up our visiting allowance for the day. It also had the advantage that Lyn was usually able to tell us in advance who was coming, which was useful as we often wanted things brought in or handed out during the visit.

We had many visits from people we didn't know, particularly from church groups in Liverpool. I was usually happy to see them, although found it difficult sometimes thinking of things to say to fill the time, small talk not being one of my greatest skills. Visits varied in length according to how busy the visiting room was, and it was very frustrating when a friend or family member who'd travelled for hours to be there was ushered out after only fifteen minutes.

My parents made the long journey from Suffolk several times, despite finding the prison visiting routine alien and stressful. Not every parent would be happy about visiting their daughter in prison, but they were tremendously supportive of me throughout the whole process. My mother laughed as she told me the story of how an old friend had rung to say that she'd seen my name in the newspaper, but knew that it wasn't me but someone with the same name. I don't know whether her friend was more shocked that it was in fact me or that Mum was quite happy to admit to it.

We had been "adopted" by a wonderful elderly couple, Vera and Gil, who lived just a few miles from the prison and had read about the action in a newsletter from Tapol, the Indonesia human rights campaign. They visited often, and were more than happy to provide accommodation for our friends and family when they came to visit. They also transported visitors to and from the station, and usually insisted that they stay for tea as well.

It was always good to see the support group. Sometimes two or three of them would come up together, and each would visit one of us. Joint visits were not allowed, but we always waved across the room and usually managed a quick hug before an officer rushed over to tell us that fraternising with other people's visitors was against the rules.

Many of the other prisoners had apparently told their visitors about the mad aeroplane women, and we were often aware of being pointed out in the visiting room. It wasn't only us that stood out, though. On one occasion, Clare, Ricarda and Rowan were sitting in the waiting room when another visitor approached them.

"Are you visiting those aeroplane women?" she enquired. Clare said they were, and asked how she had guessed.

"It's your clothes," the woman said. "Does everyone dress like that in London?" Clearly Clare's pink dress and knee socks were not the usual fashion in the north west.

Not all our visitors were welcomed, at least by the prison. In March, Chris Cole arrived from London to visit me. I was called down to the waiting room, where I sat impatiently for ages, worrying that I was losing visiting time. Finally after half an hour or so, with other women who had arrived later than me already called in, I asked an officer what was happening. She refused to tell me, and shortly afterwards, I was taken back to the wing, having experienced my first "ghost visit" – the prison term for being stood up by a visitor.

Later that evening, when I was able to make a phone call to Lyn, I found out that Chris had been told he was banned on security grounds. Quite what they thought he was going to do – a Ploughshares action in the visiting room? – was never revealed. Since visitors didn't have to book in advance, there was no way the prison could check them out before they arrived, so they must have had a list of potential visitors who were deemed to be dangerous, Chris being one of them. The outcome of this ridiculous incident, however, was that eventually the prison apologised and revoked his ban.

They presumably also ditched their more general prohibited radicals list, as not long afterwards we were visited by four Ploughshares activist friends from the United States and Australia. One was Ciaron O'Reilly, an Australian whom I'd first met at Dorothy Day House many years earlier, who had come over to do support work around our trial. The governor relaxed the usual rules forbidding joint visits; Jo was seeing a friend but Lotta, Angie and I were able to meet all four of them at once. The officer in charge pulled two tables together, and we sat there as if at a conference, the four of them on one side, the three of us on the other.

There can never have been such a collection of Ploughshares activists all in one prison at the same time before. Our US friends – accustomed to seeing prisoners through a sheet of glass, with conversation conducted over a telephone – were astonished at the openness and informality of the visiting room. Prisoners were allowed to hug and kiss their visitors and even hold hands with them during the visit. Given that visits were an important conduit for drugs coming into the prison, I was always amazed that the prison authorities had sufficient humanity not to ban such contact altogether.

In May, I was transferred to Holloway prison in London to face another trial. This was for the action a year earlier, when Mark Chapman – another ARROW friend – and I had poured fake blood over a Hawk at a VE-Day anniversary display. I had come to the event in Hyde Park straight from a planning weekend at Angie's house, where Ricarda had helped me cook up the "blood" – a mixture of water, food colouring and cornflour – on the stove.

I was anxious about going to Holloway; my previous experience of it had been difficult, and now that I felt settled in Risley, the prospect of the upheaval was unwelcome. Thinking that it would be good to have some company, I found a way to take Jo along. She had been present when I was arrested, and if I called her as a witness, she'd have to be sent to Holloway with me. She was quite happy with the plan, being curious to see another prison and frustrated with the endless lock-up we were suffering in Risley.

We were to spend two weeks in London. My trial lasted only two days, but Risley was full up so we had to stay where we were. It turned out to be a welcome respite; Holloway had far better facilities, and we spent much less time locked up. Our brief sojourn also gave friends living in London a chance to visit us without having to make the long trip to Cheshire.

Education facilities in Holloway were far better than in Risley, but there was no point in starting classes when we were going to be there only briefly. Instead, we did full-time gym; two sessions a day of swimming, aerobics, weight training or team games. Swimming was my favourite, and ploughing up and down the pool I could almost forget I was in prison. One day I just swam and swam, happier than I'd been for ages, and when I got out the PE officer presented me with a badge to sew on my swimsuit to say that I'd swum a mile. I still have it, a souvenir of our holiday in Holloway.

For the first week we shared a dormitory with two other women. One of them, Margy, was in for burglary, and she would spend every evening telling us the most unbelievably lurid tales about her criminal career. I was quite certain she was making most of it up but it was no less amusing for that.

"Did I tell you about the time I was surrounded by three hundred armed officers?" she'd begin, bouncing up and down on her bed. Not waiting for an answer, she'd launch into the story.

"Well, I was carrying a gun, see? I found it in the bottom of the oven at my boyfriend's house and I thought, 'He'll be in trouble if the Old Bill finds him with that', so I took it away. I was just walking down the street and I had the gun in my handbag when...." The stories would go on and on, full of frankly incredible twists and turns. The other woman in the room would pull a sheet over her head and shake with silent laughter as Margy went on and on. It was quite a change from the solitary confinement of Risley, although it might eventually have driven me a little crazy.

My trial was relatively painless. The support group had encouraged people to come to court to support me, and also arranged McKenzie Friends – these are people who can sit with and advise an unrepresented defendant, but who can't address the court. Chris took the role on the first day, with Emily taking over for the second. As my legal assistants, they were allowed to visit me in the cells too, which was a welcome chance to catch up on news from outside.

I'd never been to Crown Court before, and was looking forward to it as practice for our trial. My defence was that my action was lawful as I had been using reasonable force to prevent the crime of murder in East Timor – the same defence we would use in our Ploughshares trial. Unsurprisingly, the judge disallowed it, and objected to most of my attempts to refer to East Timor. He didn't go so far as to order the jury to convict, but made it pretty clear that he thought they should do so.

The jury was out for only half an hour, before returning and announcing that they'd found me unanimously guilty. When I stood up to be sentenced, the prosecutor told the judge that I was already in prison on remand. "She is charged with a similar offence involving two million pounds worth of damage," she announced triumphantly. There was an audible gasp from the jury; they were no doubt thinking that they'd been right to convict me as I was obviously a hardened criminal. It seemed rather unfair to bring up something I hadn't been convicted of, but the judge said he would ignore it in passing sentence.

I was given two months' imprisonment, which seemed like a very steep punishment for what British Aerospace had claimed was £600 of damage to their plane, but had been washed off in ten minutes. I was sure it would have been less had the judge not known that I was already in prison.

Strangely, my sentence nearly lead me to be released by mistake. The method of calculating the time prisoners actually spend in jail is quite incomprehensible, but unbeknown to me it happened that my two-month sentence actually finished whilst I was still in Holloway, since I'd had my bail revoked some weeks earlier and therefore had only one week left to serve.

One night at lock up an officer came to tell me that I'd be going home in the morning. Assuming that by "home" she meant Risley, I asked if Jo was coming too. It turned out that she was actually telling me I was to be released. Being honest, I pointed out that I was on remand for another offence. She went away and looked it up, then returned to tell me that they had no details of any other offence and were legally obliged to release me in the morning.

There followed a sleepless night of indecision. Should I walk out? It wouldn't be as if I hadn't told them they were mistaken. I was tempted to go, and had it all planned out in my head; I'd spend the weekend with friends, before returning to British Aerospace and standing outside with a banner, thus ensuring my rearrest and return to Risley.

I smiled as I pictured the faces at Warton when they saw

me standing outside their front gate instead of securely locked away. But on the other hand, I was worried that, although technically it would be their fault, I would be the one to get into trouble, perhaps by being charged with absconding. In addition, I felt bad about dragging Jo to Holloway and then abandoning her, although she said she didn't mind.

In the end, I decided that I'd mention it once more in the morning, and if they still insisted on releasing me, I'd walk out. What actually happened was that I was almost out of the door when I mentioned to another officer that I thought they were making a mistake. She immediately rang Risley, and that was the end of my dreams of freedom. I spent the next week cursing myself for not taking the opportunity to walk out, and regret it to this day. It makes a good story, but would have been even better if I'd actually been released by mistake.

About a week later, Jo and I were finally returned to Risley. It had been an interesting and not unpleasant trip, but we were glad to be back with Angie and Lotta, to catch up on prison gossip, and really get down to preparing for trial, which was creeping up on us rapidly.

We'd talked extensively about trial during our preparation process, so the whole group could have some input. One weekend we'd had a long session with a lawyer, someone we knew and trusted, whom we plied with questions about defences and court procedure. For Lotta and Jo, it was all new. Angie and I had been on trial many times, but for me this time felt very different as there was so much more at stake than on previous occasions.

We decided to stick to our original decision about representation, which was that one of us would be represented by a barrister, and the other three would represent themselves. In an ideal world we would all have represented ourselves, but we were aware that some awkward legal issues might arise – such as whether we would be allowed to call witnesses – and if that happened, it would be wise to have a barrister to argue our case.

This decision felt very sensible, but others saw it differently. The governor and some of the senior officers made no secret of their horror that we were planning to represent ourselves on such a serious charge. Yet again, we were cast in the role of inexperienced women who didn't know what serious trouble we were in.

Each time this – increasingly boring – trope came up, I was left wondering whether it would have been different had we been a men's group. Would we have experienced the same patronising attitudes, the same implications that we had got ourselves in out of our depth, the same suggestions that we should listen to those who knew better than we did? Somehow, I doubted it.

The governor wasn't even the end of it. A few weeks before the trial we were visited by the director of a prison reform organisation, who had spent time in jail herself. "You're barmy," she said, when she heard that three of us were representing ourselves, before going into a lecture on the perils of thinking that we could take on the system. She warned that we would end up in prison for years, and told us that we were naïve and ought to listen to people such as herself who had a lot more experience than us. Needless to say, this did nothing to make us reconsider.

The main advantage of representing yourself in court is that you can communicate directly with the jury. Whilst a barrister is bound professionally to stick to the strict legal issue, defendants have more scope to at least try to talk about the politics. In many peace movement cases, people don't dispute that they did what they're accused of doing, but argue that it wasn't a crime. In most such situations, the likelihood of being convicted is overwhelming, so there's little point having a lawyer; you might as well at least have the pleasure of putting the case yourself.

Our discussion over who was to be represented went on for some time. I think probably none of us really wanted to be the one, but in the end, Jo offered and the rest of us accepted gratefully, aware that she was making a sacrifice for all of us. A minor compensation was that she would be the first one to tell her story in court, but that perhaps didn't make up for not being able to directly address the jury herself.

The work we had to get through before the trial seemed endless. Contacting expert witnesses, nailing down our defence, writing our speeches, formulating questions for the witnesses, practising what we'd say in our own evidence. Everything took ages, particularly as much of it had to be done by post via the support group. Sometimes I felt we could be in prison for the next year, and still not be ready for trial.

The four of us planned to meet at least three times a week after tea to work on trial issues, but by May we were being locked up so much that getting together had become almost impossible. We explained this to the governor who said that we could meet on the landing when the other women were at education, but that never happened because there were not enough officers to supervise us.

The problem grew worse and worse. We had taken to meeting at the far end of the landing during association, sitting on the floor near the stairs. This was to avoid the constant interruptions which we suffered on the main landing, and for several weeks it worked well. But one evening we were in our usual place, poring over prosecution evidence, when we were approached by the officer who had once snatched my notebook to prevent me taking notes in a meeting with the governor. She was furious.

"Get up! You can't sit here!" she screeched. "It's a fire hazard! Now move!"

It patently wasn't a fire hazard; we were sitting in a dead end corridor outside an empty cell. But the officer wouldn't listen. She continued to scream at us as we gathered our things, and then practically pushed us back down the landing, getting more and more worked up as she did so.

I knew immediately that this marked the end of our meetings there. The officer would obviously go to the governor and demand that we be banned, in order to avoid losing face. Sure enough, the next night we were informed that from then on we could only sit on the main landing. The sheer pettiness of it was frustrating in the extreme. But there was nothing to be done; we'd just have to make the best of it.

CHAPTER 17

"SET FREE THE DOVES OF PEACE!"

Preparation for trial became more and more difficult as we were locked up for ever-longer periods. We continued to put in complaints and to remind the governor at every opportunity that we had to meet together. Finally, in late June, there was a breakthrough.

"Get your stuff together. You're moving," announced an officer at my door one lunchtime. I was horror-struck; had they decided to split us up now, after all this time, and just a few weeks before trial? I asked where I was going. "Windsor," came the short answer. "All four of you."

After five months in Risley, it had finally been decided that it would be safe to send us to the lower security unit. Presumably after observing us for so long the prison authorities had realised that, despite what the Home Office might be telling them, we really weren't intent on causing trouble or escaping. The governor had even told us on one occasion that if the prison gates were accidentally left open, she thought the four of us would be the only ones who wouldn't make a run for it. I wasn't sure that was true, but chose not to dispute it.

Looking back later, I wondered whether my honesty in pointing out that I wasn't supposed to be released from Holloway had contributed to the decision to allow us onto Windsor. I had been given the opportunity to simply walk out of prison, and I had chosen not to. I'd like to think it did, given how long I spent kicking myself afterwards for being so stupid.

Actually getting to Windsor took most of the afternoon, involving as it did descending two flights of stairs, negotiating a long passage, and then going up another flight of stairs. By June, we'd each accumulated a lot of belongings – Angie had some fifty books, despite the prison regulation that only six were allowed – and we had to make journey after journey, each time waiting ages for a prison officer to accompany us.

At last everything was moved, and I stood surveying my new home. The cell was smaller than those on Butler, but there was more storage space. The windows were covered in metal mesh, but opened wide so there was plenty of fresh air. And there was a duvet on the bed instead of the usual green blankets; this turned out to be a mixed blessing as I always found it far too hot. My cell was painted a rather nasty shade of green, and to my disappointment faced north. I wasn't going to be enjoying lying on my bed in the sun.

But lack of sun was the least of my problems. It turned out that the real issue on that side was noise. Soon after everyone was locked up for the night a woman on Butler put a radio on her windowsill – which faced across to Windsor – and turned it up as loud as it would go. I could hear it even with my earplugs in, and work was all but impossible. Finally I gave up and went to bed, but sleep was out of the question too. Eventually, in despair when it was still blaring out past midnight, I called the night officer and asked if she could get it turned down.

Half an hour later, the noise went down a little. Shouts of "Turn it up!" immediately rang out. "I can't!" came the reply. "One of those fucking aeroplane women complained about it!"

The problem with the noise carried on every night, until I was nearly driven to distraction. I was miserable, unable to work, unable to sleep. I would lie in bed each night, fingers clamped tightly in my ears, willing the noise to stop, but it rarely did despite continued complaints.

One of the officers suggested that when a cell came up on the other side of the wing, I should move. Women moved around all the time to be near their friends or because there was a cell they liked the look of, and the officers were quite happy to allow this.

After a couple of weeks, a cell became vacant on the south side, and I asked to move. The officer on duty was new, and said she'd have to check with a senior officer to see if it was allowed. My heart sank; most of the senior officers clearly didn't like us, and I thought that once they heard that it was me who wanted to move, it would be vetoed.

I was right; the officer came back to say that prisoners weren't allowed to move cells. I pointed out that other women did it all the time, but it made no difference. I had to watch as a new woman moved into the cell I so desperately wanted.

I wasn't quite ready to give in, however. If I'd learnt one thing in prison, it was guile. Next time a cell became vacant, I went straight to a different officer and asked to move. She agreed straight away, obviously unaware that I'd been banned from doing so. I ran back to my cell and started grabbing all my belongings and bundling them up in the duvet. If one of the senior officers should see me, I knew I'd be stopped; I had to work fast.

By the time a senior officer did walk through, I was in my new cell. Nothing was ever said to me about it. From then on, things started looking up. The sunshine and the quietness of the south side of the wing improved my spirits beyond measure. From my new cell, I could look out at the exercise yard and try to spot the prison rabbit, which lived under the classrooms. This was because, according to one officer, "It used to live in the classroom but it didn't like being in a cage." She seemed not to notice any irony in this.

Windsor, in the end, was just what we needed. I was relieved to discover that the officer with the obsession about cleaning had left; we were expected to sweep and mop our cells every Saturday, and each had a cleaning job at the weekend, but apart from that there was no great pressure. Although I missed some of the friends we'd made on Butler, I found it quite a relief to be in a much quieter environment, something which seemed particularly important as the trial approached.

By the time we moved to Windsor, preparations for the trial were gearing up rapidly on the outside. In order to avoid prejudice, it had recently been moved from Preston to Liverpool, which was perfect – Jo had lots of friends and contacts there, which helped enormously in terms of mobilising support, and it also had a reputation for being somewhat of an anti-establishment city, which I thought could only be in our favour.

As soon as the location was fixed, several groups in Liverpool started organising events and publicity. The Kirkby Women's Community Action Group – a group Jo had belonged to – stepped up the awareness-raising work they'd been doing throughout our time in prison. Shortly after we were arrested, two women in the group, Maureen Dunwoody and Dot Quirk, had taken the initiative to leaflet the Northwood council ward in Kirkby, explaining to local people why their independent councillor – Jo – was now in prison. Their organising was clearly effective: shortly before the trial, a journalist for the national newspaper *The Independent on Sunday* went to Kirkby and interviewed local people. A shopkeeper said that even children from the area were discussing East Timor as a place where people were being killed by the government and the army. "And Britain is selling them weapons by the lorry-load. How do you explain that to your kids?" he asked.

Jo had for several years been part of another women's group – the Full Moon group – in Liverpool, and together with other local feminists and peace activists, they also set to work to publicise the trial, organise events, stir up the local media and much more. I didn't meet them all, but I got to know Jude Mazonowicz, Nancy Jenkins, Sue Joyce, Val Hall and Ros Hurley; they were wonderful, committed women, determined to offer whatever support they could to all of us and the support group.

Meanwhile, another group was forming, based around St Michael's Catholic Church in the inner city area of West Derby in Liverpool. Ciaron O'Reilly, who I knew from the Catholic Worker in Washington DC, arrived in Liverpool a few weeks before the trial to do support work. Jo put him in touch with Terry Egan, an active trade unionist and a parishioner of St Michael's. The priest, Father Arthur Fitzgerald – "Fitz" – and congregation were soon also on board, organising meetings and fundraisers, hosting supporters, writing to us in prison, visiting us, and rallying many of the other Catholic parishes in Liverpool. Julie Currall, Margarita Egan, Jan Harper, Eileen Lang, Josie Macfarlane and many more: all were hugely and unconditionally supportive of us. Other religious groups were similarly supportive, especially the Liverpool Justice and Peace Commission, including staff member Frank Kennedy, who went out of his way to do whatever he could to support us and spread the word about the trial.

Altogether, it was a fantastic feat of organising by a huge number of people from very different backgrounds, who did everything in their power to ensure that nobody in Liverpool could be left wondering what this trial was all about. Having these groups organising in Liverpool took a lot of pressure off the support group; they were working non-stop as it was, and clearly it made sense for local events to be organised by local people, who would have lots of contacts and networks already in place.

A couple of weeks before the trial started, Fitz hung a huge banner on the front of St Michael's – which stands on one of the main roads into the city centre – demanding, "Set free the doves of peace!" His attitude, and that of many other clergy in the city, was in stark contrast to the official reaction from the church. Just a few days before our trial, three senior church leaders in Liverpool issued a press release about our action. Whilst they opposed arms sales to Indonesia, they said, "To break the law is a serious matter, especially at a time when many people have deep fears about the breakdown of the rule of law in the face of lawlessness.... before anyone chooses to break the law they should weigh up some serious considerations. We understand their motives but we cannot support their action."

This was a terrible prejudgment, based entirely on the prosecution case, and we worried that if local papers reported it before the trial, it could seriously sway any potential jurors who might read it. Several local priests wrote to protest on our behalf, but were given short shrift. The requested retraction and apology was not forthcoming, even after we had been acquitted. It saddened me that church leaders – who are surely supposed to be upholders of morals in society – could be so short-sighted and prejudiced against us.

Meanwhile, the support group were frantically getting themselves together for the trial. Tasks had been carefully divided out, and Rowan and Ricarda – responsible for media work – spent weeks hounding reluctant journalists to take an interest in what most appeared to think was a story of little consequence. There were a few notable exceptions, individual journalists who were immensely supportive, but for most

191

it simply wasn't a story. As far as they were concerned, we'd done the damage and now we were going to go to trial, be convicted, and sent to prison. Case closed.

Others in the group were busy writing and mailing out newsletters and responding to the enquiries which continued to flood in. In order to share out the work, they developed a monthly rota for dealing with our requests from prison, which came in thick and fast as we always needed phone calls made, photocopying done, obscure facts researched, messages passed on and information sent in to us.

Having people on the outside ready to respond so quickly to our needs made our life inside very much less stressful, as it meant that we were saved a lot of battles with prison bureaucracy. Photocopying, for instance, was theoretically available in prison, but in practice it meant putting in an application and then waiting days for it to happen. I often wondered how people managed to survive in prison without a support group.

A few days before the trial, the entire support group moved to Liverpool. This was a huge task, involving as it did transporting not only themselves but also all the office equipment. Jude Mazonowicz, Jo's friend from the Full Moon group, had offered to house everyone during the trial. It made life much easier for the group to be all together, but chaos must have reigned at times as the whole group plus assorted partners, children and friends crowded into one small flat. For the entire period they were there, the support group was working non-stop to support us and publicise the trial, and stress levels were running high throughout.

Meanwhile, the four of us were hard at work finalising our defence. We'd asked Gareth Peirce to be our solicitor and were delighted when she agreed. She had helped the Guildford Four and the Birmingham Six to win their appeals after they had spent years in prison, wrongfully convicted of IRA-related terrorism offences. Gareth came up to visit us in prison several times, and was always a very down-to-earth and calming presence.

Gareth had also found us a barrister, Vera Baird, a woman of striking looks – very tall, with red hair – and imposing courtroom presence. She was definitely not a woman to suffer fools gladly, but outside court she had a great sense of humour and was very encouraging of us when we occasionally had doubts about our legal abilities. Many barristers might be disturbed or even affronted at the idea of appearing jointly with defendants representing themselves, but Vera seemed to have no qualms about it.

We'd already met our judge – who had the rather unfortunate name of Judge Lynch – at a hearing a few weeks before the trial was to begin. Our first meeting was far from auspicious. There were several issues we wanted to raise, the main one being that Lotta and I wanted to have McKenzie Friends to help us with notetaking. But Judge Lynch wasn't having this.

"If you need assistance in court," he declared, "you should have a barrister."

"But we want to represent ourselves," I pointed out. "We just need someone to take notes for us. We can't take notes and conduct our defence at the same time. And barristers have clerks to take notes, so it's not fair if we're not allowed to."

"You heard what I said," the judge snapped. "I'm not going to allow my courtroom to be disrupted by unrepresented defendants."

In the end, after much argument, he said that he might allow one McKenzie Friend each (despite our pointing out that if the trial lasted the expected ten days, it might not be possible to have the same person for the whole period) but that we'd have to submit their details in advance so that he could decide whether they were "suitable". He refused to say what "suitable" might mean.

We also asked if the trial could be held in a larger courtroom. The one we were in at the time seated about ten people, and if we were tried there, most of our friends and family would have to remain outside. Judge Lynch, however, saw no problem with that and refused to make a request for a larger court. His attitude was infuriating, but there was nothing to be done. We'd just have to go along with it, and hope he lightened up once he saw that we weren't interested in causing disruption.

All in all, it was a rather sobering first encounter. The judge seemed so outrageously prejudiced against us that it was difficult to believe that we might be able to get a fair trial in front of him. However, he must have thought about the issues we had raised, as a few days later we received a letter from the court saying that Lotta and I would be able to have McKenzie Friends – with no mention of vetting them – and that the trial would be held in court ten, which turned out to be one of the biggest courts in the building, seating some fifty people.

As the trial approached, we got more and more mired in the technicalities of the law. Our basic defence was that in British law (the Criminal Law Act 1967) you are allowed to use reasonable force to prevent crime. However, we couldn't quite decide what crime we were trying to prevent in strict legal terms. Was it aiding, abetting, counselling, procuring, soliciting or conspiring to commit genocide? We were a little hazy about the legal definitions of some of these, and Jo and I had many long discussions about which one was the most relevant.

A fly on the wall of our cells would have fallen off laughing had it been able to hear us sitting there saying things like, "Counselling genocide is a non-inchoate crime of secondary participation." I knew what the individual words meant, but somehow when they were all strung together they didn't make much sense. Finally, Jo rang Gareth and asked her for advice about this. She seemed surprised at the question, and said, "Well, I thought it was very simple. You were trying to prevent people being killed." We were definitely in need of a reality check every now and again.

Although work on our defence was progressing well, there were still problems. As the trial got closer, we were spending increasing amounts of time preparing and Jo started to feel that she needed more time than was available. Although she was being represented, she was doing most of the liaison with our witnesses, and was also doing as much as any of us in terms of formulating questions for prosecution and defence witnesses, laying out our defence and working out what we wanted to say in the witness box.

On Windsor, everyone was required to either take a job

or go to education full time. However, Jo had sometimes been staying in her cell and working whilst we went off to education, and for several days this appeared not to present a problem. One day, though, one of the officers decided she had to enforce the rules and told Jo she'd have to go. In education we could chose to do private study, so Jo simply picked up her law books and took them across to the classroom with her.

She'd been there five minutes when a teacher came and asked her if she was doing defence work because, she said, "I've been told you're not allowed to do that." The officer had actually rung and asked the teacher to check up on what Jo was doing. When she found that she was indeed working on our defence, the teacher demanded that she stop and suggested that she do a jigsaw instead. Jo pointed out that other women were allowed to write letters to their solicitors in education, but this cut no ice: she had to stop.

Jo had come into the artroom in tears, and she and I retreated to the toilet to talk about what had happened. Not for long though; we were soon followed in by the teacher.

"You can't stay in here," she said. "You'll have to go back to class."

"We won't be long," I replied, and made no move to leave.

"You have to go now," she insisted. Peering more closely at us in the half darkness, she suddenly noticed that Jo was crying. "You haven't been in prison before, have you?" she said patronisingly.

"Yes I have, actually," I said, determined not to let her get the better of us. She ignored me and forced us out of the toilets, and then refused to let Jo come into the art class, saying that people couldn't just come and go as they pleased. I was furious. She was employed as a teacher, not a prison officer, but apart from the lack of uniform, you couldn't tell the difference.

The outcome of this incident was that the four of us were yet again summoned to see the governor, who explained that she couldn't allow us to work on our defence in class because she had to make decisions "for the common good". She conveniently avoided the question of what common good was served by Jo being forced to do jigsaws, but went on to wheel out the excuse which we'd heard a hundred times, over virtually every issue we'd ever raised. "Other women," she said, "are jealous of the special treatment you get."

This was quite simply untrue; we'd never had the slightest hint of jealousy or animosity from any of the other women. In fact, most of them sympathised with us because they could see that we did indeed get special treatment, but in the form of harassment rather than privilege. It wasn't exactly the kind of special treatment to make anyone jealous. And why would other prisoners care if we were allowed to work on our defence in education? It was an absolute nonsense.

But there was undoubtedly a humane side to the governor, and she said that although Jo would not be allowed to work on her defence in class, she would write her a sick note saying that she needed to rest in her cell for the next few days. Obviously she knew that Jo was not physically unwell, and would spend her "sick leave" working on trial preparation, but this was a way in which she could be allowed to do that without anyone losing face.

In her anxiety to be seen to be enforcing the rules, however, the governor had called everyone on Windsor into the lounge earlier that day to hear her holding forth about how "Windsor girls" had to take a job if asked, rather than going to education. "Too many people," she said, looking round the room and perhaps lingering just slightly too long on us, "are going to education. There are certain jobs which have to be done, and you girls are expected to do them. Being on Windsor is a privilege which brings with it certain duties. If you don't want those duties, you can go back to Butler." This was very clearly directed at the four of us. We were the only ones on Windsor who were on full-time education, as most women preferred to have at least a part-time job.

Later that day, fed up with the implication that we were refusing to work, I said to the governor that I would give up education and take a job. It turned out that there were no jobs available. As with so many situations, we just couldn't win; if we went to education, we were accused of not wanting to work, but when I offered to work, there was no work available. "Alice in Wonderland strikes again", I noted in my diary that night.

CHAPTER 18

═══════════════

"I CAN LOCK THEM UP FOR
A VERY LONG TIME"

Just before moving unexpectedly to Windsor wing, we had decided to make one final bail application, as we were unable to spend enough time together preparing our defence. Once we were moved, this was less of a problem but even here prison budget cuts were biting and we were often locked up for the entire weekend. Daytimes were taken up with education, leaving only the association period – often cancelled – to work together. Given these factors, we decided to press ahead with the application.

This was to be our first serious bail application. We had asked for bail on several previous occasions, but never with the slightest thought that we might get it. This time we would be better prepared.

The support group ran round frantically amassing character references for each of us. These were most impressive and included a lord, several MPs and a retired naval commander. They also contacted anyone they could think of who might be willing to put up money for sureties – any awkwardness about asking for money set aside in the urgency of getting us out – and in the end managed to come up with well over £100,000. Surely that would be enough to secure our release?

On the day of the hearing, Angie went off to court in the morning. Jo, Lotta and I stayed in prison since we were being represented by Vera. I didn't think much about the hearing during the day, and didn't dwell on the fact that we might be released that afternoon. It seemed quite unlikely, and I didn't want to set myself up to be disappointed.

I rang Lyn late that afternoon to see if there was any news, and she'd just heard that our application for bail had been refused. She went on to say that the judge, Judge Wickham, had referred to us as "professional troublemakers". He had refused to look at the references Angie had brought and had told her that there was nothing she could have done which would have made him even consider granting bail. We had, he stated firmly – and without having heard any of the evidence – no defence.

Vera said that we were women of conscience and that if we promised to turn up in court, we would do so. Judge Wickham replied that that was exactly the problem: we were women of conscience. Whilst this appalling prejudice was quite shocking, I wasn't too disappointed to hear that our application had been refused, since I hadn't really been expecting anything else.

"Never mind," I said to Lyn. "At least he's not our trial judge." There was a momentary silence on the other end of the phone.

"I don't know how to tell you this," Lyn said. "He's

appointed himself to your trial."

It turned out that Judge Wickham was the senior judge in Liverpool, and he had decided that he wanted to try us. Whether this was because he thought the seriousness of the case merited a senior judge, or because he was so personally outraged by what we had done that he wanted to make sure we were convicted and given a long sentence, we never found out. But he had made no bones about his leanings. When Vera had pointed out that he couldn't lock us up forever, the judge had replied, "No, but I can lock them up for a very long time."

The other women, and even some of the officers, offered their condolences when they heard our news. Judge Wickham was well known to many of the prisoners and had earned the nickname "Wack'em Wickham" through his reputation for heavy sentencing. This wasn't looking good.

But there was worse to come. Angie returned to the wing that evening and told us that Vera's opinion was that if we were convicted, Judge Wickham would give us the maximum sentence: ten years.

I stared at her, horrified. Ten years? *Ten years*? That couldn't possibly be right, could it? Of course I knew that was the theoretical maximum, and certainly we'd done a lot of damage in purely monetary terms, but we were trying to prevent terrible crimes. We were nonviolent and accountable. We were nice women! Wickham couldn't give us ten years – could he?

The previous two Ploughshares actions in Britain had ended in sentences of fifteen and eight months. Whilst it would be unwise to put too much weight on this, one could be forgiven for thinking that it would be unlikely that the third such action would get much more than five years, which was the arbitrary figure I had until then kept in my head as being the probable – but unlikely – maximum. Now I had to take in the prospect of being inside for twice as long as I had anticipated.

As if all this weren't bad enough, it turned out that Vera was going to be unavailable for the first week of the trial, and Judge Wickham had refused to put the date back. That meant that we'd have to find another barrister, and it seemed unlikely that we could find anyone as good at such short notice. Suddenly, everything was going wrong.

That night was the worst I spent in prison. Unable to sleep, unable to concentrate on anything other than that terrible figure – ten – which battered itself ceaselessly against my skull, I just lay there calculating and recalculating. You had to serve two-thirds of any sentence over four years, unless you behaved yourself and professed regret for what you did, in which case you might be released on parole at the halfway point. Disregarding that possibility, we would have to serve six years and eight months, and we'd already have done six on remand, which would mean six years and two months from the end of the trial, so if we were sentenced in July 1996, we wouldn't be released until September 2002.

These figures were really fantasy; if we were sentenced to ten years, we would obviously appeal and it would be certain to be reduced. However, at that point, logic wasn't uppermost in my mind, and I lay there in the darkness, figures spinning round my head, and tears rolling down my cheeks. Finally, head aching and eyes sore from crying, I drifted off into a restless sleep.

I slept very little and woke unrested, my head splitting, still with only one thought on my mind. In the morning I wrote a quick letter to my parents telling them what had happened; I wanted them to hear it from me first. After explaining the situation, and saying that we expected that the judge might disallow our defence and our witnesses, I ended by saying, "Please don't get too despondent; we do have a chance of acquittal!" This was as much for my own sake as that of my parents; I needed to keep reminding myself of that, to prevent myself descending into complete despair.

It was a long and difficult day. In the morning we went to education, where we recounted the story to one of the more sympathetic teachers, who was as shocked as we were. Later that day, I had a visit from someone I didn't know. Normally I was happy to have such visits, but this time it was a terrible strain; I didn't feel like pouring my heart out to a stranger, and found it extremely stressful sitting there making small talk and pretending that everything was all right.

After the visit, I had to sit in the tiny waiting room for half an hour as there weren't enough officers to take prisoners back to the wing. The room was thick with smoke, my head was throbbing, and I was missing exercise. My request to be taken out because the smoke was making me feel sick was met with a sharp, "You'll just have to put up with it." All in all, it was an extremely miserable day.

That evening, Lotta and I were sitting in her cell talking quietly about the implications of a long sentence when Jo burst in, grinning from ear to ear. "Guess what?" she said. We couldn't even begin to guess what could have precipitated such delight, and asked her to continue. "Vera said we'd get two years, not ten!"

She'd just rung Gareth, who was amazed to be told the "ten year" story. She said that it must have been a misunderstanding; what Vera had actually said was that if convicted, we were likely to get two years. We all collapsed on the bed, hugging each other, unsure whether to laugh or cry. Two years was less than we'd been expecting, and whilst we took it with a pinch of salt, it was wonderful to hear that Vera thought ten years, or anything even approaching that, completely out of the question.

Having spent twenty-four hours contemplating the prospect of a ten-year sentence, two years felt like a mere slap on the wrist; it would mean only another six months to serve after trial. Whilst I didn't intend to get complacent or to put too much weight on this estimate, it was nonetheless a huge relief to hear Vera's opinion. I relaxed, and was able to get on with trial preparation without feeling as if I had the sword of Damocles hanging over my head.

The next two weeks passed quickly; we spent most of our free time working on our speeches, refining our questions to the witnesses and making sure that every aspect of our case was polished and repolished. Judge Wickham had in the end been prevailed upon to put the trial back by a day, and Vera had managed to juggle her other dates so she could be there from the start. At last I felt really confident about our ability to make this trial a success, whatever the outcome, and started to look forward to it.

There was a silent procession to the court planned for the first day, and this went ahead despite the start of the trial being delayed. Our families – my parents, Jo's parents, Angie's daughter Zina and Lotta's sister Karin – had arrived the previous day and were able to join the long line of people winding its way slowly through the centre of Liverpool. There had been almost 200 people there, and my mother especially was very moved by this huge outpouring of support for us.

We were locked up for the whole of the weekend before the trial, but by then we'd been over our case so many times that it didn't really matter. I spent the weekend writing and rewriting my speeches, practising them, timing them. Officers looking through the spyhole when they were doing a headcount must have wondered if I'd finally lost it, seeing me sitting on the bed apparently talking to myself.

On the Sunday night, we were allowed out for a few hours, and we took the opportunity to have a final ritual together. We read an account of the Santa Cruz massacre in East Timor, and letters sent to us by Timorese prisoners, to remind ourselves of why we did the action, and that what we did was right, whatever the outcome. Angie gave Jo, Lotta and me friendship bands she had made, and we each committed ourselves to getting through the trial together. We were, finally, ready for what was to come.

CHAPTER 19

"I CAN'T DISQUALIFY THE WHOLE OF KIRKBY"

By 23 July, the first day of our trial, we'd spent 176 days in custody, been to court ten times and been denied bail on three occasions. We were ready to go.

It was 25 miles from Risley to Liverpool, about an hour's bumping around in the uncomfortable prison van. We arrived shortly after nine, entering the court via the back entrance by the docks. The security guards who lead us from the van were friendly enough; they showed us into a basement cell, and offered us tea whilst we waited to be called.

I found it difficult to sit still, and my fidgeting, checking and rechecking of notes, brushing and rebrushing of hair was probably quite annoying. A few days earlier, Angie and I had been given "not guilty" haircuts by one of the officers – who insisted this would ensure our acquittal – and we were all wearing quite smart clothes. Hopefully we looked respectable enough, and would subvert the picture the prosecutor would no doubt try to paint of us as deranged and dangerous women.

Finally the keys turned in the door and a security guard

looked in and told us it was time to go. I took a deep breath and we squeezed each other's hands one last time. This was it.

We went up in a lift, and along a passage, then one of the security guards unlocked a door and we emerged into the dock. It was very bright in the court and walking in felt almost like stepping out onto a stage, with the audience arrayed in front of us, eagerly waiting for the performance to begin. The whole room was packed, with every last seat taken; as we came in, people smiled and waved at us – friends, family members, and complete strangers who had heard about our case and come along to support us. The only people not smiling were the besuited men in a row at the back of the court; I guessed they were from British Aerospace, sent to witness the spectacle of these terrible women being sent down for a very long time.

The row adjacent to us was taken up with family members. They were in the privileged position of having a seat reserved for them every day by the support group; everyone else had to put their names on a rota as there were always far more people wanting to come in than there were seats available.

We wanted to sit at a table in the body of the court; sitting in the dock was impossible as we'd be forced to balance all our papers on our knees. Having regard to Judge Wickham's reputation, we were expecting a battle over this, and had made contingency plans which were to include frequent and noisy dropping of books onto the floor.

We needn't have worried; the judge came in and agreed to our request with barely a murmur. He also agreed to our McKenzie Friends – Jen and Clare – sitting with us, and to our request to change the order in which we would be called. Could this be the same judge who only two weeks before had called us "professional troublemakers" and threatened to send us to prison for a very long time if we were convicted?

Housekeeping over, a crowd of potential jurors was ushered into the courtroom. I eyed them up closely, trying to decide – ridiculously – which ones looked like possible sympathisers. Vera had asked that jurors should be questioned about links to British Aerospace or the military; Judge Wickham agreed to this, and added a question of his own about whether any of them had ever worked in Indonesia. Only one juror was disqualified through the questioning but another stood up to ask whether he should be disqualified.

"I'm from Kirkby," he explained, "and I know one of the defendants comes from there."

"Well, I can't disqualify the whole of Kirkby," Judge Wickham replied drily, and the man sat down, smiling. I was pleased when he was selected; he looked sympathetic and I thought he would be bound to like Jo, with all her links to his area. As the names of the selected jurors were read out, each one got up and took their seat on the jury panel. At first it seemed to be all men, but then several women's names were read, and in the end it was seven men and five women.

Once they were seated, the prosecutor, Mr Pickup, stood up to open his case. He explained the charges against us and then went on to describe what happened on 29 January. He made it sound all a little sensational, like a bad action movie.

"They attacked the plane with hammers," he declared loudly, "causing over one and a half million pounds worth of damage. The defendant Kronlid was found to be in possession of a plan of the cockpit, with a note on it warning her to watch out for the ejector seat. Their motivation," he added, "is shown by the tools they were carrying, each of which was painted with a slogan proclaiming their cause."

With this, he started picking up each tool in turn, reading the messages we'd painted on them. "All life is sacred," he started sniffily. "We all have the power to disarm. Women disarming for life and justice. Disarmament is a duty not a crime." He grimaced as he picked up the heavy iron bar we'd used to smash the fire exit window, and there was a loud clunk as he put it back down on the table. I smiled as I thought about carrying that huge chunk of metal for miles across the black Lancashire fields.

There was forensic evidence, he said triumphantly. "The fingerprints of the defendant Andrea Needham were found on this lump hammer," he said, waving my beautiful blue hammer in the air. Strangely, they'd been unable to match Lotta's or Jo's fingerprints to any of the tools, and neither did any of the glass fragments found on our clothes match the glass from either the fire door or the broken panels in the cockpit. It's fortunate we're admitting it, I thought; if they had to rely on their forensic evidence there wouldn't be much of a case.

Security guards found us, Mr Pickup went on, seated on the steps of the Hawk, which he referred to as a "training aircraft" throughout his speech. He made it sound as if they'd just happened upon us, failing to mention that the only reason they knew we were there was because we'd told them so. When we were asked what we'd done, Lotta had reportedly said that we'd "de-armed" the Hawk.

Angie, he said, was arrested a week later, carrying not only a hammer and boltcutters, but – horror of horrors – a bag of seeds which she said were to spread on the next plane to be disarmed. He implied that she was the ringleader, the one who'd told us what to do and then carelessly been arrested later once she'd done the all-important media work which, he said, was the sole reason for our action: it was nothing other than a publicity stunt.

This was a damning case indeed; what a heinous crime we'd committed. However, the prosecutor obviously didn't want to come over as the big bad wolf. "There is no question," he explained to the jury, "that the defendants' views were held genuinely and sincerely, but it is not relevant for us to examine this in any detail because what they did was a criminal offence, whatever the truth or otherwise of their views." Just to underline how implausible our motivation was, he added that, "No reasonable person could or would do what they did and consider it justified."

That first day, Mr Pickup called three British Aerospace workers and our arresting officer to the witness stand. The first was Thomas Fitzpatrick, an electrician who had been working the day before the action on the Hawk we disarmed. He was asked to verify that the Hawk had been undamaged when he left it. Cross-examined by Vera, he claimed to know nothing about the weapons the plane could carry, but admitted that it had "combat capability", although he too insisted that it was primarily a training aircraft.

Lotta was determined to challenge this and quoted from a military aircraft book. "It says in this book about Hawk," she said, "that for reduced aircraft workload in a combat environment both cockpits are equipped with hands-on-throttle-and-stick, or HOTAS, controls whereby all time-critical weapon control switches are ergonomically equipped on the throttle control stick. Would you agree that is correct?" In less technical terms, this meant that firing its weapons is such an important part of operating the Hawk that the buttons and switches controlling the aircraft's missiles and guns have been put on the throttle lever and the flight control stick, which the pilot is always holding in order to fly the aircraft.

Mr Fitzpatrick looked slightly at a loss for words for a few moments before regaining his composure and confirming that this was indeed correct. It was odd to hear Lotta talking obscure technicalities like this; she was usually the one most keen to demystify such language and put it on a level that everyone could understand. But we wanted to keep pointing out throughout the case that the Hawk was not primarily a trainer, as the prosecutor was intent on having the jury believe. It was primarily an attack aircraft, and the HOTAS controls were just one element of its attack capability.

Next we had Philip Brownley, the security officer who had found us that night. British Aerospace was clearly embarrassed about the major security breach we had caused, and he was cagey and reluctant to discuss security matters. "We did a full patrol of the site at 4am," he said. "We found nothing of concern and the fence was secure." He was adamant that the door to the hangar had not been damaged at that point, although we'd actually broken in over an hour earlier.

Later evidence would show that the first phone call we'd made from the hangar was at 4.26am. This meant – if the security guard was correct – that we had cut the fence, walked to the hangar, tried to break into one door, walked round the hangar, broken into another door, hammered extensively on the plane, hung up our banners, stuck our photographs to the wing, scattered our seeds and located a phone, all in the space of some twenty minutes. This was extremely implausible, but there wasn't much point disputing it; it wouldn't advance our case and would detract from the main point – the disarmament of the plane.

In cross-examination, Mr Brownley admitted that he was aware that there was controversy surrounding the Hawk deal, but didn't know what it was about. He knew there had been protests at Warton and claimed to have seen Lotta there on a previous occasion.

"How did you know we were on the premises that night?" I asked. He was forced to admit that the source of the information was the Press Association. Lotta asked him about our demeanour and actions, and he agreed that we had been peaceful and had made no attempt to escape. That was as much as we needed to hear from him, and we moved on to the next witness.

Cross-examination was a lengthy procedure, with Vera going first on behalf of Jo, followed by Angie, me, and finally Lotta. Some of the witnesses were rather uncomfortable with this lengthy interrogation, and it must have been quite daunting for them to be cross-examined by no fewer than four different people, three of them defendants.

After the security officer had given evidence, it was time for lunch. We were hustled back downstairs – the security guards were always anxious to get us out of court as quickly as possible and got very cross when we lingered to chat with friends and family – and put back in our little cell. Lunch was a real treat; being quite at a loss as to what to feed four vegans, the guards gave us wholemeal bread, tomatoes, and four pieces of fruit each. They apologised for the food, but we assured them that it was exactly what we wanted, as we greedily tucked into varieties of fruit we hadn't seen for six months.

That afternoon, we heard evidence from the site manager at Warton, Geoffrey Mountain. We asked him about the 1978 Hawk deal with Indonesia; he denied that the Hawks had been fitted out as warplanes after delivery, and said they weren't used for ground attack, although he agreed that they could carry weapons including cluster bombs. He said he was aware of the campaign against the deal, but took little notice of it as he didn't believe that the Hawks were being used in East Timor.

The most significant evidence from Mr Mountain came when we questioned him closely about the Hawk we had disarmed. He prevaricated when asked whether the plane we had disarmed had been delivered on time.

"Tell me where that aeroplane is now," Vera asked.

"It is still in the UK," he replied.

"So does that amount to a delay in it being exported to Indonesia?"

"You could not describe it as a delay, no."

"Has it caused a delay?"

"Caused a delay in what?"

"Delivering this Hawk to Indonesia."

"It is simply going in a different order."

"It has been delayed, has it not?"

"As a single aeroplane, yes." Finally, the answer we wanted.

Mr Mountain seemed uncomfortable, almost evasive, throughout the cross-examination, and the relief on his face when he was finally allowed to step down from the stand was evident.

Our first day on trial was over. All day long, people had been standing outside the court with banners and leaflets, bearing witness to what was going on both with us and in East Timor. Father Fitzgerald sat on the concrete slabs, praying silently, whilst nearby, Buddhist monks and nuns were drumming and repeating their mantra.

Every day, there was a procession to the court from a church in the city centre which had been bombed in the Blitz and stood empty and ruined, a stark reminder of the power of bombs dropped from above on civilian populations. The dignity and power of the procession was overwhelming; a video made of it shows dozens of people walking silently, many dressed in black, holding crosses with the names of people killed in the Santa Cruz massacre. There are people of all ages; people from all over the country and the world; friends and family; and people who didn't know any of us personally but were moved to come to Liverpool to witness this extraordinary event. The only sound is a single drumbeat and a plaintive song about the tragedy of East Timor.

CHAPTER 20

"IT IS NOT BRITISH AEROSPACE THAT IS ON TRIAL HERE, IS IT?"

In my diary for the second day of the trial, I noted that Judge Wickham spent the day "switching from totally outrageous to utterly reasonable in the blink of an eye (but always utterly reasonable in front of the jury)". He had a chameleon-like quality whereby he could appear terribly prejudiced when the jury was out, but as soon as they came in he would be fairness personified. It was quite a thing to watch.

The jury spent much of that morning out of court as various legal arguments went on. The main one – conducted by Vera on our behalf – centred around the estimate of the damage. British Aerospace had put the costs at nearly £1.7m – down from an original £2.4m – but had refused to allow an independent assessment, citing "security" reasons. Vera felt that they were simply being obstructive and trying to hide the fact that they'd massively overinflated their damage claim.

She told the judge that, based on her independent assessor's examination of photographs of the plane, £1.7m was a gross overestimate, and that the correct figure should be nearer £500,000. Judge Wickham was unmoved.

"The only thing that matters," he said, "is that the damage was substantial. If the defendants are convicted, I will sentence them on the basis that it was between half and three-quarters of a million pounds."

However, although he made great play of how reasonable he was being by setting a lower figure for sentencing purposes, this was not allowed to be communicated to the jury. They were left thinking that the damage was actually £1.7m when it fact it was probably considerably less. But there was no point pursuing the issue further; the judge had made his mind up.

Further arguments followed; should we be allowed to show our video to the jury, and should we be allowed to call expert witnesses? Mr Pickup, mindful perhaps of the effect the video had had on the magistrates at our committal hearing, protested that the video was irrelevant and the jury did not need to see it. Vera countered that it was extremely relevant because it showed our state of mind and motivation for acting as we did.

In the end, Judge Wickham decided to see it for himself, and after watching it carefully, agreed that it could be shown. I was hugely relieved; I felt sure that the jury could not fail to be moved by what they saw. In addition, the video would give them a good overview of the issue and would put the whole case into context.

In regard to expert witnesses, Judge Wickham took no time in making up his mind.

"I have a number of witnesses who will give evidence about East Timor," Vera stated.

"I do not think I shall allow that," came the judge's immediate reply. However, Vera was nothing if not tenacious, and was determined to argue the matter out. The prosecutor, for his part, said that he wasn't challenging our sincerity or beliefs and that therefore there was no need for us to call witnesses.

Technically, the defence of using reasonable force to prevent crime is subjective; it is enough for a defendant to claim that she *believed* a crime was taking place, even if objectively it can be proved that she was mistaken. Therefore, Mr Pickup said, it was not necessary for us to call witnesses to the alleged crime since whether it was happening or not was irrelevant. All that mattered was our belief that it was happening, and he was happy to concede that our belief was genuine.

"What could be fairer than that?" asked Judge Wickham.

Vera wasn't having this. She said that we needed to call witnesses in order to show the reasonableness of our belief that a crime was going to be committed with the Hawk. It's all very well, she pointed out, to claim that you thought a crime was about to happen, but if the jury thinks that your belief is totally unreasonable, they're not likely to put much weight on your defence that you were acting to prevent that crime. As an example, she pointed out that the prosecutor had consistently referred to the Hawk as a trainer, which would suggest to the jury that although we might genuinely *believe* that it was an attack plane, we were in fact mistaken.

"He cannot accept," Vera said, "that it was in Joanna Wilson's mind that these planes are predominantly lethal weapons and then call evidence that they are actually only trainers."

"It is a trainer plane that can be used as a military plane," Judge Wickham stated.

"Yes, but Mr Pickup used the word 'trainer' twice in his opening. There has not been a witness from British Aerospace who has not sought to call it a trainer at every available opportunity."

"That is why there are two cockpits," the judge said, speaking more slowly than usual and emphasising each word. "It is a trainer plane. You don't need two cockpits. A Spitfire didn't have two cockpits."

He and the prosecutor continued to insist that as long as they conceded that we genuinely believed the Hawk was a lethal weapon which would be used in East Timor, it was unnecessary for us to call evidence to prove the point. But Vera was tenacious.

"A lot of people," she said, "genuinely and sincerely believe in things which the jury just would not tolerate as a reason for taking a step that damaged somebody else's property because they would think that it was ill-founded."

In his response, Judge Wickham perhaps revealed what he really thought of our case. "They may certainly think," he said, "that this genuine and sincere belief is no excuse for breaking into somebody else's property and doing extensive damage."

The argument dragged on and on. Finally the judge could stand it no longer and backed down, trying to save a little face as he did so. "If you've got witnesses here that can walk through the door and tell us," he said somewhat scathingly, "you can call them. But if you are going to expect the State to pay for witnesses to be brought from East Timor, you've got another think coming." Vera assured him that she expected no such thing, and the jury was called back in.

The first witness to be called that day was grandly titled "Manufacturing manager, development flight". Christopher Foster had been responsible for assessing the disarmed Hawk and deciding whether each damaged item needed to be replaced or could just be repaired. In his evidence he said the Hawk was not normally kept in that hangar; it was only there temporarily whilst it was having certain tests done, and would normally be stored elsewhere. It was no wonder the police had thought we had inside information.

Like the other British Aerospace witnesses, he said that he was aware that there was controversy over the Hawk deal.

"Were you aware of allegations that Hawks from an earlier deal had been used to bomb civilians in East Timor?" Vera asked.

"I understand there were some allegations."

"The allegations were that the Hawks from the previous deal had been put to a murderous rather than a military use. That was the case, was it not?"

"That may be one interpretation." He was not going to concede the point.

Mr Foster consistently referred to the Hawk as a trainer, going to some lengths to avoid admitting what we hoped was very clear to the jury by that point: the Hawk was an attack aircraft.

"It says here," I said when it was my turn, quoting from a military aircraft book, "'The Hawk's potential weapons fit and avionics make it not primarily a trainer but a light combat aircraft ideal for real attack sorties.' Would you agree with that statement?"

"That could be one possibility in certain scenarios," he replied, "but on every aircraft the pilot has to be trained."

"Obviously, but what are the pilots being trained for?"

"The basic handling qualities of the aircraft."

"Once they have been trained, then what do they do?"

"They can either train other pilots or they can use the aircraft in its secondary role."

"Which is?"

"Which is a military role, an offensive role if you wish to call it that."

I certainly wished to call it that, but he was most reluctant to do so, and continued referring to the plane as a trainer throughout his evidence. Judge Wickham, though, had made up his mind, and interjected with his own position, which was contrary to all the evidence we had heard. "It is principally a trainer but can be used as a fighter," he declared. The reality of course was that it was principally a fighter but could be used as a trainer.

The prosecutor had grilled Mr Foster at some length over the damage to the plane, and we had been treated to a long list of items allegedly beyond repair. The jury looked more and more bored as he droned on and on. "Pitot probe", "vortex generators", "side-mounted unit rear fin", "starboard outboard wing fence", "tailplane trailing edge". We had apparently hammered on all of them.

As the list grew longer and the names more

incomprehensible, I started to feel quite sick with the evidence we were hearing. Here they were, going on and on about the damage to bits of metal, but what about the people, the children, women and men who would have been on the receiving end of this weapon? Didn't anyone care about them?

During my cross-examination, I said to Mr Foster, "You're obviously greatly concerned about the damage we did to the Hawk. Do you have any concern about the damage which would be done to people in East Timor if this plane were delivered?"

He looked straight at me, and uttered a single word: "No."

Perhaps this was a turning point in the case, the point where the jury could for the first time see what lay at the very heart of our action: that British Aerospace were not being accountable and didn't care if their weapons were used to kill civilians whose misfortune it was to live in a country under occupation.

On the local radio news that evening, the report about the day's events started, "A senior British Aerospace manager has admitted in court to having no concern for people who may have been killed by Hawk aircraft which have been sold to the Indonesian government." It was a moment of real clarity in a trial where so many people were conspiring to hide the truth behind obfuscation and technical jargon.

Later that day we heard evidence from three police officers. The first one was the scenes of crime officer, whose role was to describe the hangar at Warton and produce the tools he had found around the Hawk. He also brought out the booklet we had left in the cockpit, and Vera asked for each jury member to be given a copy of the booklet. The prosecutor immediately objected.

"My concern is the propaganda, in effect the content of those booklets. It contains a lot of materials – "

Judge Wickham interrupted. "I think the jury are sensible enough to be able to read this if they wish," he said, and the matter was closed.

The second police witness was Detective Sergeant Lee, in charge of the case against us, who had arrested Angie that snowy night in Preston. He looked quite different – and not entirely comfortable – in his smart blue suit, and he shifted nervously as he was questioned.

Angie wanted to make it clear that she had not tried to evade arrest, but Sergeant Lee wasn't keen to put this interpretation on her actions.

"Is it true that I phoned you of my own free will on the morning of 6 February?"

"Yes."

"And is it true that I did not hide from you my intention to attend the Preston meeting?"

"That is right, you did not."

"And that I actually invited you to meet me?"

"You expressed your intention to go to Preston."

"And that I came with the tools in my briefcase knowing that you would probably be there to arrest me?"

"You did not know that because the weather was bad and you had no way of knowing whether I would be able to get there or not."

"But it was likely that I knew I would be arrested?"

"I cannot comment on that."

Angie wanted to know whether Sergeant Lee had taken any steps to investigate the allegation she had made that British Aerospace were in breach of the Genocide Act. Under questioning, he said that he was aware that genocide is a crime in British law.

"Do you have the same responsibility to investigate genocide as any other crime?" Angie asked.

"Not personally, no. As a detective sergeant, my responsibility is to investigate alleged crime which occurs in my area."

"But we did allege that a crime was being committed in your area. We were alleging that aiding and abetting genocide was occurring at the Warton factory and we gave you the information about that. What I want to know is why you did not investigate our allegation?"

"Basically because that is not for me. Somebody at the level of a detective sergeant is not going to start investigating genocide against a company such as British Aerospace."

"But now that you are aware of the law, will you actually do something to try and make sure that those crimes are stopped?"

"All I can comment on is the action that I took against the four people that are accused here today. It is not British Aerospace that is on trial here, is it?"

"But anybody would think it was," the judge interjected loudly, bringing Sergeant Lee's evidence to a close.

The third police witness was the exhibits officer. He produced all the evidence seized from us when we were arrested, describing each item as he took it out of tatty

Flyposting on the Department of Trade and Industry during the anti-Hawks campaign calling for the prosecution of BAe's executives for aiding and abetting genocide in East Timor.

cardboard boxes carried from a cupboard at the back of the court. Here were our overalls, our woolly hats, our torches, our shoes. It wasn't clear what the shoes were meant to prove, although perhaps my filthy and disintegrating boots constituted a crime against footwear. I was glad to see that the police hadn't lost them, and looked forward to having them returned to me at some point.

This officer had searched Jo's flat after our arrest. He had found nothing of relevance belonging to Jo, but in my bedroom had found a poster I had made accusing British Aerospace of genocide, and two dividend cheques from my shareholding in the company.

Campaign Against Arms Trade had for several years distributed single shares in British Aerospace to supporters, allowing them entrance to the Annual General Meeting. Once inside, some people tried to call the company to account by asking searching questions about arms sales to repressive regimes. This was of limited success as the board always expected such questions and had their glib non-answers ready. Others of us took a more direct approach, and preferred to unfurl banners, sing, climb onto the stage, or whatever else came to mind, until we were dragged out by security guards. It had become a bit of an annual ritual, and a good chance to catch up with friends as well as to protest against British Aerospace's nasty business.

Each year I received a dividend cheque from my shareholding, none of which I'd ever cashed. The police officer presented these cheques to the court with a great flourish, as if they were evidence of terrible hypocrisy on my part. Here I was, condemning British Aerospace for selling Hawks to Indonesia, whilst all the time profiting from such sales.

Judge Wickham sat up and asked to see the cheques. His face fell when he saw that one was for six pence, the other for four pence. "This doesn't suggest she has a very large holding," he commented drily, causing a ripple of laughter through the public gallery. The cheques were not mentioned again.

The other piece of evidence to emerge that day was the transcript of an interview which Angie had given to Radio

Lancashire shortly after Jo, Lotta and I were arrested. This, Mr Pickup explained solemnly, was evidence of the conspiracy charge against her. In point of fact, we were not disputing that we'd conspired; what we were denying was that what we had conspired to do was criminal.

The interviewer was a particularly obnoxious woman who wanted only to talk about jobs; she had no interest in the issue of people being killed in East Timor. She referred to "so-called genocide", and when Angie said that ordinary people were being bombed, she replied, "I don't think we're being bombed by Hawk aircraft, are we?" Angie managed to hold her own against this onslaught of trivialisation, and when asked whether any more "attacks" were being planned, said, "Yes, I myself am part of this group and I will go in and do the same thing as soon as I can." This, then, was the evidence that she too was guilty of the terrible crime of conspiracy.

That was nearly the end of the prosecution case. The following morning we heard more evidence of the damage from a British Aerospace "cost estimator"; again, the jury were not told that the amount the company was claiming was likely to be substantially overestimated. The grand total, according to this witness, was £1,680,480. Leaving that huge figure ringing in the ears of the jury, the prosecutor announced that he had concluded his case. Now it was our turn.

CHAPTER 21

"A LANDSCAPE OF CROSSES"

"Slashing someone's tyres," Vera said to the jury in her opening speech, "would usually be an act of criminal damage. But supposing that you slashed the tyres of the car carrying the recent IRA bomb which exploded in Manchester. That would not be criminal damage because you would have the lawful excuse of acting to prevent crime."

We were charged under the Criminal Damage Act 1971, which makes it an offence to destroy or damage property "without lawful excuse". On that three word rider hung our whole case. The jury would not be asked to decide whether we had caused the damage to the plane – of course we had – but whether we had done it without a lawful excuse. Our excuse, we would say, was that of using reasonable force to prevent crime, as allowed by the Criminal Law Act 1967.

Having explained the law, Vera went on to show the jury our video. The prosecutor, perhaps peeved at the judge's decision to allow it, fiddled with his papers as it played, not deigning to dignify it as proper evidence by paying attention. Most of the jurors, however, were rapt, several of them leaning forwards and staring intently at the screen as the whole unedifying history of British complicity in genocide was laid out before them. Now, I thought, whatever else happened, at least they knew why we'd disarmed the Hawk.

Video over, Vera called Jo to the witness stand. During her evidence she was confronted frequently by Judge Wickham – particularly tetchy that morning – who stopped her at every opportunity to scold her for answering Vera's questions at too great a length.

"I think you had better control the witness," he instructed Vera, and then turned to Jo and said, "We will get on very much better if you answer the questions and restrict yourself to answering the questions."

Undeterred, she ploughed on. She talked about her involvement in the Hawk campaign, and about the Timorese refugees she had met whose personal stories of Indonesian oppression had spurred her to further action. The court was silent as she described in detail what had happened on 29 January; there was barely a stir as she told the tale of that strange night.

Being the first to give evidence, Jo bore the brunt of the prosecutor's cross-examination. Mr Pickup questioned her for well over an hour, asking around a hundred separate questions. He seemed determined to get her to admit once again – in case the jury was in any doubt – everything that she'd just said.

"So you admit damaging the plane?" he asked.

"I admit that I disarmed it," Jo replied. "I wanted to disarm it to prevent it from killing people in East Timor."

"And it was your intention to cause damage?"

"It was my intention to disarm it."

"And you take full personal responsibility for your action?"

"Yes." To further underline her moral degeneracy, the prosecutor asked if she regretted what she'd done. "No, not at all," came her very firm answer.

Mr Pickup was determined to prove his case that we had disarmed the Hawk as a publicity stunt rather than an act of crime prevention. Why else would we have painted messages on our tools, made banners, rung up the Press Association? Why else was Angie giving interviews immediately after the action?

He seized on the fact that we had made the video and written our personal statements some months in advance as evidence that we were intent on damaging the Hawk regardless of what happened politically, and would have gone ahead even if the deal had been cancelled. It wasn't something we only decided to do right at the last moment, he said, but something we'd been planning for nearly a year.

"But why would we want to go ahead if the Hawk deal had already been stopped?" Jo asked. She pointed out that we'd prepared well in advance because when it came to the point where delivery was imminent, immediate action would be necessary. It was always our hope, she said, that the deal would be stopped by other means and we wouldn't have to disarm the Hawk.

In the middle of the prosecutor's questioning, Judge Wickham suddenly sat up and motioned for Jo to stop talking.

"Just pause one moment," he said in a tone of some

agitation, glaring at the public gallery. "Members of the public," he announced, "are allowed in the court only so long as they keep quiet and poker-faced. Anybody else nods or reacts in any way, he is out. I hope that is clear." There were to be no signs of support for us in his courtroom.

The prosecutor pressed on, accusing Jo of wanting to be arrested, prosecuted and tried simply for publicity purposes.

Jo wasn't having this. "I did not want to be arrested," she said. "I believe what I did was lawful. I had no desire to enter the whole criminal justice system." According to Mr Pickup's logic, our remaining at British Aerospace after we had hammered the Hawk proved that our sole intention was to be arrested and draw publicity. This was his main contention, and he was took every opportunity to drum it home to the jury.

Finally he got to the issue of safety. This had nothing to do with our supposed motivation and was thus irrelevant, but seemed designed to paint a picture of us as irresponsible women who had put other people's lives at risk.

"Did you consider whether the plane had fuel in it?" Mr Pickup asked.

"It was very important to us that the action was peaceful and safe," Jo replied. "We'd made an assessment of safety factors, and asked acquaintances for more information. We knew that the action would be safe whether or not the plane had fuel in it."

"So you knew where the fuel tanks were?"

"We knew that hammering on the external panels would be completely safe. We wouldn't have done anything that wasn't safe," Jo said firmly.

We had anticipated questions about safety, as it had been a big issue in the local media after our arrest. The *Lancashire Evening Post* had run an article quoting the union representative at Warton saying, "If you hammer on a fully-fuelled plane you risk fracturing the fuel tank and if that happens it will only take one spark to ignite it... the devastation would have been astronomical, and they would certainly have killed themselves and probably other people as well". This kind of newspaper coverage was one of the reasons we had wanted the trial moved from Preston, where many potential jurors would have heard about our supposed nonchalance about blowing up the entire factory.

In fact, what Mr Pickup was suggesting was nonsense. We had read and consulted widely before we did the action, and were quite clear that hammering on the fuselage of a plane could not cause the fuel tank to fracture. This was, after all, an attack plane which might come under live fire; if a simple hammer blow could fracture its fuel tanks, there wouldn't be much hope for it in a real battle situation.

"Do you not accept," the prosecutor asked finally, "that what you did was a very, very irresponsible thing to do?"

"Not at all," Jo replied. "What is irresponsible is selling weapons to a regime which Amnesty International has described as casual about mass murder." The prosecutor sat down, perhaps wishing he hadn't asked that question.

After Jo's evidence, Vera called her first witness, John Pilger. Having visited East Timor clandestinely, made a documentary and written extensively on western complicity in the genocide, he was well qualified to tell the court exactly what was happening there, and he didn't mince his words.

"I had never seen anything like East Timor," he said, "although I have reported from war zones all over the world. I found a place that was a landscape of crosses, like a vast cemetery. Massacres had gone on in which whole families had been wiped out in the space of a day, whole communities wiped out in the space of a week."

He went on to talk about massacres he had been told about, but Judge Wickham objected to this evidence on the grounds that it was hearsay. This reminded me of the endless protestations we'd heard from the government over the years, that eyewitness accounts of Hawks bombing East Timorese villages could not be proved. The Timorese, apparently, could not be trusted to tell the truth, whether about killings on the ground or from the air.

Vera moved on to ask about Hawks and whether there was evidence that they were used in East Timor.

"It is the most distinctive type of fighter aircraft that I have seen," John replied. "It has a particular nose that sets it aside from other types of fighter aircraft and it makes a particular sound as it dives. There is absolutely no doubt that Hawks are used and used often in East Timor."

When Vera had finished her questioning, Angie, Lotta and I each had a turn to ask questions. Angie pursued the subject of genocide, asking John whether an ordinary person visiting East Timor would conclude that what was going on there was genocide. His answer was unequivocal.

"It would be impossible for any ordinary person not to see that it was genocide," he said. "Going into East Timor is like going into one of the Nazi death camps at the end of the war. The piles of bodies may be missing but all the artefacts and evidence of horror and extermination are there. There are graveyards everywhere and the entire population is terrorised."

I asked John why the world had ignored the plight of East Timor. His answer gave Judge Wickham the perfect opportunity to put in one of his asides.

"East Timor is a very difficult and dangerous place to get into," John explained. "Also, I have to say that the media usually works in fashion and for many years East Timor was well and truly out of fashion."

"It needed a spot of publicity?" asked Judge Wickham. He was clearly of the same opinion as the prosecutor: our action was simply a publicity stunt.

Finally, I asked John to comment on recent assertions from the British government that the human rights situation in East Timor was improving. "That assertion is just ridiculous and offensive to all the suffering people that I and others who have been to East Timor have seen," he stated. "It is the equivalent of denying a small holocaust."

The prosecutor, having objected to our calling witnesses at all, didn't deign to validate John's presence by asking him any questions. We passed on to the final witness of the day, José Ramos Horta, the Timorese resistance representative to the UN, who would many years later become the East Timorese president. Exiled from his own country because of his political activities, he had been tirelessly working for self-determination for over twenty years.

Shortly after we arrived in Risley, we had received a letter from José. In it he said, "In twenty years of resistance we were never able to shoot down an aircraft. You did it without even firing a single shot and without hurting the pilot".

José talked in his evidence about how whole tribes in East Timor had been wiped out and thousands of people slaughtered indiscriminately or "disappeared" in a campaign which he said amounted to genocide. Vera asked what the response of the British government had been to these atrocities.

"The British government," José replied, "has been one of the key supporters of the Indonesian regime. The people of East Timor very much fear the new Hawk deal."

"But the Indonesians have given assurances that the planes will not be used in East Timor," Vera said. José dismissed these as so much propaganda.

"The word of an Indonesian official is worthless," he declared.

When it was my turn, I asked José what would happen if someone in Indonesia or East Timor tried to disarm a Hawk in the way we had done. His answer was blunt: "They would be shot on sight."

The day ended with Vera calling two character witnesses for Jo. We had talked at length about character witnesses, and in the end decided that only Jo should have them. If you call witnesses to your good character, the prosecutor can then call evidence to malign it, and we didn't want to give him the opportunity to trot out all Angie's and my previous convictions. However, we hoped that Jo's witnesses would reflect on all of us; surely with her flawless character, she wouldn't associate with us if we really were criminals?

The witnesses were a Catholic priest and an Anglican woman vicar. Both were clearly very fond of Jo, and more than happy to sing her praises; she was honest, had great integrity, was very dedicated to her work. They spoke at length about all the community work she had done in Kirkby. The overall impression was of a very caring, responsible woman who would not commit herself to something like this unless she had thought about it very deeply and was absolutely convinced it was the right thing to do. Vera left the jury with those thoughts, and announced that she had concluded her case.

That was the end of day three. Already, I was feeling quite worn out and looking forward to the weekend and a chance to have a break from the pressure of being on trial. Many of our supporters must have been as tired as we were; not only were they spending the days in court or standing in vigil outside, but the local support groups had also organised an extensive programme of evening events. One night there was a public meeting with some of our witnesses, on other nights supporters could have attended a ceilidh, a talent night, or even a rave. It all sounded quite exhausting. Given the choice between prison and a rave, I'd choose prison every time, so probably it was just as well we hadn't been granted bail.

CHAPTER 22

"I'M NOT BREAKING THE LAW, I'M UPHOLDING IT"

Angie was the first to speak on Friday, the fourth day. She gave a brief opening speech, then took the witness stand to explain her part of the action. Unlike Jo – who had to be questioned by Vera – Angie, Lotta and I could just stand up in the witness box and speak freely. We'd prepared questions which the others could ask if we got stuck, but they weren't really necessary. The judge allowed each of us to refer to notes, and for the most part we each spoke without any need for prompting.

Angie talked about international law and the UN resolutions which had been passed condemning Indonesia's occupation of East Timor, but Judge Wickham drew the line at her giving the jury copies of the export guidelines on arms exports which were, she explained, being breached in the case of the Hawk deal.

"I am not having these guidelines distributed," he announced, "because this is really getting miles away from the case that the jury have to decide. They cannot be expected to read through all this material."

"But this is a very complex case," Angie said. "We are talking about a government department and a huge company that are breaking major laws."

"You are making it into a complex case. It is a perfectly simple case."

The judge had made his mind up, but we still got the evidence in. When it was Lotta's turn to put questions, she asked about the guidelines, and Angie explained that the sale of Hawks to Indonesia was in breach of a clause prohibiting the export of weapons likely to prolong or aggravate an existing armed conflict, and another that weapons should not be sold where they might be used for internal repression.

After a similar cross-examination from the prosecutor to that which Jo had faced, Angie called her witness, Dr Paul Rogers from Bradford University. He was head of the department of peace studies and his credentials included lecturing to the RAF and NATO. Angie wanted him to counter the prosecutor's claim that the Hawk was primarily a training aircraft.

Paul dismissed the government's claim that the Hawks sold in 1978 were trainers and unsuitable for ground attack and made it clear that the plane was in fact a combat aircraft, perfect for attack missions in mountainous and forested areas like East Timor.

"The Hawk," he said, "can carry more weapons than any other plane of that type. It can carry many different kinds of weapons including cluster bombs which explode and scatter a third of a million pieces of shrapnel over an area of an acre."

In case anyone was left in any doubt as to the effect of a cluster bomb, Paul added that it was "like razor blades raining down". He also described how it could carry fuel-air explosives, which are extremely effective against what are euphemistically known as "soft targets" – that is, people.

Expert witness notwithstanding, the prosecutor and the judge stubbornly continued to refer to the Hawk as a trainer throughout the rest of the trial.

Then it was my turn. The walk to the witness box, security guard following closely behind, seemed very long – although it was actually only a few feet – and I was suddenly aware of how many people were in the courtroom. I was nervous, but sure of what I wanted to say; I had practised it so many times that my notes were hardly necessary.

A couple of weeks before trial we had been visited in Risley by a solicitor who came up from London to answer various legal questions for us. Marcia was full of energy and laughter, and told us that we should at all times picture the judge surrounded by light. We should only think of him positively, she said, and he would have no choice but to succumb. And we should take our shoes off in court, she added, to make us feel grounded. Remembering this advice now, I leant down in the witness box and slipped off my sandals, before straightening up and starting my story.

Like the others, I told the jury about what had led me to the point where I felt I had to take the risk of this action. I talked about the three years of campaigning I had done beforehand, and showed the jury the letters I had written – over fifty of them, to British Aerospace, to my MP, to government departments and ministers – asking for the Hawk deal to be cancelled. I wanted the jurors to be clear that this was a last resort, that we had done everything in our power to stop the deal some other way.

I talked about East Timor, and why what was happening there had affected me so deeply. Describing the 1991 massacre in the Santa Cruz cemetery, I said that what had truly chilled me about that terrible event was that mass graves had been dug outside Dili several days before the planned procession. The Indonesian claim that this tragedy was due to a few officers acting against orders was an outright lie; the whole operation had been planned, and the graves dug to send a message to the Timorese that this was their likely destination if they participated in the demonstration. Despite this, many thousands still took part; they were willing to risk their lives to resist the Indonesian occupation.

I didn't say much about disarming the Hawk; Jo had told the story in full so it didn't seem necessary to repeat everything. When I had finished, Mr Pickup stood up. He was keen to question my contention that we had not only had the intention of preventing crime, but that we had actually prevented crime.

"You knew the plane would be repaired and sent to Indonesia. You didn't prevent a crime at all, did you?" he said

"That plane hasn't left for Indonesia yet, so we prevented the crimes it would have committed in the time it's been delayed," I replied. "We don't know whether that plane will ever be sent to Indonesia. I hoped that the deal would be stopped before it was delivered."

Mr Pickup was trying to cover all the bases: trying to prove that we were motivated by publicity rather than crime prevention, but at the same time arguing that even if crime prevention were our motivation, we were still guilty because we weren't effective enough. We just couldn't win.

Returning to the publicity stunt angle, the prosecutor said that we had only carried out this action in order to force British Aerospace into court.

"You wanted British Aerospace witnesses to come to court and give evidence that you did not challenge," he said accusingly.

"Well, I didn't call them," I pointed out. "You called the British Aerospace witnesses, not me."

"That's because you wouldn't agree to their evidence being read out."

"But people have to take responsibility for their actions and these people are making a living out of selling products that kill people. I think they need to be held accountable for that."

"You wanted them brought to court to make them accountable?"

"I wanted them to be brought to court so that I could ask them, 'Why are you doing this? Does it not concern you?' We had an answer from a senior manager that it didn't concern him that people were being killed."

"Didn't you use the trial as a vehicle to get your views and opinions across to the public?"

"I would have been more than happy not to have been put on trial," I replied. "I would have been more than happy not to have spent the last six months in prison. It wasn't my choice."

My witness was Carmel Budiardjo, the founder of TAPOL, the Indonesia human rights campaign. She had been a political prisoner in Indonesia from 1968-71, held without charge in appalling conditions, at the time of the "anti-communist" crackdown shortly after President Suharto seized power. Her campaigning activities in Britain had led her to become a figure of hate for the Suharto regime, and the Indonesian press even went so far as to blame her for our action, reporting our trial under the headline "Four women who were influenced by Budiardjo".

Carmel said that TAPOL had run a campaign against the 1978 deal to sell Hawks to Indonesia, predicting – correctly – that they would be used in East Timor. The Labour government had dismissed their claims and allowed the deal to go ahead. She had also been closely involved with the campaign against the current deal, and had been part of a delegation which went to the government to raise their concerns about the Hawk deal.

"But we were ignored," Carmel said. "They said that they had assurances that the Hawks would not be used in East Timor, but we simply do not accept those assurances."

"What effect would the cancellation of the Hawk deal have on the situation in East Timor?" I asked Carmel.

"It would have a major effect," she replied. "It would be almost impossible for the Indonesians to maintain their occupation without the use of ground-attack planes."

"And how would it affect the people there?"

"It would lift an enormous burden from them," Carmel replied. This was the signal for Judge Wickham to put his oar in.

"Would nobody else step in?" he asked. "Would the French not sell them?" This was a line Mr Pickup had carelessly overlooked: our action could not be said to have prevented crime because if Britain didn't sell the planes, someone else would. It was lucky the judge was there to do the prosecutor's job for him.

Finally it was Lotta's turn to give evidence. She told the jury that she felt quite at home in Liverpool; it was, she said, not unlike her home city of Gothenburg, with its big river and declining docks. She talked about how she had joined the campaign against the Hawk deal whilst she was living in Oxford, then described the events of 29 January.

She had always found it odd to be in the village of Warton, she said. "On all the occasions when I have been in Warton, it always strikes me how everything is very normal. You see houses everywhere and you know that ordinary good people are going to work there and despite this, there is assistance to genocide going on. It is nothing against the people who do it. It is just hard to reconcile this image of normality and decency."

Lotta told the jury about a report from an Indonesian newspaper before our action which concluded that a new phase must start in East Timor. "All Timorese resistance to the occupation must be totally eliminated", it stated.

"We knew," Lotta explained, "that this meant bombing raids on people in the mountains, and that would be the task of the Hawks when they were delivered. We could not come to any other conclusion."

Being the last, Lotta was given the shortest cross-examination, but Mr Pickup was keen to make her restate what she'd already said: yes, she'd hammered on the plane and intended to hammer on the plane.

"And do you believe that it was right to take the law into your own hands and go and attack someone else's property?" the prosecutor asked.

"I think the people who have taken the law into their own hands are British Aerospace and the British government. They are blatantly breaching the Genocide Act. I'm not breaking the law, I'm upholding it."

"You consider it reasonable to go and smash a plane with a hammer?"

"Yes. What else could I do?"

Judge Wickham seemed to like Lotta and sat smiling benignly through her evidence. He appeared to have decided that she and Jo were the innocent party, dragged into this criminal endeavour by the guile and persuasiveness of those of us with more experience of such activities.

"You knew that the likely outcome would be that you would be arrested and prosecuted, didn't you?" the prosecutor continued.

"It's hard to judge likelihoods," Lotta replied. "I was always hoping that people would see that what we did wasn't a crime. But there was a certain risk."

"You didn't expect the police to come along and say, 'Well done', did you?"

"I was hoping they would."

"Did you expect them to do so?"

"It's hard to know. To expect people, you have to know

them, and I didn't know the police."

"And would you expect British Aerospace to say, 'Oh dear, never mind, go away'?" The prosecutor was becoming increasingly sarcastic.

"You never know. You always have to live in hope."

"But you had already had a dialogue with British Aerospace. You knew what their view was going to be."

"Are you suggesting that we should give up on them? I don't think we should. We should always believe that they'll see what's right."

The prosecutor finished with his endlessly repeated theory of our motivation.

"You went in there, hammered on a plane for thirty minutes, left banners and said, 'Arrest me. There will be a big trial and everybody will know about East Timor.'"

"I never did that," said Lotta firmly. "I never said that, and I didn't even think it."

It was mid-afternoon when Lotta stepped out of the witness box, but to my relief the judge said that he'd adjourn at that point, and summing up would start after the weekend. I was exhausted after four days in court, and was looking forward to a relaxed weekend to recuperate and gather my strength for the final part of the trial.

In our pile of mail when we arrived back at Risley late that afternoon was a letter from a Timorese prisoner in an Indonesian jail. "Be assured, dear friends," it said, "that your action has deeply touched our hearts and that the hardships you are now suffering are an inspiration to me and all the other Timorese prisoners as well as all the people of East

Timor. The warmth that your example has given us will be an inspiration in moments of weakness and grief. You are in our hearts and in our thoughts."

❖

We were locked up for most of that final weekend, and saw very little of each other. However, I was so tired that it didn't seem a great hardship. All I wanted to do was to practise my summing up a few more times and then just rest and gather my thoughts. It was a strange time; all I could think about was that in a few days we might be free, or we might be starting a jail sentence of several years. It's very rare in life to be faced with two such starkly different paths over which you have no control. It was at the same time freeing – I've done all I can, and now it's up to someone else to decide – and terrifying.

We'd discussed at length what we'd do if we were convicted and given a long jail sentence. We'd researched which prisons we might be sent to, in the hope that we would be able to make a request for a particular one, although we were aware that our "security risk" categorisation might affect where we would go. Jo and I wanted to stay in the north of the country, whilst Angie and Lotta wanted to move south, to be nearer friends and family. I was very keen to be somewhere with the possibility of outside work, perhaps in one of the prisons with its own farm.

However, I still couldn't really imagine how it would be, even at that point so near the end of the trial. I was caught between my head telling me that conviction was quite likely, and my gut asking how anyone could possibly convict us for what was so clearly a right and just action. It was a curious place to be, a kind of transitional state where the only things that I could relate to were the here and now, the familiar routines of prison life, the wondering what we were going to have for tea, the staring out of the window and hoping for exercise.

On Saturday afternoon, I had a visit from my parents, who were completely exhausted from the mental and physical stresses of the past few days. It was a strained kind of meeting; all of us were too tired to talk much, and at one point my mother apologised but said she would simply have to put her head down on the table, unable to hold it up a minute longer.

We talked a little about the trial, but mostly stayed off the subject, and chatted instead about Liverpool, about my sister's forthcoming wedding and other family news. We didn't discuss the possibility of a conviction and a long sentence; I think we all barely had the emotional energy left to get us through the remaining days of the trial. I had decided that I would deal with whatever happened when it happened, and my parents were no doubt thinking the same.

On the Sunday, I went to church. As usual it was very dull, but it was at least a chance to get out of my cell for an hour, to walk outside to the chapel and to chat to other women. The priest always stood by the door as we filed out, shaking our hands and exchanging greetings. On this occasion he said to me, "Are you expecting to be JRed?" "JR" – judge's remand – is the term for being remanded in custody after conviction whilst pre-sentence reports are prepared for the judge.

I was offended by his assumption that we were going to be convicted. Here was a man who could believe in the resurrection of Christ – which some might say requires quite a leap of faith – and yet he couldn't believe that we might not be found guilty. I held my head up high and answered, "No, I'm expecting to be acquitted." He looked shocked and muttered some kind of apology – although he was obviously thinking that I must be slightly deranged – and I gave him a big smile and walked on.

By Sunday night, I had been over my closing speech so many times that I could practically deliver all thirty minutes of it without reference to notes. Lying in bed that night, I was tempted several times to get up and make minor alterations to it, but finally convinced myself that it was as good as it was going to get, and drifted off into an uneasy sleep. By the time the morning arrived, I just wanted to get it over with and to face whatever the next day would bring.

CHAPTER 23

"WE ARE FOUR ORDINARY WOMEN"

As Judge Wickham settled into his seat on Monday morning, the prosecutor rose to his feet and started his summing up. As usual, the courtroom was packed, with new faces mixed in with the old. That morning, over a hundred people had walked in silent procession to the court, where they had held a ceremony to remember those killed in East Timor. The case had been extensively reported in the local press, and tens of thousands of leaflets had been handed out in Liverpool. The jury could not fail to be aware of the gravity of the issue they were being asked to decide.

Mr Pickup's summing up was quite short. Perhaps he was sure that the case was open and shut: we'd admitted the damage, our defence was obviously nonsense, therefore the jury was bound to convict and he simply had to go through the motions.

He started by giving the jury his definition of a Ploughshares action. "Effectively," he stated, "it is damaging property belonging to somebody else." This was stretching the point somewhat; by his definition, somebody vandalising a phone box could claim to be carrying out a Ploughshares action.

"You or I," he went on, "would call what these women did damage or vandalism, but you recall how the defendants did not like such words. They did not like the word 'damage'. They resisted any suggestions that there was an attack. They preferred to use the phrase 'disarm'. That gives you, members of the jury, a clue to their fanaticism, their self-delusion that what they were doing was in some way justified."

This seemed a little unnecessary, but I felt that the jury could see that we were simply four ordinary women, deeply concerned about an issue of injustice. As for being deluded, we had called many reputable and entirely credible witnesses who had confirmed that we were absolutely justified in our beliefs about the situation in East Timor.

The prosecutor went through all the evidence, showing how, in his view, it all proved that our action was done simply for the media. The video, he said, was "deliberately contrived" to become part of the prosecution case and be shown in court; there was no purpose for it other than "pure propaganda". The banners, too, were made only for publicity reasons. "We even went through the farce," he declared, "of having prosecution witnesses hold the banners up in court so we could all see their slogans." One of Judge Wickham's asides gave him further ammunition. "You heard John Pilger agree with his Lordship's suggestion that it was perhaps time that East Timor had a boost," he stated.

Summarising this line of reasoning, he argued, "There is nothing in this case, members of the jury, that has not been done to maximise the publicity angle and the cause which they sincerely believe in. They speak of wishing to take responsibility for their action, yet only one of the defendants admitted to the police that she was actually there. Why? Because they prefer to tell the world and tell you in court, to the point of calling witnesses to tell us second hand what is happening in East Timor."

Mr Pickup's case was probably not helped by his attitude towards us. "If you think about it, members of the jury," he said, "the best that any sensible person could possibly hope for – perhaps a sensible person would not have done this – but the best that any intelligent person could have hoped for would be a delay in the supply of one of these aircraft whilst it is repaired. They surely knew that they could not and would not have prevented this aircraft from leaving."

There was more. "What they did," Mr Pickup explained gravely, "was very, very irresponsible, in fact possibly dangerous. These defendants in a democratic and free society have the right to protest. The law grants that right. What the law does not permit is for people to set about enforcing their views on you and me and everyone else by destroying or damaging property. Where would it end? Members of the jury, we would become a nation of vigilantes." If vigilantism meant disarming weapons, I thought, that might not be a bad thing.

In order to show he was entirely fair-minded, however, the prosecutor ended by making it clear that he wasn't disputing our beliefs. "These defendants are genuine and sincere in their opinions," he said, "but they did what no reasonable law-abiding person could consider to be justified. They have to be dealt with according to the evidence. Members of the jury, the only way of dealing with that is to apply the common sense and the reason you have and return a verdict of guilty."

"Members of the jury," Vera immediately countered as she stood up to deliver her closing speech, "You are not here to apply any of those things. You are here to apply the law, and I am going to tell you what it is. The prosecution have not got within a million miles of even attempting to rebut the defence of using reasonable force to prevent a crime."

With this, Vera explained again the basis of our defence under the Criminal Law Act. She pointed out that the prosecutor had not argued that the amount of force we used was unreasonable in the situation. She also pointed out that if the prosecutor was correct in his assertion that our motivation was publicity rather than crime prevention, it meant that we had each been lying throughout the trial.

"The Crown," explained Vera, "say that they accept the sincerity of these women when it comes to the question of believing about planes and the situation in East Timor, but as to the rest of what these women say, the Crown say that they are unmitigated liars from start to finish. Let us make no bones about it, it is their case that this is a fraud and that these women could not reasonably have thought that they were preventing a crime."

Did the jury think, she asked, that Jo had been lying to them in her evidence? Jo, she pointed out, had been described in glowing terms by her character witnesses as a woman of great integrity. Is it likely, she asked, that she was in fact lying when she said she was acting to prevent crime?

In summary, Vera said, "I invite you to just simply and clearly see the sincerity of these women, the keenness and accuracy of their purpose, that it succeeded and that they are not guilty of criminal damage without a lawful excuse. They have raised their lawful excuse for you, and the Crown cannot say that it is wrong."

Angie concentrated on international law in her summing up. "Governments and companies such as British Aerospace," she explained, "are often treated as if they're above the law. Their crimes are usually unrecognised. This is the point of international law: to control the worst excesses of such bodies."

She talked about the Nuremberg and Tokyo war tribunals held after the Second World War, which established the principle of individuals having to be held accountable for their breaches of international law, and read out to the jury the conclusion of the Tokyo tribunal, which found that, "Anyone with knowledge of illegal activity and an opportunity to do something about it, is a potential criminal under international law unless they take measures to prevent the commission of the crimes". In other words, she explained, it's not enough for each of us not to commit crimes ourselves; we also have a responsibility to act to prevent crime when we see it happening.

Angie finished by telling the jury about the Zyklon B case. During the Second World War, she explained, two German industrialists sold the pesticide Zyklon B to the Nazis, who wanted it for the gas chambers rather than for killing rats. After the war, the industrialists were put on trial for supplying the poison. In their defence, they argued that it had a legitimate

– as well as an unlawful – use and could therefore be sold in the same way as any other product. The tribunal, however, ruled that Zyklon B was being used for the criminal purpose of exterminating people, therefore its supply was a war crime.

This case was not dissimilar to that of the sale of Hawks to Indonesia, Angie said. British Aerospace and the government claimed that there was a legitimate purpose to the Hawks – training pilots – and therefore it was acceptable to sell them. However, they knew quite well that they were likely to be used for criminal purposes in East Timor, and the sale was therefore not only immoral, it was also illegal. No objective person, she added, would think that it would have been a crime to try to stop the Zyklon B from reaching the concentration camps, or to have destroyed the gas chambers, and in the same way, what we had done was not a crime, and we should be found not guilty.

She finished by addressing the prosecutor's remarks about our action not being capable of stopping crime, and the judge's comments that if we didn't sell them, the French would. "We're not on trial," she reminded the jury, "for not being more effective. We're not on trial for not stopping more crimes. Just as no police officers are punished for not stopping all the crimes in their area, neither should we be punished for not being more effective. We did what we could."

After lunch, it was my turn to sum up. I started and finished my speech with a quote from a Timorese witness to the Indonesian occupation. I wanted to remind the jury about why we were here, to make them remember that this trial was not about what the four of us had done, but why we had done it. Our action could not be divorced from the terrible events still being played out in East Timor.

The first quote was an eyewitness account of a massacre at Lacluta in East Timor, during which some 500 people had been killed:

*Indonesian soldiers took hold of the legs of small children and threw them around in the air a number of times and smashed their heads against a rock. There was one who asked for one of the children to be given to her... the army person did not want to hear her pleadings and in front of everyone destroyed the body of this small child, who had done no wrong. And then this soldier opened his mouth, showing his teeth with a smile, and said, "When you clean your fields, don't you kill all the snakes, the small and large alike?"** *

The point about this, I explained to the jury, was that this was not an isolated incident, caused by a few ill-disciplined soldiers; it was part of a sustained campaign of killing that was still going on. I said that I could not apologise for the shocking words I was reading to them; it was reality, and it was important that they knew the nature of the regime to which Britain was selling weapons.

I went on to sum up the facts that had been brought out in the trial. The figure of 200,000 dead had been raised again and again, but perhaps that didn't mean much to the jury. Explaining that 200,000 equated to one in three of the Timorese population, I asked the jury to try to imagine that

* Michele Turner, *Telling East Timor: Personal Testimonies 1942–1992*, New South Wales University Press 1992.

one in every three people they knew – their families, friends, workmates, neighbours – was dead, killed by an occupying power. Clearly it was beyond imagination, but for the people of East Timor it didn't require any imagination; it was reality. And I reminded the jury of what José Ramos Horta had said to them: that the very survival of the Timorese depended on international solidarity and support.

I talked about the campaign we had carried on against the Hawk deal for the three years prior to our arrests, and the dozens of letters I had written to try to stop it. I quoted from the last letter I had received from the Department of Trade and Industry, just ten days before our action. The message is blunt: "You appear to be advocating a total embargo on the sale of defence equipment to Indonesia. We have nothing further to add to previous correspondence on this matter." "It was the government," I pointed out, "that closed that avenue of communication, not us."

Vera had talked to us about making our evidence to the jury relevant to them, relating it to their lives. I made an analogy with the Blitz during the Second World War, which had caused terrible destruction in Liverpool. Several of the jurors were certainly old enough to remember it; many of the others had probably heard stories about it from parents or grandparents. "Imagine," I said, "that someone living in Germany at that time thought it wrong that ordinary people in Liverpool should be killed. Supposing that person had nonviolently disarmed a German warplane so that it could no longer be used to kill civilians. Would you think that person had committed a crime and should be imprisoned?"

"But we have been imprisoned for six months already, and we're facing a sentence of up to ten years if we're convicted." Vera had advised us that whilst it would not be professional for a barrister to mention the possible sentence to a jury, there was nothing to stop an unrepresented defendant from doing so. We assumed that they knew that we'd been in prison for six months, since our case had been widely reported locally, but we found out later that they hadn't known, and were shocked when they heard it.

Addressing the conspiracy charge, I explained that if the jury found us not guilty of criminal damage, they must also find us not guilty of conspiracy to commit criminal damage. If the act itself was lawful – because we had the lawful excuse of acting to prevent crime – then it followed that the planning, or conspiracy, to carry out the act must also have been lawful. I wanted to explain this very clearly, as I had concerns that the jury might grasp the lawful excuse defence and find us not guilty of the damage, but decide that since we had – as we freely admitted – conspired to do what we did, we must therefore be guilty of conspiracy.

I added that all four of us were equally responsible for the entire action, and that the jury should reach the same verdict for each one of us. We were anxious to make it clear that we had acted as equals, especially since we suspected that the judge had made up his mind as to who the "ringleaders" were – certainly Angie, probably me – and was likely to communicate that to the jury in his summing up.

I finished as I had started, with the words of a woman from East Timor. Describing the Indonesian occupation, she says:

We have nothing left to lose. We are human beings and they have treated us like insects. We will never accept them here. Even if we have to die resisting, we will resist.

Later that day, one of the security guards who had been sitting in court accused me of "emotional blackmail" in my speech. I replied that I'd call it telling it like it is; how can you talk about the deaths of 200,000 people, about torture, rape, mass starvation, indiscriminate slaughter, without being emotional? Even if we had wanted to, it would have been impossible to keep emotion out of the issue, and I certainly wasn't about to apologise for bringing it in.

Lotta was the last to sum up. "We are four ordinary women," she said. "In East Timor, ordinary people – people like us, people like you – are being killed in a systematic but indiscriminate genocide." She went on to talk about the situation we were placed in when deciding whether to carry out this action.

"We were faced with a choice," she went on, "of either standing back and saying, 'We have done all we can now' and letting the Hawk leave Warton for Indonesia and for bombing raids over East Timor, for more deaths, yet more pain inflicted upon a people which for over twenty years have suffered inexpressibly. Or we could take our simple household hammers, our shaky legs, our longing for justice and our hope that the East Timorese will know peace – we could take all this with us to Warton and ourselves disarm the warplanes."

I could see that Lotta was shaking slightly as she delivered her speech, but it came out so clearly and with such conviction that only the most hard-hearted of people could have failed to have been moved by it. The jury was listening intently, a few of them leaning forward slightly, all of them by now having lost that vacant, slightly benumbed expression which had haunted me for the first few days.

Lotta left them in no doubt as to the importance of their role. She told them that they had an absolute right to find us not guilty, regardless of any instructions they were given to the contrary, and finished by saying, "You the jury have been called here to act as the conscience of the community.... I ask you to look beyond the superficial appearance of shattered glass and of holes in an expensive aeroplane and to know what the purpose of that Hawk was. Ultimately we acted in order to save lives of people, people like you, people like us. What can be more right, more just than that? For justice to be done, I ask you to return a verdict of 'not guilty.'"

As soon as Lotta had finished, the judge announced that he would adjourn for the day, and he would sum up in the morning. We waved a quick goodbye to our friends in court, and were taken back to the cells.

Finally, it was over. That is, our part in the proceedings was over; now it was up to the jury. We had done our absolute best, and now all there was to do was to wait.

Arriving back in Risley that evening, we spent some time in reception chatting to a new arrival. She was from Liverpool, and on hearing what we were in for, said, "Everyone in Liverpool's talking about you. Everyone's behind you." I hoped fervently she was right.

Back on the wing, we described the day's events to the other women, had our tea, then settled down to a relaxed evening in front of the television. Our happy mood was shattered by the arrival back from court of a friend, with the news that she had been given seven years for a drugs offence. It was her first offence, she had pleaded guilty, and was expecting four years at the very worst. Needless to say, she was absolutely devastated. Everyone was shocked and a sombre atmosphere descended on the room. We all lived so closely together that it was impossible not to be affected by someone else's tragedy, and at times like this everyone was suddenly cast down, reflecting perhaps on their own situation.

I couldn't help wondering if this depressing scenario was going to be repeated the following night. Would it be the four of us walking in, announcing that we'd just been given a huge sentence? I tried to put the thought out of my head, but it kept pushing itself back in, despite all my best attempts to concentrate on something else.

Going to bed that night was rather strange. We wouldn't see any of the other women in the morning, as we'd be gone before they were woken up, yet it didn't seem quite right to say goodbye to them. I'm not superstitious, but saying goodbye felt like tempting fate, as if to invite our return the following evening.

It seemed sensible, however, to make a few practical preparations in case we didn't return, and to that end we each packed up our belongings and put them in storage – there was too much to take to court, and we could return for it if we were released – whilst I delivered my extensive supplies of stationery to a friend, with instructions to share it around if we didn't come back. She laughed and said, "Now we don't want to see you back here, do you understand?", and I assured her that the feeling was mutual. If I never set foot in Risley again, I would be more than happy.

CHAPTER 24

"THERE'S A VERDICT"

"All right girls?" said one of the officers in reception the next morning. "All ready for the verdict, are we?" We assured her that we were. She had obviously made up her mind about what the verdict would be, and objected when I said that I wanted to take a bag of clothing with me rather than leaving everything in the prison as we normally did. "I'll need them if we're released," I said stubbornly. She was clearly thinking, "Yes, and pigs might fly", but eventually she gave in and let me take them.

A couple of hours later, we were sitting in our cell in the basement of the court when the door was unlocked and another woman came in. We knew her from Risley; she'd been overlooked that morning and had been brought to court separately. She told us that one of the officers in reception had been talking about us, and had said that she hoped we were sent down for a very long time.

We knew who it was, as she had made no secret of her animosity towards us. Whilst there were probably several others who felt the same way, they weren't – I thought – representative of most of the officers, who might have thought we were a bit of a nuisance but didn't bear us any overt ill will. Nonetheless, I found it disturbing that this officer felt so strongly about what we had done that she wanted to see us behind bars for years.

Judge Wickham took about an hour to sum up that morning, taking time going over both sides of the argument and putting our defence to the jury. By that stage of the trial, having allowed us to bring witnesses and to talk extensively about East Timor, it would have been almost unthinkable for him to have disallowed our defence, but I still breathed a sigh of relief when we actually heard it from his own lips. The question for the jury, he said, was whether we were acting to prevent crime, as we claimed, or out of some other motivation such as the desire for publicity for our cause. If the jury decided that we were acting to prevent crime, the next question was whether what we did was reasonable in the circumstances.

He made it pretty clear that he personally felt that the prosecutor was correct in his assertion that our action was simply a publicity stunt. "Why did they stay there after they had done the damage?" he asked. "Why did they ring the Press Association? Why did they wait for arrest rather than run away as they could have done? Did they really believe that they were preventing crime? They knew the plane would be repaired, they must have known that all the planes in the contract would be delivered eventually. You may think common sense would have told them that."

Moving on to the question of whether we genuinely

believed that what we did would actually prevent crime, Judge Wickham again made his own position clear. "If Hawks were being used to commit crime in East Timor, did they really for one moment think that they could stop that by damaging a plane? Did they really think that they could stop the government of Indonesia from doing just what they wanted to do?" He was similarly scathing about whether what we did was in any case reasonable, even if the jury were so credulous as to accept that our intention was to prevent crime and that we genuinely believed that our actions would have that effect.

The judge lingered for some time on the financial loss suffered by British Aerospace, and repeated the figure of £1.7m damage, even though he had earlier promised that if we were convicted, he would sentence us on the basis that the damage was between half and three-quarters of a million pounds. Perhaps to avoid being accused of misleading the jury, he hastened to add that, "You may think it does not matter whether it was £1,500,00, £1m or £500,000. It very clearly was substantial damage to the plane."

Our pointing out that the maximum sentence for this offence was ten years' imprisonment – and that we had already spent six months locked up – had clearly needled the judge. He looked sternly at the jury as he warned them not to be swayed by what he intimated was emotional manipulation on our part.

Finally, he took the opportunity of putting his own particular spin on events. In his mind, Angie was the ringleader, masterminding events from outside whilst Jo, Lotta and I – all younger and less experienced – went in to do the damage.

"You may think," he said, "in spite of what they say about them all being equal, you may think she was the organiser." Lotta, perhaps because she was the youngest – albeit only by a couple of years – was painted as the innocent party. "You may think," he said gravely, "that she perhaps is a girl who has been influenced by people with stronger personalities than her own."

Clearly he didn't know Lotta, a woman who very much knew her own mind. All four of us frowned and shook our heads vigorously. By that point, however, I felt that the jury had heard enough to understand that there was no ringleader, no innocent dupe; we were each equally responsible, despite anything the judge might suggest.

At 11.40am, the judge drew his speech to a close. He told the jury that it was time for them to go away and deliberate, with the aim of reaching a unanimous verdict. They filed out, looking suitably serious at the task in front of them, and we were hustled back to the cells.

The next few hours passed slowly. We spent the time sitting with our legal team, discussing what we would say in mitigation if we were convicted. Every time a guard approached we would all stiffen and hold our breath, wondering if there was a verdict. Each time they passed without stopping, we'd all breathe out again.

As the time ticked away, I started to feel a little more confident. If the jury were going to reach a unanimous guilty verdict, I reasoned, they'd surely have done it by now. The passing hours must mean that at least one person was holding out. Maybe we'd get a hung jury?

There was precedent for it; Chris's Ploughshares trial had ended in a hung jury and a subsequent retrial. If two trials end in a hung jury, it's usual for the prosecution to offer no further evidence and for the case to be dropped. Whilst this would certainly be better than being convicted, the prospect of going through the whole trial all over again was far from inviting. Anyway, we wanted to be acquitted outright, not released because a jury couldn't reach a verdict.

Finally at 3.45pm, a guard came to the door and told us we had to go back to court as the jury had a question for the judge. The courtroom was packed when we came in; unwilling to risk missing the verdict, people had decided simply to sit there for as long as it took, rather than wait for the announcement over the tannoy that the court was reconvening.

It must have been a very long afternoon, sitting there in the hot courtroom waiting and waiting for something to happen. Outside the court, dozens of people were standing in vigil. A few miles away, a convent of Carmelite nuns – a silent, cloistered order – were spending the day praying for us. Meanwhile, other people all over the world were holding support vigils, from Washington DC to Dublin, Australia to Portugal. It was an incredible outpouring of solidarity, which carried with it a strongly expressed demand for justice for the people of East Timor.

The question for the judge turned out to be a request to be allowed to bring in a majority – rather than unanimous – verdict, as the jury had decided that they were not going to be able to reach agreement. They had deliberated for well over the minimum time stipulated before a majority verdict is allowed – two hours – so the judge agreed to their request and we were sent back to the cells.

An hour later, we heard the familiar rattle of keys that signified the approach of a guard. It was quite late in the afternoon by then, so we assumed we were being called back to court so that the judge could send the jury home, to reconvene the following morning. The guard swung open the door and stuck his head into the cell. "There's a verdict," he announced.

Suddenly, I was really scared. Until that moment I had been able to remain quite calm, secure in the knowledge that our fate was not yet decided. Now it was decided, and all that remained was for us to hear what it would be. I pressed my fingernails hard into my palms and took some deep breaths as we went out to hear our fate.

Going up in the lift, we were accompanied by four guards instead of the usual two. I asked them whether they thought we were going to do a runner if we were convicted, but they just laughed and said it was routine.

As we entered the court, the most noticeable difference from usual was the faces of people in the public gallery. Normally everyone would be smiling, trying to catch our eye, giving us a thumbs-up or a wave. This time, all I could see was row upon row of serious faces and furrowed brows. The press box, normally occupied by only one or two journalists, was packed, reporters squeezed in tightly in order to hear the verdicts first-hand.

As the jury filed in, they too were grim-faced. Often they would come in chatting in low voices, exchanging a few words, smiling at each other. This time they were silent, unsmiling. None of them looked at us. Prison wisdom had it that if the jurors don't look at the defendants when they come in, it means a guilty verdict. My stomach churned.

Our agony was to be prolonged; Vera had disappeared. We waited and waited whilst runners were sent around the building to look for her, and announcements made over the tannoy appealing for her return. After ten long minutes, she was finally tracked down; she had been in the law library, looking up sentencing guidelines. That didn't feel like a great vote of confidence, but I knew that she was simply looking to do the best for us should we be convicted.

Finally everyone was present. The jury foreman stood up from his seat in the front row of the jury box, and a vacuum-like silence filled the room. The four of us sat holding hands tightly, sweaty palms pressed together. I couldn't look at the foreman, but sat with my head down, eyes shut, every muscle in my body tensed. I could feel my breath coming faster, and I pushed my feet hard to the floor to stop my legs shaking, just as I had on that night six months earlier as we'd sat on the steps of the Hawk, waiting to be discovered.

I repeated to myself that the verdict didn't really matter; what we had done was right, and nothing could change that. It became almost like a mantra, and I tried to use it to block out the feelings of fear which were flooding over me. If we get five years, or even more, I told myself, I'll deal with it. We were right, and we know that even if the court can't see it.

It was one of the strangest and most emotional moments of my life. In a few seconds, the course of the next few years of our lives would be determined. It had been decided by twelve complete strangers, twelve people who knew no more about us than we had chosen to reveal to them, who knew nothing of our hopes and fears, our weaknesses and strengths, our loves, our lives. Yet they alone were responsible for our fate.

There were seven verdicts to be read; criminal damage charges against Lotta, Jo and me, and conspiracy charges against all four of us.

"Do you find the defendant, Lotta Kronlid, guilty or not guilty on count one of the indictment, conspiracy to damage property?" asked the clerk.

The foreman's words rang out around the courtroom.

"Not guilty."

There was a gasp from the public gallery. Judge Wickham turned and announced sharply that if people couldn't be silent in the courtroom, they'd have to leave. We squeezed hands even tighter. I kept my head down, aware only of the foreman's voice and the press of Angie's and Lotta's hands in mine.

The next five verdicts came quickly, tumbling over each other and echoing round the silent courtroom. Not guilty, not guilty, not guilty, not guilty, not guilty. Were there ever such beautiful words? As each one came out, it seemed more and more likely that we would be acquitted on all counts, but none of us dared relax until the last one was read.

"Do you find the defendant, Joanna Wilson, guilty or not guilty on count two of the indictment, damaging property?" asked the clerk.

"Not guilty."

Suddenly it was all over; a story which involved a year of planning, six months in prison, and a gruelling trial had ended in the course of just a few minutes. Ricarda, who'd been standing at the back of the courtroom, dashed out to bring the good news to those waiting patiently outside. Much of what happened in Liverpool was filmed, and there's a wonderful clip of her rushing out of the door into the courtyard, her arms outstretched, tears running down her face, crying, "Not guilty! Not guilty on all charges!" The crowd immediately erupts into huge cheers, with people hugging each other and waving white ribbons.

Inside the court, pandemonium was also about to break out. The judge, ashen-faced, announced that we could be released then almost ran out of the court. The moment he left, the room erupted. Everyone was cheering, hugging each other, crying. Jo's mother climbed over the barrier separating us from the public gallery to gather Jo in her arms. The jury, meanwhile, were grinning broadly – with one or two exceptions, one assumes – and appeared as delighted with their verdict as everyone else.

The guards were anxious to get rid of us, and told us sharply to get moving, back down to the cells to collect our belongings. In the corridor behind the court the four of us gathered in a collective hug, not sure whether to laugh or cry. It was a moment of pure joy. We had been vindicated.

After the trial, we were asked over and over again how it felt when we heard the verdict. I found it impossible to sum up the emotions; I think it's something which someone who hasn't been in that position could never really understand.

Only when you have your freedom taken away do you realise how precious it is, and how much we take it for granted in the normal course of life. And only when you have it restored to you can you perhaps really understand what freedom means.

A few minutes later, we were being let out of the cells. It was a strangely abrupt and almost banal exit. For six months we'd been prisoners, accompanied everywhere we went by officers, handcuffed whenever we went outside the prison walls, searched at regular intervals, presumed to be criminals and treated as such. Suddenly our status had changed utterly. In the few seconds it took for the security guard to unlock the door from the cell block and usher us out, our lives were transformed, and would perhaps never be quite the same again.

We were almost running as we climbed the stairs from the basement. I felt as if I couldn't get out of there fast enough; perhaps subconsciously I was worrying that there'd been a mistake, and that we had to escape before they realised and came after us. Finally, we reached the revolving door leading outside. As we came out, we were hit by an enormous wave of excitement as people in the assembled crowd started whooping, applauding and dashing forward to greet us.

The first person to reach us was a rather dubious character in a grubby white suit, who stepped forward and thrust a thick brown envelope at each of us, muttering something about our being sent to prison if we didn't comply. Suspecting – rightly as it turned out – that this was a furious British Aerospace issuing us with injunctions to stay away from their property, I declined to accept mine. Undeterred, the man simply dropped it at my feet, where it was seized by delighted supporters who proceeded to ceremoniously tear it into pieces.

Injunctions delivered, the man disappeared and the four of us were immediately engulfed by a throng of journalists, who surged forward, pushing microphones and cameras in our faces, shouting out questions, manoeuvring for a better angle. To say it was overwhelming would be an understatement. Being released suddenly from prison after six months, with no chance to prepare ourselves for the occasion, was shocking enough, but suddenly being the centre of so much attention was almost too much.

For a while we stood in a line with our arms around each other's shoulders, each one of us being interrogated by journalists from a different direction. After a few minutes, however, I decided that I'd had enough of answering questions. It was almost impossible, anyway, to know what to say. "How do you feel?" the journalists kept asking. I just couldn't answer that, other than with a glib "Wonderful" or "Amazing." It was all too emotional; words seemed inadequate. We could have been sent to jail for years, but instead we were free. How could I possibly explain how that feels?

In London, several ARROW members had gathered outside the Houses of Parliament to hold a vigil for us. Emily's mother Susan had a tiny radio, and at 5pm she put the news on, not really expecting that we'd be on it. In fact, it was the first item: four women had been acquitted of damaging a Hawk jet. We had made the national news. British Aerospace's offices were nearby, so the vigil reconvened there, no doubt to the great annoyance of the company. Although they had prepared the injunctions just in case, I'm sure they had not thought there was any real prospect of our being acquitted.

In Liverpool, I had slipped away from the journalists and was walking around the square outside the court looking for my parents. Complete strangers were grabbing my hand, hugging me, spinning me round. People were dancing and crying, laughing and smiling, or simply standing silently in shocked but delighted contemplation. Other people joined hands to form a long human chain, which twisted around the square, in and out of the small knots of excited people discussing the verdict and the television crews trying to film this extraordinary event. Someone had a microphone and people were taking turns to make speeches, but they could barely be heard above the hubbub.

I found my parents sitting on a wall near the entrance to the court, somewhat overwhelmed by the situation. They were almost as overcome as I was by the verdict. They'd supported me unwaveringly throughout our imprisonment and trial, and had come to terms with the fact that I might be locked up for several more years. It was so good to suddenly be together, to be able to talk freely without the restrictions of the prison visiting room, and to know that a prison officer wasn't going to come along and drag me away in the middle of our conversation.

The support group were no less emotional than the four of us. We hugged and laughed and cried, barely able to find words to express our feelings. From the very beginning, we had all been in this together, and their constant and loving support – which we knew would always be there for us, despite occasional conflicts – was hugely important. The celebration belonged not just to the four of us, but to the whole group, and beyond that to the thousands of people who had been with us in spirit throughout the process.

It was a very sudden ending. Justice, when it came, came swiftly. For us, it was over – a jury had seen the rightness of our actions, and justice had been done. Ordinary people in Liverpool had acted in solidarity with the people of a tiny country on the other side of the world. They had recognised that we can't turn our backs on situations such as East Timor's, and that we have a duty to peacefully resist our government's complicity in evil.

And more than that, perhaps they had recognised that by acting boldly for justice – whether by disarming a plane or bringing in a brave and truthful verdict – we all become more human. That's all we can ask of ourselves.

CHAPTER 25

"WHAT KIND OF LIFE MUST YOU HAVE?"

Four months after we came out of Liverpool Crown Court to cheering crowds, I found myself sitting in a cell in the basement of the Houses of Parliament with my friend John. We had gone into the Strangers' Gallery during Prime Minister's question time, with the aim of throwing "blood money" – photocopied banknotes splashed with red paint – down into the chamber. Unfortunately for us, we were not the first protesters during that week of action against the Hawk deal and the moment we got up from our seats, we were jumped on by very large security guards and dragged down to the cells to cool our heels for a few hours.

It wasn't my first arrest since the trial (that came very early on, when an overzealous police officer arrested me for doing nothing more than walking along a road near British Aerospace in Warton) but the first time I'd taken part in an action where I knew arrest was likely. It felt good: this was me, this was what I did, this was what I knew. And since the Hawk deal was continuing, of course I had to continue to oppose it.

I'd stayed in Liverpool for a few months after the trial, then moved back to London. I loved Liverpool, and had got to know many wonderful people there – particularly those involved with St Michael's church – but I wanted to be back with ARROW, the affinity group which had been such a large part of my life for so many years. I had been kept up to date with what ARROW had been up to while we were in prison by regular letters from Emily and Lyn, and was itching to be back in the group again.

I moved into a community in the East End, found a job at a hostel for homeless people, and resumed the life I'd lived before my move to Manchester a year and a half earlier.

But although I was back in London, back with ARROW, life had changed. Our acquittal had provoked a huge storm of publicity, which went on for many months afterwards. The support group had been trying to interest the mainstream media in our action throughout the time we were in prison, but with only limited success. This was not due to any failure on their part; as far as the media were concerned, we'd done a lot of damage, admitted to it, and would eventually be found guilty and sent to prison. That wasn't much of a story.

But when the four of us walked out of Liverpool Crown Court on 30 July, acquitted of all charges, everything changed. We were on the front page of national newspapers, on the TV and radio, being interviewed by journalists from all over the world. It was quite surreal: one morning being in prison, contemplating the possibility of a sentence of several years, and that evening being on national TV. It was such a sudden transition, and one which I was not really prepared for. We had certainly considered that we might be acquitted, and as the trial went on, and our defence was allowed, that possibility seemed to grow, but I don't think any of us was expecting to suddenly be thrust into the spotlight like this.

The media response to our acquittal was very mixed. Some, particularly the local and right-wing papers, were outraged. The Blackpool *Evening Gazette*'s editorial the next day was titled "Taking a hammer to justice". The *Lancashire Evening Post* went with a single word, in huge type on the front page: "Unbelievable". The *Daily Express* had a cartoon of two muggers confronting a victim in front of a newsstand reporting our acquittal. They were saying, "Just hand over your wallet pal... while we think of a lawful excuse".

Some papers even went so far as to call for an enquiry into how the jury had managed to reach their verdict in the face of all the evidence against us. The MP for the Warton area, Michael Jack, had echoed the call, saying that he would be discussing our acquittal with the Attorney General. That the jury might have listened to the evidence, applied the law, and reached the logical conclusion that we were not guilty, was clearly not a possibility they wanted to consider.

The *Daily Mail* ran an article, "We're so proud, say the Hawk wreckers", in which we "gloated" about our acquittal, "boasted" about our action, and used our sudden notoriety to "launch a political tirade". We even went so far, allegedly, as to claim that god was on our side. There were amusing attacks on our personal lives: Jo and I appeared to be living together (as a couple, it was implied) in a council flat and living off "state handouts". We ticked all their boxes: left-wing, law-breaking, welfare scroungers, probably lesbians. One of us wasn't even British.

Other papers were more supportive. The *Guardian* ran an article titled "The girls done good", which lauded our action but misunderstood the reason for our acquittal, calling it "a triumph of emotion over legislation". The *Observer* had an editorial in which it compared the media's response to the Dunblane massacre (of children at a school in Scotland, while we were in prison) with its reaction to our acquittal. Whilst much of the right-wing media had screamed for a handgun ban following the killings in Scotland, the same papers had been outraged at our disarming of weapons to prevent massacres in East Timor.

Although we were kept busy immediately after the trial with the many demands of the media, there was still time to relish the simple delight of just being free. I could get up when I wanted, do what I wanted, go where I wanted, eat what I wanted. Most of the group stayed in Liverpool for a few days after the verdict, and it was wonderful to be able to spend time together properly, unconstrained by visiting hours and prison officers, with all the strains and difficulties around the trial finally over. Whilst the support group had not had to put up with the unpleasantness of prison, the past half-year had been stressful for them in a different way. Supporting us practically and emotionally, working to spread the word about the action, responding to supporters; the sheer volume of work required inevitably caused tensions and frustrations. It had been a long six months for all of us.

A couple of days after the trial ended, Jo, Lotta and I went back to Risley to collect our belongings. Even though we had only just left, being there as visitors rather than prisoners felt very strange. I have a photograph of the three of us standing outside the gates, behind a huge trolley piled high with prison service bags. Next to us is Mrs Barton, an older officer who could often be heard yelling from one end of the wing to the other. Although we're all smiling, I can still feel the awkwardness about the situation, not quite knowing how to negotiate the sudden change in our relationships.

I remembered Mrs Barton once telling me that all prisoners – convicted or not – must be guilty, otherwise they wouldn't be in prison. I wondered how she was feeling about our acquittal, but she clearly didn't want to talk about it. Never usually at a loss for words, on this occasion she bid us a quick farewell and hurried back inside, the big door slamming loudly behind her. It was good to be on the other side of it.

A few days after the verdict, we all went our separate ways, back to our homes, our jobs, our families, our normal lives. Later that summer, we had a final gathering at Angie's house, to evaluate the action, wind up the group, and say our goodbyes. It was an emotional time for me: the group had been absolutely central to my life for a year and a half. I remember having quite a mixture of feelings that weekend: happy that we had completed the action, with an outcome that we had barely dared hope for, but sad that the community we had formed over the past eighteen months was no longer going to be part of my life. Of course we would still see each other from time to time, but there would no longer be the intensity, the shared purpose, the sense that we were doing something crucially important. But our group of ten strong and dedicated women had done something amazing together, and now it was time to move on.

The immediate flurry of news stories didn't last long, but was replaced with requests to appear on discussion programmes, take part in documentaries about protest and the arms trade, write comment pieces. A folk band, Seize the Day, wrote a powerful song – "With My Hammer" – about our action. A Merseyside playwright, John Fay, wrote a play, *A Hammer in the Hand*. An Irish production company made a documentary, *Grounding a Hawk with a Hammer*. There were requests for us to speak at meetings and events all over the country, as well as in Ireland, the US and Canada.

Looking in my diary for the last few months of 1996, there is hardly a week without a speaking or media engagement. And I have to admit that whilst I probably presented the ongoing demands of it as a chore, in reality I liked it, not just for the chance it gave to get the issue across, but also – and rather to my shame – how it made me feel about me. I was important, people wanted to talk to me, to know my opinion. It was exciting tripping off to a TV studio and sitting under the bright lights whilst famous presenters asked me questions. Few activists are thrust into the spotlight in this way, and I think most of the media work we did was worthwhile, but there were certainly a few questionable projects later on which in retrospect added little to the campaign but probably much to my ego. Celebrity can indeed be corrosive.

As well as all the speaking and media work, I was doing a job which required me to work shifts – weekdays, weekends, nights – and I was also trying to fit in ongoing meetings, vigils, demonstrations, trial support for other people. I was frantically busy most of the time and, looking back, I wonder whether I was subconsciously trying to fill the space in my life that had for so long been occupied by Seeds of Hope. Planning the action and being in prison had felt constructive, purposeful, important. Now that it was all over, I was left feeling quite empty. The only way to continue to justify my existence was to keep campaigning.

The campaign against arms sales to Indonesia went on for several more years. The Conservative government continued to claim that they had assurances from the Indonesians that the Hawks would not be used in East Timor. By contrast, Labour's Shadow Foreign Secretary Robin Cook had spoken in Parliament in 1994 about the use of Hawks by the Indonesian air force, saying that they had been "observed on bombing runs in East Timor in most years since 1984". Given Cook's speech, and his party's much-vaunted commitment to an "ethical foreign policy", it would not have been unreasonable to expect that Labour might institute an arms embargo on Indonesia if they won the 1997 election.

I was sceptical, however. I'd had an article published in a national newspaper not long after our trial, in which I'd said that Robin Cook had not replied to any of my four letters to him about his party's policy on arms sales. Pointing out that one of British Aerospace's board members was a Labour peer, I'd suggested that it was unlikely things would change if they came to power.

My article had obviously needled Robin Cook, who invited me to discuss the issues with him at the Labour party conference in Blackpool in late September. It was a day of torrential rain and howling gales, and I arrived at the conference centre frozen and soaked through. Sitting in the meeting with Cook and his aides, wet and windswept, my clothes slowly dripping onto the fancy carpet, I felt like a complete outsider. I'm sure Cook felt the same about me: I was the typical scruffy activist, the sort of person who doesn't understand the harsh realities of foreign policy.

Although he had been indignant about the article I'd written, Cook refused to say that Labour would put an arms embargo on Indonesia. He insisted they'd have an ethical foreign policy, but almost in the same breath was making the same excuses I'd been hearing for years: everyone has a right to self-defence, the Hawk is really a trainer, if we don't sell them someone else will. Even when I pointed out that he had himself claimed a couple of years earlier that the Hawks had been used to bomb East Timor, he was unmoved, saying that he was happy with the assurances the Indonesians had now given about the use of British equipment.

How much of this was really Cook's opinion, and how much was the party line, is hard to say. In his 2003 memoirs, Cook talked about Tony Blair's very close relationship with British Aerospace during his time in office, writing, "I came to learn that the Chairman of British Aerospace appeared to have the key to the garden door to Number 10 [Downing Street]."*

---

* Robin Cook, *Point of Departure*, Simon & Schuster, 2003.

Blair later stepped in to thwart a corruption investigation into British Aerospace over its dealings with Saudi Arabia. In his eyes, it would appear, British Aerospace could do no wrong.

I was not surprised, therefore, that when Labour won the general election in May 1997, they refused to cancel the Indonesian export licences, saying it would not be "realistic or practical". They even went on to agree more Hawk sales, exposing Labour's "ethical foreign policy" for the sham it was.

Although I expected this, I was angry: the hypocrisy of crowing about having some morals whilst at the same time selling weapons to a genocidal dictatorship was simply staggering. If genocide wasn't enough reason to institute an embargo, then what could possibly be? It confirmed my cynicism about many political parties: they'll say what they think people want to hear in order to get elected. Once elected, they'll do exactly what they want.

British Aerospace was determined that nothing should threaten their profits. They wanted to clamp down on those they saw as the ringleaders of the campaign, and issued lifetime injunctions to thirteen of us, including Jo, Lotta, Angie and me as well as Chris and Mil from ARROW, Ciaron, and various other ne'er-do-wells. The injunctions ordered us not to enter the British Aerospace sites it listed, or encourage others to do so.

Breaking the injunction carried a maximum sentence of two years' imprisonment, so was not something to be undertaken lightly. Chris had been convicted of breaching his injunction the previous year, for attending – and writing a leaflet about – a trespass at British Aerospace, and had been sentenced to six months in prison. I was not anxious to return to prison at that point, and consequently had to become a little more circumspect in my opposition to British Aerospace's activities. There was plenty of opportunity to protest – at arms fairs, AGMs, conferences – without risking imprisonment.

At the end of 1996, the situation in East Timor was highlighted when José Ramos Horta and Bishop Carlos Felipe Ximenes Belo were jointly awarded the Nobel Peace Prize. Bishop Belo, who had been Bishop of East Timor since 1989, had been very outspoken in recent years about the Indonesian occupation, and had called repeatedly for a referendum on independence. He had written to UN Secretary General Perez de Cuellar shortly after his inauguration, setting the situation out very starkly: "We are dying as a people and a nation".

The Indonesian government was very unhappy about the peace prize. Foreign Minister Ali Alatas said he was "astounded" and accused Ramos Horta of being a "political adventurist". The deputy governor of East Timor tried to play the whole incident down, saying that, "This is just a conscience massage for the liberal West.... The Nobel prizes are like the Oscars, and, as with Hollywood, they are partly removed from reality."* But it was clear that the government had been stung, and was worried about the effect the award might have on Indonesia's image in the world.

To add to Suharto's troubles, the Asian financial crisis of 1997 led to huge political upheaval in Indonesia. The value of the rupiah plummeted, there were large outflows of capital, and many companies went bankrupt. The ensuing

---

* *Washington Post* Foreign Service, 12 October 1996.

unemployment and poverty led to mass unrest, with riots and demonstrations around the country. Suharto appointed many members of his family to office later that year, after elections which were widely believed to be rigged, and this led to further insurrections. By 1998, the country was in chaos, with unrest and riots breaking out regularly. In May, students occupied the parliament building in Jakarta and demanded Suharto's resignation. A few days later, having failed to win the support of his former political colleagues, Suharto resigned after 31 years in power.

The downfall of Suharto created a space for a change of policy on East Timor, which by now had become a very thorny issue for the Indonesian government. The international solidarity movement was growing, other countries were increasingly vocal about the situation in East Timor, and there had been the embarrassment of the Nobel Peace Prize. After the Dili massacre, Foreign Minister Alatas had remarked to a Portuguese journalist that East Timor was "a pebble in the shoe": annoying, but not a big problem. But the pebble had grown over the intervening years, and by now had become what Alatas later referred to as "a veritable boulder": the situation had become unsustainable.

BJ Habibie, Suharto's replacement, announced that the people of East Timor would be allowed to vote on their future: they could choose between independence and being an autonomous province of Indonesia. He obviously favoured the latter, but was under pressure to show that the people of East Timor were being offered a genuine choice.

The Indonesian military, however, was not willing to let

East Timor go so easily. There were secessionist movements in various parts of the vast archipelago that makes up Indonesia, and the military was concerned that if East Timor became independent, other minorities might decide they'd like to go their own way too. The folly of choosing independence needed to be clearly demonstrated.

Leaked Indonesian documents show that, months before the vote, the military was already putting plans into place – "Operation Global Clean Sweep" – to deal with East Timor in the wake of a vote for independence. One such document stated, "Massacres should be carried out from village to village after the announcement of the ballot if the pro-independence supporters win."* Militias were recruited throughout the country, often by undercover Indonesian soldiers. Arms were stockpiled. The country was split into four "killing zones". East Timor was going to be taught a lesson.

The violence began even before the vote took place, with militias going on the rampage in a campaign to show the Timorese people what they could expect if they chose independence. When the people did just that, in August 1999, the violence escalated. According to Noam Chomsky, a close observer of the situation, "In one month, this massive military operation murdered some 2,000 people, raped hundreds of women and girls, displaced three-quarters of the population, and demolished 75% of the country's infrastructure."**

The appalling violence led the US and EU to impose arms embargoes on Indonesia in September 1999. Announcing the

* *Guardian*, 12 September 1999.
** Appeal by Noam Chomsky, ETAN [East Timor and Indonesia Action Network] website, December 2001.

suspension of arms exports, including Hawks, Robin Cook said, "It is right that we should bring home to the Indonesian army the horror of the whole world at the brutalities they have visited on East Timor."* He presented it as a moral decision, failing to note that his government had been supporting those brutalities for many years. By the following January, the EU embargo had been lifted, and Britain immediately resumed its arms exports.

At home, I followed the news closely, watching with horror the dreadful scenes on my television screen. After almost a quarter of a century of bloody occupation, it was appalling that the path to independence should also be drenched in blood. Around the world, solidarity activists started organising; rallies and vigils were held in many countries, with huge turnouts in Australia and Portugal, where the whole country stopped for three minutes, and people formed a 10km human chain in Lisbon, standing in silence while the sirens of fire trucks blared in solidarity. In London, Timorese activists and supporters held a vigil at the gates of 10 Downing Street calling for the UN to intervene. In Jakarta, protesters marched to the state parliament building, where they were fired on by police.

The US and Australia could have put intense diplomatic pressure on Indonesia to stop the violence, but for some time they sat on their hands, unwilling as ever to upset the Indonesian government. However, the pressure from people on the streets continued to grow, forcing the Australian government – worried that the demonstrations would get

***

** *Independent*, 11 September 1999.

even larger and turn into a political crisis – to finally take action, lobbying the US to put pressure on Indonesia to allow an international force into East Timor. With the US and Australia in support, the UN authorised the formation of a multinational force and in late September INTERFET (International Force for East Timor) entered East Timor, led by Australia.

Although Dili was secured relatively quickly, it took many more weeks to end the attacks in more remote parts of the country. Had the west acted earlier to put diplomatic pressure on Indonesia, and to form an intervention force ready to tackle the violence which they knew was planned, much of the slaughter and destruction could have been avoided. But, craven as ever, Indonesia's friends, including Britain, held back, not wanting to disrupt their cosy relationship with the regime.

Eventually, an uneasy peace prevailed and the UN took over administration of the country. In May 2002, East Timor's independence was finally formalised, with former resistance fighter Xanana Gusmao sworn in as the first president. The years since then have been difficult; high levels of poverty, the mass destruction of infrastructure after the 1999 vote, having to set up a new government from scratch, a fragile economy, ongoing disputes with Australia over oil revenues from the Timor Gap, the sea between the two countries.

But the people of East Timor are resilient. They resisted Indonesian occupation for years upon years, and voted for independence despite knowing that appalling violence was likely to follow. And their struggle has been the struggle of solidarity campaigns around the world which worked to raise awareness of the situation, and to pressurise their own governments to cut diplomatic and business links with Indonesia and to demand a withdrawal from East Timor.

Daily Mail, Thursday, August 1, 1996.

Page 25

We're so proud, say the Hawk wreckers

By STEPHEN OLDFIELD and NICK HOPKINS

FOUR women who walked free from court after £1.7million damage was caused to a Hawk jet gloated over their acquittal yesterday.

Flanked by supporters, applauding and cheering their comments, the activists boasted of what they had done and used the platform to launch a political tirade. They revelled in their past as demonstrators and agitators and claimed

The cleared four: From left, Needham, Kronlid, Wilson and Zelter. They claimed God was on their side

Two days after we were acquitted, the *Daily Mail* had published an article by Richard Littlejohn, one of their most reactionary columnists. He wrote, "On the scale of faraway places of which we know little, East Timor wins the gold medal. What kind of life must you have to spend it worrying about East Timor?"* What kind of life, indeed? Perhaps the kind of life in which everyone matters, where our shared humanity means that if my government is complicit in atrocities abroad, it is my responsibility to speak out and to stand with the victims. Not the kind of life lived by Richard Littlejohn, where people can be arbitrarily written off because they don't live next door. The kind of life you must have is one where you strive to be human.

---

*Daily Mail, 1 August 1996.

❖

It has been almost twenty years since our action, and I can still feel the reverberations. In my life, I can identify a certain restlessness, a reluctance to be tied down, a feeling that I always have to be ready to take action. I've had various jobs over the years – nurse, support worker, a local council post, a bit of journalism, office work – but none of them has developed into anything approaching a career. I look back now, at 50, to what might have been – I could be a very senior nurse, I could be doing any number of responsible jobs, I would certainly be very much better off – and sometimes feel a regret that I made choices in life which excluded these possibilities.

But the reality is that it's very difficult to combine "ordinary" work with activism. Over the years, I've been sacked from a nursing job (when the agency I worked for changed hands and the new owners didn't want anyone with a criminal record), been thrown out of voluntary work, found it impossible to get insurance, struggled to get beyond the application stage of jobs where you have to disclose your criminal convictions. These are not insuperable problems, but do militate against a settled, stable, comfortably-off life.

Perhaps I could have chosen another life, one of being on the margins of resistance, of going to protests when I could but having a career at the same time. A lot of people do it, but for me I don't think it would have been enough. There were plenty of people who wanted to do important jobs like nursing, but few who were willing to risk arrest and imprisonment. Once I'd established that I was one of those people – perhaps when I took that very first step into Pennsylvania Avenue all those years earlier – it seemed imperative that I continue down that path. I was willing to do it, had no responsibilities that would prevent me from doing it, and therefore it was my responsibility – and privilege – to do it.

I gave many talks about our action in the years after we were acquitted. At meetings ranging from tiny peace groups in church halls, to huge gatherings of international activists, there was one question which would always come up: "Are you disappointed that your action didn't stop the Hawk deal?"

It was true that all 24 Hawks were eventually delivered to Indonesia, along with many other weapons. But whilst our household hammers didn't stop the deal, I believe that what we did contributed in some small way to the goal of turning the pebble of East Timor into a boulder. We can't always measure the outcome of our actions, but have to trust that, if we're doing the right thing, then ultimately it will be for the good. In the end, Indonesia came to see that the combination of resistance and solidarity was too much: this troublesome people, and their supporters around the world, would not be silenced. Granting East Timor its independence was the only way of getting the boulder out of the shoe.

Over the next few years, I continued to be very politically active. ARROW kept going for several more years, until 2003, focussing on various issues but particularly sanctions on Iraq which were causing a mass humanitarian crisis. We held a weekly vigil outside the Foreign Office for twelve years, and several of us made trips to Iraq, symbolically breaking the sanctions by taking medical equipment without an export licence. Over that period, I was arrested many more times, spent a couple of short periods in prison, and continued to juggle work and activism, with varying degrees of success.

In 2004, my daughter Esme was born, heralding a period of much quieter activism – meetings and rallies rather than direct action and arrest. As she grows up, it gets easier to do more. While writing this book, I've been very involved in campaigns against road-building. Esme has been coming to protests since she was a few weeks old and has turned out to be a natural activist. With two parents who have long been involved in activism, and have each spent time in jail for their beliefs – her father Gabriel Carlyle is a campaigner on peace and environmental issues – it was almost inevitable she wasn't going to accept the status quo. Esme is remarkably tolerant of sitting in the back of political meetings with a book, happy to venture out to muddy fields at the crack of dawn to confront road-builders and police, and always willing to tread the streets delivering leaflets.

She has also developed her own activist skills. I recently told her that I was thinking of cutting down the apple tree in our garden. It was a very sad little tree that had hardly grown since it was planted, bore no fruit, and was diseased. I suggested we replace it with something more suited to the dry soil. Esme was outraged. She marched upstairs and a little while later I noticed her in the garden, hanging protest banners on the tree. Needless to say, the tree is still there. And Esme was right: as I was finishing this book, it had a big crop of apples. It just goes to show that activism can change the world.

WITH MY HAMMER

================

SHANNON SMY/SEIZE THE DAY

You who see injustice all around
But have not the courage or the will to fight

or stand your ground

We who see but are too scared
There are not enough of us prepared
To put our lives at risk time and again
And then comes a drop of rain
To the parched lips of a world
That needs to feel hope again

We are dying as a people and a nation
A third of our people have been killed in 21 years
Of illegal occupation
Ten UN resolutions
Requesting Indonesia to withdraw
They chose to ignore
And a woman cried
If you are really human
You'll stop them sending these weapons to our shores

CHORUS
With my hammer I break the chain
I will not remain in silence
I will stand and I will defend
My right to fight against violence
No prison can contain
The freedom that we gain
When we move through fear – here

Laws of our civilised land are quite clear
Selling weapons to dictators who murder, starve, rape
                                          and torture is illegal
But there is timber, there is oil, on Indonesian soil
And there's money to be made from the arms trade
Our boys need jobs, you shouted from the rooftops
But not one word of the lives lost or destroyed
I cannot believe you continue to deceive yourselves in this way
Or the people that you pay to make the jet fighters

CHORUS

To think, to plan they took a year
To build trust, to work through fear
At 3am on a cold January morning
At BAe Warton, no one saw them, no one gave the warning
Hawk jet ZH 955 came alive to the sound of singing hammers,
the hanging of banners,
the scattering of seeds and ashes on its wings
And the women waited to see what justice brings

For 2.4 million damage done
Thirteen million for a new one
We are not martyrs or heroines
We owe so much to our friends
Who held our courage in their hands

   CHORUS

And after half a year in jail
They came before a court of law
And the truth the jury heard and saw
Stunned them into silence
And when the verdict came (not guilty)
Justice had been done, the celebrating could begin again
Dancing laughing praying weeping crying
And in East Timor they danced and laughed
                     and cried some more
And as the seeds of hope begin to settle on the ground
A gentle rain begins to fall

   CHORUS

With my hammer I broke the chain
I did not remain in silence

AFTERWARDS

All the Seeds of Hope women were offered the opportunity to have a brief bio of their life since 1996 included here. Some chose not to do so.

JO BLACKMAN

Jo remained in Liverpool for many years after Seeds of Hope, working for a global education project. She now lives in a low-impact community in Shropshire with her partner and son, and is a tutor for the Workers' Educational Association, teaching courses on sustainability, eco-psychology and permaculture.

LYN BLISS

Lyn returned to her job at the London School of Hygiene and Tropical Medicine, until she was injured in a bicycle accident in 2002. She then worked for War Resisters International and *Peace News*, and was active in CAAT and Trident Ploughshares. Lyn lived in Portugal between 2006–2010. She now lives in Luton and spends a lot of time looking after her grandchildren, as well as being active in her local residents' group.

EMILY JOHNS
Emily has combined activism and art, travelling to Iran twice for "Drawing Paradise on the Axis of Evil", and, while working for *Peace News,* celebrating the people and movements that opposed the First World War in "The World is My Country". Other subjects have included genetic engineering, road building and the oil industry. She lives in St Leonards-on-Sea.

LOTTA KRONLID
Lotta moved back to Gothenburg soon after Seeds of Hope, and undertook training in gardening and tree surgery. She has worked as a gardener for many years, and started a workers' co-op of gardeners. In the last few years, she has become active in peace work again.

ANDREA NEEDHAM
Andrea continued campaigning against the Hawk deal after Seeds of Hope. She also worked on other campaigns including sanctions on Iraq, twice breaking the sanctions by delivering medical equipment to Iraq without an export licence. She lives in Hastings with her 11-year-old daughter, and works on anti-roads campaigns.

JEN PARKER
After Seeds of Hope, Jen continued campaigning work for ten years, especially resistance to ecological destruction. She then moved to the Peak District and worked in outdoor education before relocating to New Zealand, where she lives with her partner and two children.

RICARDA STEINBRECHER

Ricarda has been working as a geneticist since 2000 for EcoNexus, a non-profit scientific research organisation which investigates genetic modification and other technologies for their impacts on ecosystems and health. She has been an advisor and consultant to civil society and environmental organisations in the UK and internationally, and been involved in UN processes.

ROWAN TILLY

Rowan co-founded the genetiX snowball campaign which used Ploughshares methods to pull up GM crops until GM plantings in the UK were withdrawn in 2003. She is currently training for ordination within the Triratna Buddhist Order, participating in direct actions against climate change and training activists in direct action. Rowan lives in Oxford with Ricarda and two cats.

ANGIE ZELTER

Angie continues to be involved in nonviolent direct action, and has engaged in solidarity actions all over the world. She was a founder of Trident Ploughshares, the International Women's Peace Service – Palestine, and Faslane 365, and has written several books on nonviolent activism. At the time of going to press, she is co-ordinating two groups, PICAT (Public Interest Cases Against Trident), and the Knighton Tree Allotment Trust in mid-Wales where she lives.

SEEDS OF HOPE PREPARATION

ISSUES WE EXPLORED/DISCUSSED/AGREED:
- Purpose/aims of the action.
- Key principles of the action eg nonviolence, accountability, women's action, all group members to be equally involved in all decisions etc.
- Membership of the group and how to recruit.
- Establishing roles within the group: hammerers and support members.
- How the action relates to and supports the wider campaign against the Hawk deal and arms sales to Indonesia.
- Timeframe of the action.
- Do we see the action as civil disobedience and/or upholding the law?
- How secret/open do we want the action to be?
- Are we aspiring to do minimum/symbolic or maximum/unlimited damage?
- What symbols can we use to illustrate the purpose of the action?
- Degree of non/co-operation with the police.
- Our fears relating to the action and strategies for coping/managing fears.
- Other more philosophical topics such as: militarism and patriarchy, women and Ploughshares, when is it right to break the law?

PRACTICAL TASKS
- Research the use of Hawks to maintain the Indonesian occupation

of East Timor and the role of British Aerospace and the British Government in enabling this.

● Write an indictment of British Aerospace and the British Government's role.

● Prepare evidence of the need for our action, eg a booklet to leave at the site of the action (including the indictment).

● Plan and make a film – also to be left at the site of the action.

● Make banners – to hang on disarmed Hawk(s).

● Prepare material for the second wave of the action: "laying an information" at a magistrate's court and seeking an injunction to prevent the delivery of the Hawks.

● Research into target: how to identify the Hawk reliably (identifying the particular Hawks due to be sold to Indonesia).

● Research, discuss and agree which parts of the Hawk to disarm.

● Research the layout of the site via observations and recces/trespass actions.

● Research the security of the site – fences, alarms, cameras, doors, patrols, dogs?

● Obtain and decorate tools (hammers, crowbars, bolt-cutters etc).

● Draw up detailed plan: how to get to site, how to break in, what to do.

● Discuss different scenarios and make contingency plans.

● Discuss safety, and roleplay what to do when discovered.

● Brief selves on arrest procedure and roleplay police interview.

● Decide on phone number for hammerers to contact after arrest.

● Agree a support group member to go to police station after hammerers arrested.

● Discuss and prepare for possibility of house raids (remove any sensitive information).

● Find witnesses to be present if houses are raided.

ENSURING THE SAFETY OF ALL GROUP MEMBERS
● Discuss and plan how to make it obvious that we are a nonviolent group.

● Discuss and agree safety procedures, eg regarding use of phone.

● Plan how hammerers can inform support group about the action – and if possible, its outcome – in a way that does not put support members at risk, eg by leaving a letter for the support group to open after the action explaining the background to the action and asking for support.

● Create relevant cover stories for support group members, eg why they are ready to launch into presswork immediately after the arrest of the hammerers.

● Create and use codenames.

● Destroy duplicate notes before action, leaving just one set with trusted friend for safekeeping.

MEDIA-RELATED WORK

● Decide who are to be main press liaison people and which phone numbers to use as a contact point for the press/media.

● Compile list of press/media contacts – mainstream and alternative.

● Prepare press releases (draft first press release before the action so that it's ready to go).

● Take photos of hammerers as a group for use in press/media work

● Make list of awkward media questions and discuss possible answers.

● Roleplay press/media interviews.

● Pro-actively approach the press/media.

● Monitor and collect/record press/media coverage.

MAKING LINKS WITH THE WIDER CAMPAIGN AND OTHER GROUPS

● Produce and distribute a general leaflet about the action (draft this before the action so that it's ready to go) and regular newsletters.

● Compile a list of sympathetic groups to contact after the action.

● Liaise with wider campaign and other sympathetic groups.

● Make a list of people willing to give talks to groups.

● Respond to requests for speakers and maybe pro-actively offer speakers to groups.

● Organise/support/liaise with solidarity actions.

LEGAL MATTERS

- Seek off-the-record legal advice before the action on likely charges for hammerers and the risks for support group members, possible legal defences, possible sentences (including the minimum time which has to be served), risks of deportation etc.
- Consider how to minimize risks for support group, eg of conspiracy/aiding and abetting.
- Research and prepare different legal defences, eg Criminal Law Act 1967, international law and the defence of necessity.
- Discuss approach towards bail: Apply or not? Accept or not? What if some people offered bail and not others?
- Consider: sureties, fixed addresses, undertakings to court.
- Brief selves on court process – different hearings, transfer to Crown Court, trial etc.
- Discuss and agree approach towards representation in court.
- Appoint solicitor/barrister? (After the action!)
- Support group members to act as McKenzie Friends?
- Investigate eligibility for legal aid and make application.
- Research and approach possible expert witnesses.
- Prepare lists of questions to ask witnesses.
- Roleplay giving evidence in court.
- Consider and raise any issues which may be prejudicial to a fair trial, eg the trial taking place near a BAe site; members of the jury being BAe employees etc.
- Make contingency plans for protest actions/non-co-operation if court process is unfair/flawed, eg if defendants are not allowed to call witnesses or to have McKenzie Friends.

ORGANISING AROUND THE TRIAL
AND OTHER COURT HEARINGS

- Mobilise people locally to attend court hearings and/or to hold vigils outside court.
- Find local groups to work with on organising and support.
- Hand out leaflets outside court and/or in city centre.

- Organise events/actions in the run up to the trial as well as during the trial to raise awareness of the issues.
- Hold speaker meetings, eg inviting expert witnesses to give a public talk.
- Organise accommodation for expert witnesses and supporters coming from out of town.
- Press/media work (as above) – especially focussing on local media.

PREPARATION FOR PRISON (BEFORE THE ACTION)

- Share experiences and expectations of prison; talk to other activists who've been in prison.
- Share fears about prison and explore strategies for coping/managing fears.
- Explore how to respond if those imprisoned are treated differently, eg are sent to different prisons, or get different sentences.
- Research into what possessions are allowed in prison, visiting regimes, sending/receiving letters, etc.
- Hammerers to leave items with support group to be sent/handed in and to make list of other things they might like, eg particular books.
- Explore what type of support hammerers might like and who might be able to offer this.
- Appoint prison visits scheduler (to avoid double-booking visiting slots etc).
- Make plans to ensure empty homes are secure and bills paid.
- Make lists of family and friends to be contacted after arrest/detention.

PRISON SUPPORT

- Co-ordinate/arrange visits to hammerers.
- Respond to requests from hammerers, eg for things to be sent/handed in.
- Respond to enquiries from supporters about what support the hammerers need.
- Receive and pass on donations to hammerers, eg money, stamps.

● Act as go-betweens, passing on messages to/from prison.

ADMINISTRATIVE TASKS

● Set dates/venues for group meetings and arrange travel pools (ie share out the travel costs).

● Prepare an initial mailing to go out to family/friends and sympathetic organisations and individuals after hammerers arrested (prepare this before the action).

● Produce regular newsletters.

● Compile mailing lists.

● Discuss and agree fundraising strategies.

● Set up a bank account – in what name? which bank? (Don't set up until after action because of risk of conspiracy charges)

● Appoint treasurer to keep accounts.

● Appoint archivist to keep records of decisions, press coverage etc.

● Ensure that necessary IT support is in place.

Thanks to Jo Blackman for helping to compile this list.

ACKNOWLEDGEMENTS

THANKS FOR THE ACTION

Our action would not have been what it was without the help of the many, many people who supported us, donated money to the campaign, offered accommodation for our visitors, opened up their homes – and churches – to strangers during the trial, and a thousand other things that made it all more possible. Thank you to all the hundreds of people from around the world who wrote to us in prison; mail time was always the highlight of my day, and your letters kept me going through many dark hours.

The Seeds of Hope action affected not only the ten of us in the group, but also partners and children: thanks are due to Pete Bliss, Carrie Bliss, Milan Rai and Arkady Johns for their forbearance.

I'm grateful to Zoe Broughton and Jamie Hartzell, who made the video we left in the plane and helped distribute it far and wide; and to our legal team, Gareth Peirce, Vera Baird and Marcia Willis Stewart; and to Mike Schwarz for invaluable legal advice.

Thanks to Vera and Gil (with apologies for forgetting your surname) for hosting our prison visitors and to Kay (likewise), the Quaker chaplain in Risley, who was endlessly supportive.

In Manchester, members of Stop the Hawk Deal supported us with organising and attending court hearings: thanks in particular to Tricia Allen, Michael Bane, Stuart Cooper and Adam. In Oxford, Emma Westwood, Stephen Hancock and Mike Hutchinson did a great deal of support work and publicity, whilst in Sweden, Kajsa Svensson, Stellan Vinthagen and Per Herngren did likewise.

Our trial in Liverpool would have been a very different affair without the incredible support from local people. Thanks are due to Father Arthur Fitzgerald and the parishioners of St Michael's Catholic Church in West Derby, including but not only Julie Currall, Terry Egan, Margarita Egan, Jan Harper, Eileen Lang and Josie Macfarlane. Ciaron O'Reilly put in a great deal of organising work around the trial, in Liverpool and elsewhere.

Other groups very involved in organising in Liverpool were the Kirkby Women's Community Action Group, particularly Maureen Dunwoody and Dot Quirk, and the women's "Full Moon" group, including Jude Mazonowicz (who also hosted the entire support group during the trial), Nancy Jenkins, Sue Joyce, Val Hall, Ros Hurley, Jackie Doran and Fiona Jenkins. Others who offered a great deal of support in Liverpool include Frank Kennedy, Greg Dropkin, Kate Wise, Gareth Williams, and Kolin Mazonowicz and his schoolmates.

A crucial element of our trial was the evidence of expert witnesses, who brought the truth about East Timor into the courtroom and enabled the jury to see the rightness of our action. A huge thank you to Carmel Budiardjo, José Ramos

Horta, John Pilger, and Paul Rogers for their invaluable contributions.

Thanks are due to the wonderful Seize the Day band for "With My Hammer", a truly beautiful song about Seeds of Hope, with special thanks to Shannon Smy for writing the song and allowing me to reprint the lyrics.

And finally, to my parents, Janet and Duncan Needham, who supported me throughout the process: thank you.

Inevitably, there will be people who contributed in some way to the Seeds of Hope action who have inadvertently been missed off this list. Please forgive me if you think you've been forgotten. Your name may not be here, but your contribution is remembered.

❖

THANKS FOR THE BOOK

There are many people who have helped me with getting this book (the first draft of which had been in a file under my bed for eighteen years) into a publishable state, and I am grateful to all of them. At times I found the whole process of writing and rewriting incredibly stressful, but the support of a few key people made me believe that it was worth persisting with the project. I hope they will agree.

Huge thanks are due to Milan Rai, my long-suffering editor, for pushing me along with such patience and good humour, and suffering my many arguments about grammar. Without him, this book would not have seen the light of day. Thanks to Gabriel Carlyle for his persistence in telling me

I should write the book (and his invaluable assistance with the Kickstarter fundraising campaign); and to friends and family who believed I could do it and encouraged me even when I thought I'd never finish it, in particular Emily Johns, Jo Blackman, Virginia Moffatt, Chris Cole, Siobhan Watson, Jenny Allan and Steve Amos. John Pilger took a very early interest in my book, and offered much practical help.

Thanks are very much due to the other nine Seeds of Hope women, who may have felt inundated with requests from me, but were very generous in offering the information I needed. Jo Blackman, Lyn Bliss, Clare Fearnley, Emily Johns, Lotta Kronlid, Jen Parker, Ricarda Steinbrecher, Rowan Tilly and Angie Zelter: thank you all (with particular thanks to Jo, who helped enormously – and patiently – with my last-minute frantic requests for information).

I am very grateful to *Peace News*, for publishing my book, and to all those who kindly read it and offered an endorsement: Micato Fernandes Alves, Carmel Budiardjo, Chris Cole, Pat Gaffney, Bella Galhos, José Ramos Horta, Rachel Julian, Hannah Lewis, Caroline Lucas, Virginia Moffatt, Rob Newman, John Pilger, Paul Rogers, Mike Schwarz, and Benjamin Zephaniah.

I am indebted to those who laboured to get the book into a publishable form: Erica Smith for the cover, Emily Johns for the typesetting and Susan Johns for proofreading.

Many thanks to all those who contributed to the Kickstarter campaign, or who donated directly, making the whole project possible. Thanks especially to Tom Barns and everyone at CAAT for your generous contribution. In no particular order,

I'd like to thank the following individual supporters: Joaquim Barreto, Lyn Setchell, Lotte Reimer, Marian Lester, Gabriel Vogt, Julia Timothy, Red Notes Choir, Lizzie Jones, Jonathan Harvey, Maggie Holdsworth, Craig Meulen, Nicholas Cooper, Karen Mack, Martin Cooper, Julie Thornton, Sara Kristine Nes, Ken Harvey, Juha Penttila, Stuart Hamilton, Nick Ballantine-Drake, Emma Sangster, Jessica Davies, Claire Poyner, Vron Ware, Martin Newell, Anton Hack, Ky Sinclair, Julie Gidlow, Jo Blackman, Kathryn Tulip, Marie Walsh, Paul Libreri, Miriam Burns, Glenn Bassett, Steve Amos, Clive Fudge, Ian Prichard, Dr Hilda Kean, Philip Crow, Alan Cottey, Ruth Stavris, Freda Carlyle, Maggie Lyons, Beatrice Millar, Matthew Bell, Susanne Levin, Kristina Goodwin Jones, Brian Jones, Lyn Bliss, Gill Allmond, Ros Dunlop, Mark Blacklock, Penny McKeague, Alice Smith, Chris Spyrou, Jim Wright, Matthew Butcher, Joe McAllister, Jeff Jenkins, Pat Gaffney, Clare Danby, Matt Atkinson, Peter Cox, Ian Blunt, Phil, Patrick Nicholson, Fiona Brown, Mark Brown, Peter Jorgensen, Kerris Casey-St.Pierre, John McTague, Robert Bromley, Richard Halvorsen, Tom Humphrey, Matthew Behrens, Bob Banks, Glen Rangwala, Judith Needham, Rebecca Lush, John Lynes, Virginia Moffatt, Chris Cole, Fiona Wright, Alan Wright, Marylouise Kidd, Georgina Smith, Rosie Hopkins, Helen Dickson, Sarah Sweet, RS and Kerry Brogan. Your support is enormously appreciated.

And finally, and especially, thanks to my daughter Esme Needham, for her positivity and encouragement, and for putting up with me on all those days when I said I was too busy to have fun.

PEACE NEWS

Peace News works for a nonviolent world – where war has been abolished and the roots of war pulled up, including the silent, routine violence of hunger, oppression and ecological devastation. Making such a world will require a nonviolent revolution in every area of society, transforming relationships based on domination and exclusion into ones based on mutual respect.

We need a nonviolent revolution in women's relationships with men, in children's relationships with adults, in relationships between races, between disabled people and non-disabled people, between animals and humans, between nature and the human race. *Peace News* believes in a nonviolent revolution in our economic and political lives, subordinating work and politics to human need, not human greed; to freedom and co-operation, not hierarchy and power.

Peace News is not just about the values that we campaign for, it is also about the way that we campaign, how we treat each other, and the way that we live. *Peace News* is for people who are trying to be the change they want to see in the world.

We reject organised violence, which perpetuates structures and relationships based on privilege, hierarchy and destruction. We urge collective nonviolent action to exert another kind of force, based on solidarity and empowerment and the ability of people to regain control of their lives.

Take out a subscription today!
Peace News   0207 278 3344   http://peacenews.info